NATIONAL CHARACTER

IN

SOUTH AFRICAN

ENGLISH

CHILDREN'S

LITERATURE

CHILDREN'S LITERATURE AND CULTURE

Jack Zipes, Series Editor

NATIONAL CHARACTER IN SOUTH AFRICAN ENGLISH CHILDREN'S LITERATURE

Elwyn Jenkins

Routledge
Taylor & Francis Group
NEW YORK AND LONDON

Routledge
Taylor & Francis Group
711 Third Avenue,
New York, NY 10017

Routledge
Taylor & Francis Group
2 Park Square
Milton Park, Abingdon
Oxfordshire OX14 4RN

First issued in paperback 2014

Routledge is an imprint of the Taylor and Francis Group, an informa business

© 2006 by Taylor & Francis Group, LLC

International Standard Book Number 13: 978-0-415-97676-3 (hbk)
International Standard Book Number 13: 978-1-138-83332-6 (pbk)

Visit the Taylor & Francis Web site at
http://www.taylorandfrancis.com

and the Routledge Web site at
http://www.routledge-ny.com

CONTENTS

LIST OF ILLUSTRATIONS

ACKNOWLEDGMENTS

Some parts of this book include revised versions or parts of previously published articles by the author, which are reproduced by kind permission of the publishers: "The Growth of a National Children's Literature in English," *The English Academy Review* 18 (2001): 140–149; "Is *Platkops Children* a Children's Book?" *English in Africa* 28(2) (October 2001): 135–140; "Nudity, Clothing and Cultural Identity," *English in Africa* 30(1) (May 2003): 88–104; "English South African Children's Literature and the Environment," *Literator* 25(3) (December 2004): 107–123; "Fairies on the Veld," in *Comedy, Fantasy and Colonialism*, Ed. Graham Harper (London and New York: Continuum, 2002): 89–103; "Adult Agendas in Publishing South African Folktales for Children," reproduced by kind permission of Springer Science and Business Media from *Children's Literature and Education* 33(4) (December 2002): 269–284, © Human Sciences Press, Inc.; "The Millennial Message of Peter Slingsby's *The Joining*," *Current Writing* 12(1) (April 2000): 31–41; "Images of the San," in *Other Worlds, Other Lives*, Eds. Myrna Machet, Sandra Olën and Thomas van der Walt (Pretoria: Unisa Press, 1996): Vol. 1, 270–296.

Illustrations have been reproduced from the following books by kind permission of the publishers: *The King who Loved Birds*, by Patricia Pinnock (Grahamstown: African Sun, 1992); *The Fairies in the Mealie Patch*, by G.M. Rogers (Cape Town: Juta, n.d.); and *Dance Idols*, by Anne Schlebusch (Cape Town: New Africa Books, 2003). The following illustrations have been reproduced by kind permission of Maskew Miller Longman: from *Song of Be*, by Lesley Beake (Cape Town: Maskew Miller Longman, 1991) and *Tongelo* by Catherine Annandale

(Johannesburg: Perskor, 1976). The following have been reproduced by kind permission of NB Publishers: from *Tales of the Trickster Boy*, by Jack Cope (Cape Town: Tafelberg, 1990); *Not So Fast, Songololo*, by Niki Daly (Cape Town: Human & Rousseau, 1985); and *The White Arrow*, by Pieter Grobbelaar (Cape Town: Tafelberg, 1974).

INTRODUCTION

In a continent where national borders were arbitrarily created by colonial powers and colonists in the nineteenth century, in a country in which literary histories that seek a grand narrative of national emergence have been discredited, in the twenty-first century, when globalization is making the concept of the nation state increasingly problematic, the use of the term "national character" in a new book needs explanation.

When Nigerian Nobel laureate Wole Soyinka visited South Africa in July 2005, he replied to a question about divided societies, "There will always be differences within society. There can be several national characters, within one nation, that sometimes seem to be at war with one another." South Africa, he said, was handling this multiplicity well.[1] Participants from several African countries at a writers' conference in Pretoria in 2003 were adamant that to try to define a national literature was a false problem, and that "national consciousness" was a romantic, poetic notion. Problems that writers encountered, they said, were the problems of *writers*, not *Africans* — *blacks* or *whites*. National consciousness was a jigsaw puzzle, an ongoing project of liberation. They warned against chauvinism, saying that what was important was that writers should voice their experiences.[2]

Most children's books in South Africa have been written by white people in English or Afrikaans, with relatively few by black writers. A significant proportion of them are versions of indigenous folktales. Some are written in the languages of black South Africans, and some that were written by whites have also been translated into these languages.

In this book I consider only children's books written in English. Following Soyinka and the writers at the conference, I regard them as simply *some* literary versions of what it was or is like to live in South Africa and be a South African.

In my search for national character in English-language children's books, I go back to the earliest written by South Africans, beginning with Mrs. Mary Carey-Hobson's *The Farm in the Karoo* (1883)[3] but really taking off in the 1890s, and I give considerable space to those published up to the 1950s. I do this deliberately, because until recently it was common to read or hear that almost no English-language children's books had been published in South Africa until after the Second World War.

Since I wrote in *Children of the Sun* in 1993, "We are not yet ready for a critical history — a complete survey — of South African children's literature in English, for we have too few critical signposts,"[4] a number of scholars have worked on documentation and historical and critical studies, there have been many exhibitions that have entailed a critical selection and a recent book on Afrikaans children's literature has provided a much-needed source for comparison and explication.[5] Book illustrators and picture books have been particularly well attended to. Critical studies of young adult fiction have concentrated on its political content from the 1970s onward, during the last years of apartheid and the country's transition to democracy. Studies of adult South African literature provide a further frame of reference for the study of juvenile literature. These developments in scholarship have freed me from the expectation to be comprehensive in the present book, so that in the limited space available I can explore some byways and topics that have not received much attention.

Cape Town, Johannesburg, Durban, Bloemfontein and Pretoria are the cities that nurtured the publication of children's literature in English in the first half of the twentieth century, being the home of publishers such as Juta, Maskew Miller, Voortrekker Pers, Knox, A.C. White, van Schaik, Afrikaanse Pers-Boekhandel, Unie-Volkspers and many small presses now forgotten. Far less English literature would have appeared if it had not been for Afrikaans publishers, who were the strongest in the country because they were community driven and were often subvented by the government. Translating books from English into Afrikaans and vice versa has long been a lifesaver for children's books in this country, with translations into other African languages joining them in recent years, adding to their economic viability.

Some of the earliest South African children's literature appeared in English-language papers in the late nineteenth century at the same time the magazine *Ons Klyntji* was pioneering writing for children in Afrikaans. Much is owed to the newspapers and magazines which, until the 1950s, published children's stories and poems, many of which were republished in book form. Their names form an honorable roll call: *Cape Times, The State, The Argus, The Star, Rand Daily Mail, Standard and West Rand Review, Sunday Express, Natal Advertiser, Sunday Times, Advertiser, The South African Woman, The Capetonian, Diamond Fields Advertiser, The Outspan.* The South African Broadcasting Corporation ran children's programs and serials that first broadcast material that was later published. No doubt the very existence of these channels served as an incentive for people to try their hands at writing.

The books were often illustrated by well-known artists, some of them associated with public projects or the popular art of their day that embodied the essence of white South African culture: Cythna Letty, the botanical artist who later designed the flower motifs for the country's first decimal coins (see Figure 5); wild-life artists C.T. Astley Maberly and Hilda Stevenson-Hamilton; Sydney Carter, popular artist of typical South African landscapes, especially his bluegum trees; Ernest Ullman, sculptor and painter of art works for public buildings such as the foyer of Auden House, headquarters of the South African Institute of Race Relations; Ivan Mitford-Barberton, sculptor of public works such as the monument to the 1820 settlers in Grahamstown and the statue of Jan Smuts in Adderley Street, Cape Town; Walter Battiss, innovator and *enfant terrible* of the art scene for years, who gave respectability to the rock art of the San; Townley Johnson, an artist who was also well known for his copies of San rock paintings; and Dorelle, artist of the covers of the books of Lawrence Green, the prolific writer of popular books on the history, people and places of the country. Jan Juta, son of the Judge President of the Cape, Sir Henry Juta — both of whom wrote a children's book — was a prominent artist whose most famous murals were those for South Africa House in London and the Cunard liner *Queen Mary*. Sima Eliovson, popular author and illustrator of books on wild flowers and gardens, wrote and illustrated her own children's picture book.

Many of the illustrators also have a reputation as artists in their own right, among the significant ones being Gerard Bhengu, the pioneer black artist of traditional rural domestic life whose reputation is greatly respected today; Frans Claerhout, a Roman Catholic priest of Flemish origin, known for his expressionist and naive paintings, murals and stained glass windows featuring African people. Azaria Mbatha, famous for his linocuts (see Figure 6), and Durant Sihlali, a founder member of the Fuba Academy for training black artists, have both had their work exhibited in many countries overseas. In recent years, children's book illustration and picture books have been dominated by professional illustrators whose work can be found in books of all languages.

As if all this South African background were not enough, from the nineteenth century until the present, the peritexts of South African books are packed with background information and messages from clergymen and politicians substantiating their authenticity as truly South African products.

In the first half of the twentieth century, prefaces were provided by people such as the bishop who signed himself "Arthur Johannesburg." Since the Second World War, writers, illustrators and publishers have been far less homogeneous, but the hankering after authenticity continues. Black writers have assured us that they heard their traditional tales from their grandmothers; white retellers of indigenous folktales have invoked Alan Paton, Mangosuthu Buthelezi and Archbishop Desmond Tutu to vouch for their authenticity, and the publisher of the novelist Jane Rosenthal recently assured readers that she is "a South African with, as she puts it, 'ancestors born, married and buried in dorps from Jo'burg to Cape Town'."[6] Perhaps in the twenty-first century this lingering insecurity will pass away, and South Africans will write and publish without any need to defend themselves.

In the 1920s the prominent Cape Town publishing house of Juta, which concentrated on educational books, published a series of storybooks for young children called Juta's Juvenile Library. The title page for each book was decorated with the same design of a frame of pictures that provides a template for the literary expression of national character by white English-speaking writers for children in the first half of the twentieth century. (See Figure 1)

The motifs of the frame are a combination of European and African elements. Three of the four corner ones are European: an old woman in archaic mobcap and shawl, telling stories to children at her feet before a hearth; a mythical, serpentlike monster; and a faun. In the bottom center is the radiating sun rising behind a range of hills.

The last two of these images are among the popular international design motifs of the 1920s that Bevis Hillier identifies in *The Style of the Century*.[7] After mentioning, among others, the faun, Hillier goes on, "And above all the sun-ray, which appeared on almost anything from gramophone needle boxes to suburban garden gates. This last motif no doubt had its origins in the sun-bathing, sun-worshipping craze which began in the early 1920s ... but the motif came to have a wider, more political symbolism. It was the symbol of New Dawns (whether fascist or communist), and also evokes worthy 1930s hikers, the gambolling nordic nudes at Hitler Youth camps, and the Nazi Strength through Joy movement" (Hillier, 90).

South Africa shared in the universal spirit of the age — it had its share of Nazi sympathizers — but it also naturalized this image: the sunburst

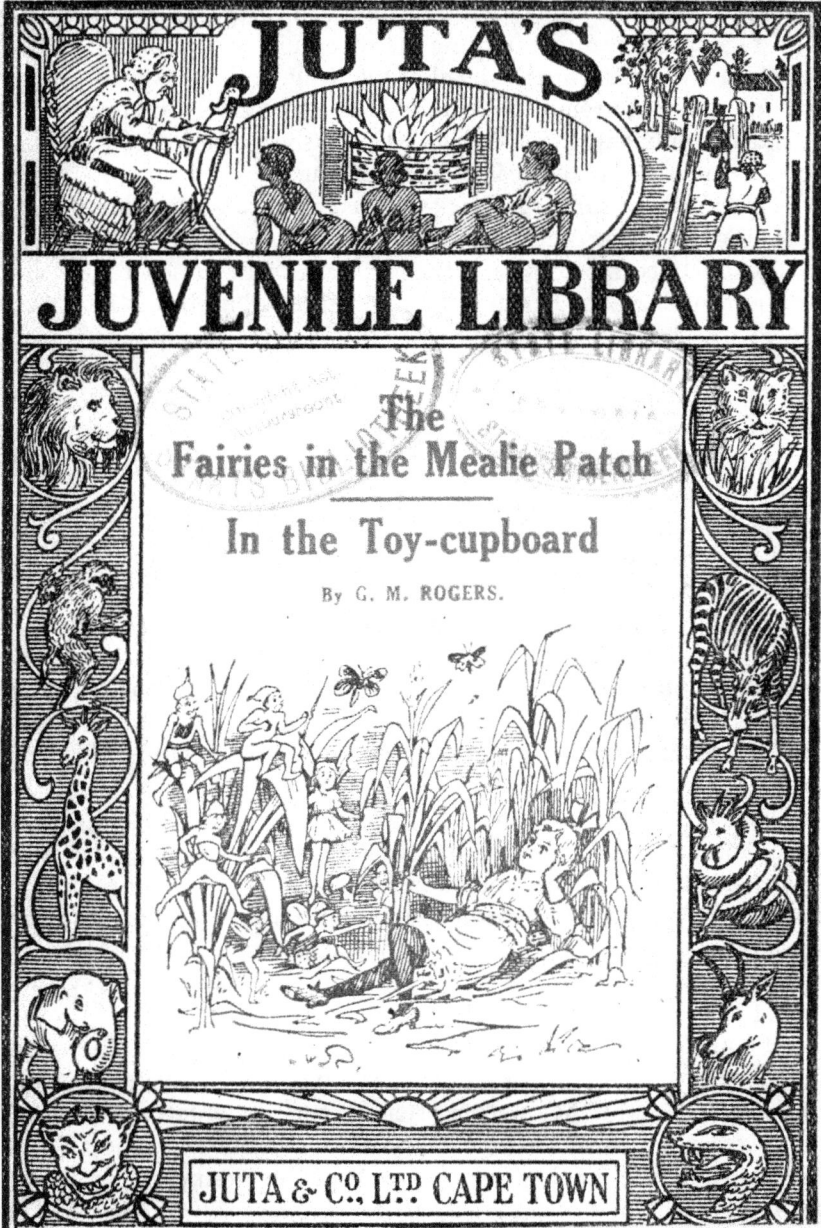

1 Title page from *The Fairies in the Mealie Patch* by G.M. Rogers and title page design for the Juta's Juvenile Library series (Cape Town: Juta, 192-), n.p.

was the logo for the popular Sunrise toffees, it was part of the design for a postage stamp commemorating the silver jubilee of Union in 1935 in which rays radiate from the head of the King, and it was incorporated in garden gates, burglar guards and window and glass door frames. The Afrikaans publishing house HAUM published a series of Afrikaans school readers for many years called the Dagbreek ("daybreak") series, which featured a full-page black-and-red picture on the cover of the radiating sun rising over the veld.

The fourth corner picture in the Juta frame shows a slave and a slave bell in front of a Cape Dutch house. The building, in the distinct "Cape Dutch" vernacular architectural tradition, gives prominence to the Western Cape and Cape Town, the "Mother City," as the home of Juta and South African white culture. Down each side is a small selection of some wild animals of Africa: only two of what the modern tourist industry has decided are the "Big Five," namely lions (shown twice) and an elephant; the colorful giraffe and zebra; an antelope; a monkey to suggest mischief, though it is not a very common animal in South African stories; and a python crushing a buck, suggesting the sensational animal world of wildest Africa. None of the birds or smaller animals that feature so frequently in South African stories are included. Most markedly, no Africans are to be seen in the entire design.

These motifs, the themes that they represent, and the gaps and silences between them, are recurrent reference points in this book, not only for the literature of the first half of the twentieth century but to the present day.

I look at children's and young adult literature in relation to the physical country, its landscapes, flora and fauna and economic exploitation; books and authors that public opinion has decided are important or famous; the past, national symbols and myths; patterns of possession of the land, domicile and population movement; oral and written literary traditions; architecture, towns and cities; material culture; the symbolism of cultural identity; schooling, books and the arts.

Of course, much of the literature that I am looking at is slight. The books were written for little children or some vaguely conceived young readership. Usually they were written for fun and entertainment, and they were often badly written by unskilled writers and crudely illustrated. Many are ideologically naive. Whether nonfiction or fiction, many have an obvious didactic purpose. Whatever their quality, they are the record of how, from the end of the nineteenth century to the beginning of the twenty-first century, certain individuals conveyed in writing and illustration to young readers their interpretation of life in a complex society.

SERIES EDITOR'S FOREWORD

Dedicated to furthering original research in children's literature and culture, the Children's Literature and Culture series includes monographs on individual authors and illustrators, historical examinations of different periods, literary analyses of genres and comparative studies on literature and the mass media. The series is international in scope and is intended to encourage innovative research in children's literature with a focus on interdisciplinary methodology.

Children's literature and culture are understood in the broadest sense of the term "children" to encompass the period of childhood up through adolescence. Because the notion of childhood has changed so much since the origination of children's literature, this Routledge series is particularly concerned with transformations in children's culture and how they have affected the representation and socialization of children. While the emphasis of the series is on children's literature, all types of studies that deal with children's radio, film, television and art are included in an endeavor to grasp the aesthetics and values of children's culture. Not only have there been momentous changes in children's culture in the last fifty years, but there have been radical shifts in the scholarship that deals with these changes. In this regard, the goal of the Children's Literature and Culture series is to enhance research in this field and, at the same time, point to new directions that bring together the best scholarly work throughout the world.

Jack Zipes

1

COUNTRY CHILDREN

In 1926, Annette Joelson opened a story for children, "In the very heart of the Cape Karoo, which again is the very heart of South Africa, where the sunshine is ever bright and warm, and skies are always blue, there lived a little girl in a very big farm-house, on a very, very big farm."[1]

Until late in the twentieth century, there were only two significant contenders for the spiritual heartland of English-speaking white South Africans: the Karoo, a semidesert region of plains and flat-topped hills covering most of central South Africa, and the bushveld of the north and northeast. Early British writers, relying on their reading, set their adventures in the Karoo. Typically, in 1856 Thomas Mayne Reid wrote *The Bush Boys; or, The History and Adventures of a Cape Farmer and his Family in the Wild Karoos of Southern Africa*.[2] A century later, its reputation continued in England: an English writer, Jane Shaw, who sends an English family to settle in Johannesburg in *Venture to South Africa* (1960), has them drive from Cape Town through "the famous Karoo."[3]

The South African children's writers who took over from the British turned the Karoo, or more broadly the wide open veld, with its blazing sky, its droughts, its windmills, its thunderstorms and its veld fires, from a setting into a mystic homeland. The very first full-length children's novel written by a South African was called *The Farm in the Karoo* (1883).[4] Mabel Waugh, author of *Verses for Tiny South Africans* (1923), apostrophizes it in "The Karroo" (using an alternative spelling):

> Great, big, wide Karroo,
> How *did* you get rolled out so flat…
> A farm, a kopje, or a windmill
> Are the only things higher at all…

And when I stand in the midst of you—oh
Do you know that I feel *very* small.[5]

Sally Starke gave the title *The Young Karoo* (1950) to her book of verses reprinted from the *Cape Times* and opens with the title poem,

Are you young?
How young are you?
  Old and ageless,
Broad Karoo?
        As young as new veld
        Breaking through.[6]

Hers is a theme that was dear to Guy Butler, born in the Karoo and one of its leading poets, who saw the geological ages of Africa as metaphysically interconnected with the youth and vigor of the country's inhabitants.[7]

Maude Bidwell wrote a children's fantasy called *Breath of the Veld* (1923) that was clearly inspired by the allegories *Dreams* (1890) and *Dream Life and Real Life* (1893) by Olive Schreiner, the most celebrated writer of the Karoo. She opens with the dedication:

Sweet memories are writ across my heart
And of my very being form a part
  Of thee, beloved Veld.[8]

The archetypal passage is to be found in the boy's story *Backveld Born* (1943) by E. Owen Wright, whose credentials are sworn to in the foreword by another writer whose name is synonymous with the veld, Leonard Flemming, author of such books as *The Call of the Veld* (1924): "He was born and bred and brought up on a remote farm in the heart of the backveld — in the lonely Karoo."[9] Wright enthuses in a meditation by the boy hero on his feelings on entering the school chapel:

One felt that way when alone on the vast Karroo veld silvered by the bright, aloof moon; and when the soft dawn breeze and the blushing East awakened the languid veld choir to herald the coming sun; and, perhaps most, when a scorching summer sun had climbed to the highest point of the steel blue heavens, had hushed the voices of the veld, stilled the winds, and made the very plants bow down their heads. The vastness, the aloneness, the silence, held one in thrall, dwarfed one's body, hushed one's voice, magnified one's spirit, and set it free to roam the vast unpeopled veld, to soar through the clear, sunwashed air of the Karroo days, and to mingle with the burnished stars of the haunting Karroo nights.

(*Backveld*, 119)

A wider view of the South African landscape was presented by Juliet Konig (who later wrote as Juliet Marais Louw) in her much admired collection of verse, *South Wind* (1945). The prefatory poem extends to the Cape coast and tropical Indian Ocean shore, but the Karoo still takes center stage:

The Southwind sings—
It brings a song
Of sunbaked lands where the grass is long,
Of sundried rivers and sunflecked seas
And scarlet flowers on tropical trees;
Little lost towns in the silent heat
Where children play in the dusty street;
Farms forgotten and far away,
Lonely huts, where the black folk stay;
Sunward ever the vulture wings,
  These are the songs
  The Southwind brings.[10]

The Karoo and the veld dotted with Free State koppies (the Afrikaans/English word for hills, also spelled *kopje*) were not entirely empty. Part of the allure was the cosy life on the farms, which Konig describes in her poems: fruit bottling, making butter, baking, and meal times.

Lights

Here and there on the veld at night
Fitfully gleams a little lost light.

Every light in the wintry gloom
Is a lamp in a dim, low-ceilinged room,

Which shines on tables and forks and knives
And supper for farmers and farmer's wives.

(*South Wind*, 41)

Many of her poems describe black people at work or in their homes.

Huts

Huts in the hills, huts in the hills,
Makanda says there's nothing fills
His heart, like the huts in the rolling hills,
Where his wife, with a little brown boy on her back,
Swings up the long, pink cattle-track.

(*South Wind*, 13)

Compared with most of her white contemporaries, who thoughtlessly wrote about black people in racist language and clichés, her writing is always humane:

Shepherd Boys

The moon is rising,
The hills are steep,
Piccanin
Is watching the sheep.

Squats in the firelight
All night long,
Twangs his fiddle
And sings a song.

Just the same
When the moon was low,
And the cedars shadowy
Long ago,

Red-cheeked David,
The shepherd's son,
Sang in the shadow
Of Lebanon.

Led his sheep
By silent streams,
Plucked his harp
And dreamed his dreams.

(*South Wind*, 18)

Juliet (Konig) Marais Louw was one of the most respected women of letters in children's literature in South Africa in the twentieth century. She wrote in English, although German had been her mother tongue as a child. As well as writing poetry, novels, plays, history and autobiography, she broadcast on radio programs for children and coedited influential school poetry anthologies that introduced children to local writers and gave prominence to women writers. Some of her books were translated into Xhosa and Afrikaans. She also had an international awareness: as early as 1945 she published a volume of verse about the children of the Holocaust. She is the only children's writer to have been awarded the Gold Medal of the English Academy of Southern Africa. She died in 2001 at the age of 91.

The farm buildings that writers liked to describe were rondavels — round buildings usually situated in the farm yard and traditionally occupied by schoolboys during the holidays. They were probably favorites because of both their design and their name, which were uniquely South African: "The big rondavel was built of stone, and thatched. It was a cosy room."[11]

The traditional African huts on which they were based, round and with conical roofs, featured often in texts and illustrations, but sometimes more for stimulating fantasy than realistic consideration of the occupants: Sally Starke named her book about toadstools that fairies build in the night *Little Huts That Grow in the Veld* (1943),[12] and Norah Perkins wrote a poem about

> Three brown thatched huts, rondavels of the south,
> Looking like giant mushrooms in the dusk....[13]

Far less often a setting for children's stories and verse were country villages, or *dorps*, Juliet Konig's "Little lost towns in the silent heat,/ Where children play in the dusty street." Detailed descriptions of towns and their buildings are rare. In *Children of the Camdeboo*, C.M. Stimie, writing in 1964, captures precisely a type of school architecture dating back to the First World War that was ubiquitous across the country.[14] Camdeboo High School takes its name from the ancient Khoi name for a region of the Karoo, and its signs date from the time before Afrikaans replaced High Dutch in the 1920s.

> It was a single storey with a wide, high front, a steep red corrugated roof and an entrance on either side. The bottom part of the walls was of dressed hard sandstone common in the area, the rest of bricks, plastered and whitewashed. Above each entrance there was a mock Cape Dutch gable from which the cream-coloured paint was peeling in ugly blotches. On the left gable, as one approached, huge letters spelt out the word "CAMDEBOO" with below it, in smaller lettering, "BOYS – JONGENS." The gable on the right was

decorated with the words "HIGH SCHOOL – HOGERE SKOOL" and below these, again in smaller letters, "GIRLS – MEISJES."

(*Camdeboo*, 39)

This is the Cape Dutch architectural style which is singled out for illustration in the title page frame for Juta's Juvenile Library. (See Figure 1.) It was what white people considered for three centuries and more to be the most important South African style.

Edith King's poem, "The Stoep," from her collection *Veld Rhymes for Children*, written in Bloemfontein in 1911, is also true of many a dorp:

Of all the places in the house
  We love the stoep the best;
It is a bowery sitting-room,
Where all the choicest flowers bloom,
  And there's a swallow's nest....
A creeper, like a curtain, shades
  From sun and dust and heat:
It is a cosy place for tea;
No prying passer-by can see
  When walking down the street.[15]

While the interior plateau of South Africa continued unabated as a setting until the 1960s, the Bushveld gradually gained popularity among children's writers. In children's literature, "Bushveld" refers specifically to the Lowveld of what is now the province of Mpumalanga, rather than broadly the countryside of the extreme north and northeast of South Africa, which also sometimes bears this name.[16] It is the setting of one of the favorite books of English-speakers, considered by many to be the only South African children's classic: *Jock of the Bushveld*, by Sir Percy FitzPatrick (1907).[17] Encouraged by his friend Rudyard Kipling, who overheard him telling his children bedtime stories of his adventures, FitzPatrick wrote this semi-fictionalized account, recalling his experiences as a young man with his dog, traveling by wagon and shooting wild animals in what is now partly the Kruger National Park. Subsequent writers for children make intertextual reference to it, expecting their young readers to appreciate the tradition it established.

The significance of the Bushveld was that it represented the primeval unspoilt African continent as it had been in ancient times, when the land swarmed with animals. It lay on the edge of South Africa, as Werner Heyns suggests in the opening of his story of an African boy who lives there, *Ramini of the Bushveld* (1963): "In a far, far corner of the Bushveld, where the Klaserie River makes a big bend, there lived a herd of seven elephant."[18] Only as the Lowveld became more accessible to visitors, especially after the Kruger National Park opened in 1926, did the Bushveld become an alternative setting for children's stories, parallel with adult fiction and nonfiction about it. The sociopolitical background to this development is considered in Chapter 3.

Other settings for children's books were scattered around the country, often apparently chosen because of their familiarity to the writer, but sometimes arbitrary. Yvonne Jooste, for example, began a story called "The Rain Fairies" (1943), "Once upon a time there was a little girl called Lalie. She lived with her mother and father in a small town far away in the heart of the Bushveld"; but the story has no sense of place, and the trees she drew for illustration look very English.[19] "Far away" suggests that Jooste simply intended to set her story beyond the Karoo homeland.

Sometimes books entailing a journey had maps to give readers a sense of geographical space. *Papa Baboon* by F.A. Donnolly (1933), which was published in Pretoria and indubitably intended for local readers, has a map on the end papers showing the route from Cape Town to Pretoria, marking incidents along the way,[20] and *Candy Finds a Clue* by Maud Reed (1958), published in England and intended for English readers, includes a map of the route followed by children from South Africa through the Kruger National Park to Rhodesia.[21]

The Cape Peninsula featured fairly often, but not with any suggestion that the place might have spiritual power. Rather, it is the home of different wild creatures and provides a coastline and ocean that have potential for different sorts of adventures to those of the interior. Next in popularity was the province now called KwaZulu-Natal, where the Drakensberg Mountains, the tropical coast and the far Lebombo Mountains provided scope for adventure and encounters with strange people, flora and fauna.

In the second half of the twentieth century the choice of country settings widened further, reflecting places that the writers knew and wrote about with love: Peter Slingsby in the Western Cape interior; Beryl Bowie, Hjalmar Thesen and Marguerite Poland in the Eastern Cape; Felicity Keats in the KwaZulu-Natal Midlands, and Brenda Munitich in the Msinga area of the remote interior of that province.

The predominance of the countryside and wilderness in the children's literature of English-speaking white South Africans does not parallel the demographic reality. Since the British occupation of the Cape in the early nineteenth century, the immigration schemes of 1820 and the mid-nineteenth century, and the diamond and gold rushes in the second half of the nineteenth century, they have always been predominantly urban people who, even if they initially settled in the country, moved to towns and cities or the mines. In 1936, only (95,000) out of the total of 992,000 English-speakers lived in villages or on farms, compared with 585,000 rural Afrikaners out of 1,121,000. Not many English-speakers could have been farmers: at that time there were only 104,249 farming units in the country, of which the majority were run by Afrikaners, and the number decreased to 45,818 by 2002. In 1974, only five percent of English speakers lived on farms or in villages, and their average age was older than that of the urban population.[22]

Children's literature historian Andreé-Jeanne Tötemeyer observes, "The rural roots of the Afrikaner remained evident in juvenile literature until well into the seventies."[23] But if English-speakers did not share these roots, why did they share with Afrikaners the "farm or wilderness background" in their stories? The population figures suggest that children's literature has played a complicated part in the relationship between English-speakers and the countryside, which is one of the elements this book sets out to explore.

South African farm stories for children first appeared in the 1890s, the distinction for the first going to *Jack and His Ostrich* by Eleanor Stredder (1890).[24] The novel deals with relations between English-speaking and Afrikaans neighbors, and although some of the Boers are shown in a bad light as ignorant, backward people who treat their black servants badly, the message of the story is that they can get along together, and the little hero later marries an Afrikaans girl. Nevertheless, the opening paragraph is ambivalent about his allegiance:

> Jack Treeby loved to say that he was an English boy, although he had never seen the dear old mother country of which his father so often talked; for he was born among the wide South African plains, where through the parching summer the sun-rays burn like fire, where the dry leaves shrivel with the heat, and the flowers can only bloom in sheltered places. Yet he was the proudest and happiest of boys when his father stroked his curly head and called him a "true-born Briton."

> *(Jack, 7)*

No wonder his Boer neighbors accepted him with reservations, one might think.

Jane Spettigue, who lived in South Africa for some time, included in her output two children's books set in this country. One is a historical romance, *A Trek and a Laager* (c. 1900)[25] but the other, *An Africander Trio* (1898), is the real forerunner of the farm genre.[26] In it, three farm children entertain an aunt on a visit from England and have amusing, innocuous adventures, with none of the mysteries, crime or natural disaster that enlivened many later farm stories.

A variety of children feature in the country stories before the 1960s. If they are white, some, perhaps most, live on farms, even if they go to boarding school and come home only in the holidays. Sally Starke wrote a poem about them in 1950:

Farm Boys

We go to town by lorry,
We go to town by car,
We go in the lucerne wagon,
We ride, if it's not too far.

We put on shoes and socks, and shirts
That button to the chin,
We wear a hat and all that
And a *visiting* grin.

We go to see a cinema,
We look in all the shops,
We count the newest motor-cars
And buy some lollipops.

We really need a haircut,
And after that is done,
We wonder where the grown-ups are
And when, O when, they'll come!

Before we go to town we talk
For days and weeks about it,
But when we're there we wouldn't care
If we had done without it.

O, town's all right and each new sight
Has some especial charm,
But the best of the day will be jogging away
Back to the veld and the farm.

(*Young Karoo*, n.p.)

Others are town children visiting a farm, usually that of an uncle and aunt, or staying at a holiday destination such as a beach cottage:

A journey in a train to some far siding,
An uncle, tanned, and seamed, and khaki-clad,
A trip by car to where the farm is hiding.[27]

A frequent theme in stories about child visitors to farms is that they learn the values and wisdom of the country folk and absorb the rural integrity of the countryside, often being healed of some character flaw or troubling problem. As late as 1991, Felicity Keats kept to this formula when she wrote a story, *Rudolph's Valley*, about a girl spending her holidays with an elderly uncle and aunt.[28] She is apprehensive of the uncle who fetches her at the station, and on the drive to the farm absorbs every strange detail, such as, "A small boy wearing a long khaki shirt leaped down the hill and pulled the hand-made wire loop off the upright pole. Carefully he drew the stranded wire gate wide so that the oxen and the cart could carry on down the road" (*Rudolph's Valley*, 8). This accuracy of detail, Keats writes in a postscript, is drawn from her own childhood holidays on the same farm.

Common to almost all the farm and holiday stories until the 1950s is their banality of plot, characters and style. They were not alone in this; in their history of South African literature, A.J. Coetzee, Tim Couzens and Stephen Gray point out that in general the English literature of the country from the First World War until the 1950s was mediocre — these were "years of literary dearth."[29] Historians of the children's literature of Canada and Australia, countries that parallel South Africa in their history in many ways, record the same banality in this period. In Canada after 1906, Sheila Egoff and Judith Saltman lament, "only a few books of the next thirty years are worthy of mention,"[30] while Brenda Niall is no more complimentary about Australia, which had its share of holiday adventures catching smugglers: "In the late 1920s Australian writing for children reached new levels of mindlessness. The next two decades did not do much better."[31]

Well known South African examples are W.M. Levick's *Dry River Farm* (1955) and its sequel, *River Camp* (1960), set, archetypally, on a farm and at a family holiday camp respectively;[32] and *Friends of the Bushveld* (1954), by a prolific writer in all sorts of genres for adults and children, Fay King (later Fay Goldie).[33]

Typically, the structure is episodic and the characters a group of children or a family with no single focalizer and little interiority in the characterization. The atmosphere is one of cosy domesticity, conveyed by a great deal of dialogue, much of it devoted to food and punctuated with children's exclamations such as "Gosh, that's topping" from a Natal boy in 1946[34] and "'Hurrah! Hurrah! Hurrah!' shouted Tessa" (when she hears they are going on holiday) — this from one of the most hackneyed, *Caravan Caravel* by Marie Philip, which came out as late as 1973.[35] Enid Blyton is never far away: "They ate a huge tea of buttered toast and scones and jam and pastries and cut fruit cake" (*Candy*, 161). Or the food clichés could be South African: "Plates of home-made bread, thickly spread with butter from the farm of one of Ouma's many sons and daughters, disappeared as if by magic, and were promptly piled high again by Lizzie. There was rice pudding and stewed fruit to finish off with, and earthen mugs of creamy milk for the children" (*Friends*, 26). The cover blurb to *River Camp* is spot on in promising the reader "children's happiness and enthusiasm and adults' good humour." Authorial digressions and Socratic dialogue between children and adults convey information about nature, life on the farm or the ways of Africans, who are always servants or farm laborers.

One of the most predictable plots for farm stories is a mystery leading to the catching of crooks. It is equally predictable that the loot of choice, or the treasure the children find, is one of South Africa's two most precious commodities, diamonds and gold, which have featured in this role in the country's fiction since they were first discovered. Daphne Rooke gives her book *The South African Twins* (1953) as South African an identity as she can by including both in her lost treasure.[36] The identity of the criminals may also reflect the era when the books were written: in Charles Hoppé's *Sons of the African Veld* (1947), they are a Portuguese halfcaste and Nazi and Japanese war criminals;[37] in *Smugglers' Cove* by Werner Heyns (1963), they are Communists led by a Jew, intent on instigating an uprising in Mozambique; and a year later in *Mystery at Rushing Waters* by Francois du Preez, they are Portuguese and French Communists.[38] The genre has not been exhausted yet; as late as 1987 Brenda Munitich wrote a farm story, *Ben's Buddy*, in which a boy catches sheep rustlers, but it differs from the superficiality of earlier adventures by dwelling on the thoughts and emotions of the boy, who is mute, as focalizer.[39]

A refreshing change from the usual male-centered story of life in the Karoo was *Tickey* by Sheila Dederick (1965), about a girl who has grown up in a country orphanage.[40] She is called Tickey because she was found as a baby with half a threepenny coin hung around her neck.

This coin had iconic status in South Africa until the 1950s. In South African English, Zulu, Xhosa, and Afrikaans, the tiny threepenny coin in use before the currency was decimalized in 1961 was called a *tickey*, a word of disputed etymology. South African English-speakers were proud of the word and enjoyed puzzling visitors with it; to them it was one of a small number of strange words current in their English that were essentially South African. Many children's authors brought the tickey into their stories in one way or another as a piece of shorthand for some local color.

In the story by Sheila Dederik, Tickey is invited by a schoolfriend to come and live with her family, the van Heerdens, on a farm. Life in the village, the orphanage and the school and on the farm is graphically brought to life. (See Figure 2) The author, like many English-speaking South Africans of that time who had any connection with farming, found that she was more at home using Afrikaans words for aspects of farm life, such as "fowl hok" for "fowl run," even though in most cases English equivalents are available. She appends a glossary, which she introduces: "As the Afrikaans words in this book will nearly all be familiar to English-speaking South Africans, they have mostly been printed like the English words. But foreign words, and where necessary some Afrikaans words, have been printed in italics" (*Tickey*, 139). Apart from solving the mystery of Tickey's parentage, the story is typical of its time in being flat: lots of dialogue and little interiority to give the reader a feeling for the girl's emotional life.

A peculiarity of South African English children's fiction up to the 1950s is that it lacked certain genres that were common in other English-language literatures and Afrikaans children's literature of the period. One of the most extraordinary differences is that Afrikaans children's and youth literature until the end of the century was filled with series, while English literature had none. A survey by Maritha Snyman lists more than 70 Afrikaans series, some of them containing scores of titles.[41] Unlike many American series, they were written by individual authors, although some of them wrote different series under different pen names. Some are famous and form the core of Afrikaans literary tradition, known to many generations of Afrikaners and republished and reread. They are key features in the formation of Afrikaans cultural identity.

Early series, says Snyman, glorified rural life. One of the first, the *Maasdorp* series by Stella Blakemore, starting in 1932, was a major series about a girls' boarding school; this was followed by the equally popular boys' boarding school series, *Keurboslaan*, in the 1940s, by the same author writing under the masculine pen name Theunis Krogh.

By the 1950s, according to Snyman, "The rise of a generation of professional white Afrikaners who increasingly did not live exclusively on farms" was reflected in series set in villages or peri-urban areas

2 Illustration by Esdon Frost from *Tickey* by Sheila Dederick .

(Snyman, 98, trans.). A popular type of story featured a small-town gang of mischief-making boys or girls, epitomized by perhaps the most famous of all, the Trompie and Saartjie stories respectively of Topsy Smith, which began in the 1950s and were still being republished (along with the Maasdorp stories) in omnibus volumes in the 1990s.

These stories were part of a wider tradition in children's literature. In the nineteenth century, America produced "Bad Boy" books, and later fiction featured the Bad Boy in ameliorated form as the "Good Bad" boys and girls who were popular in the U.S. and Canada, while Britain had its Good/Bad hero, Richmal Crompton's *Just William*. In *Making American Boys,* Kenneth B. Kidd has explained that the Bad Boy was based on an analogy between the boy and the savage, on the understanding that the white boy would outgrow his savagery; and by 1900, when the native American was seen to be vanishing, the Bad Boy took his place.[42]

It is difficult to explain why English-speaking South Africans did not write series. As for why they did not produce stories about Good Bad boys and girls, a couple of explanations can be derived from comparing the situation in other countries, but they are not entirely convincing. In South Africa, the American theory of childhood that saw the white child as savage-like had dangerous racial implications, and in any case, when it was obvious that the indigenous people were not disappearing, there was no need for this substitution. However, this would not explain why Afrikaners did, in fact, write about Good Bad white children.

A second explanation is one that Brenda Niall has given as to why the genre could not take root in Australia: "Such characters fitted best into city or small-town settings; the bush, with its harsh realities, demanded brave, hardy young settlers or explorers. The call of the bush ... must have been important in directing writers away from the everyday social settings in which a comic rebel-hero could indulge his anarchic impulses" (Niall, 133). Perhaps this applied to English-speaking white society in South Africa as well, at a time when English-speakers determinedly located their children's fiction in a rural heartland away from built-up areas.

Outside England, Afrikaans writers were the only colonial writers who really made school stories their own. Canadians had a few attempts, and Australian writers such as Lilian Pyke tried hard but unsuccessfully to transpose the English school story to Australia. South African English writers were not unaware that school stories were a very popular genre in England in the first half of the twentieth century. The first to try her hand at a local one was May Baldwin, whose *Corah's School Chums* appeared in 1912,and she certainly gave it a local flavor, because much of the usual business of these stories — rivalries, cattishness, petty crime, pranks and bullying — springs from English/Afrikaans rivalry, reflected in the lengthy political debates that the girls hold, usually taking sides about the South African Anglo-Boer War.[43] *Backveld Born* by E. Owen Wright followed, set mostly in a boys' boarding school. Both these schools were smart city schools, not small-town establishments.

Later, some Afrikaans school stories were translated into English, ranging from poor ones by C.M. Stimie and Lourens Stopforth to the well written novels of P.H. Nortje, notably *The Green Ally* (1963) and its sequel, *Wild Goose Summer* (1964), which were published in handsome editions by Oxford University Press in the U.K., illustrated by the South African artist William Papas.[44] One mediocre series was, in fact, produced: the three Meredrift School stories of George and Lorrie Raath, obviously inspired by the success of their Afrikaans counterparts and published by an Afrikaans publisher in the 1960s, which made no impact.[45] All these stories follow the events of the school year with perhaps a theft or some serious rivalry to liven things up. But, in other respects, they are unlike English school stories: they do not depend on tension between formal school rules and the informal behavioral norms of the children, the schools are coeducational, the activities are very South African (such as preparing for a military cadet parade), and they are not infused with notions of public school spirit or class distinction.

Why English-speakers did not produce girls' stories is also not easy to explain. As Chapter 5 shows, the first half of the twentieth century was dominated in South Africa by women writers, but they wrote only for children of primary school age, while other former colonies produced many series about girls growing to womanhood, such as those by Louisa May Alcott and Laura Ingalls Wilder in the U.S., Lucy Maud Montgomery in Canada, and Louise Mack, Ethel Turner and Mary Bruce in Australia. The English writer Bessie Marchant set three novels about strong, independent girls in South Africa at the same time as the Australian stories, *A Girl of Distinction* (1912), *Molly of One Tree Bend* (1910), and *Laurel the Leader* (19-), but no local writers followed suit, and her books have never been taken up as national classics, perhaps because, factually, they are ludicrously inaccurate.[46]

Farm stories often featured black children, the offspring of farm laborers, who are frequently the playmates of white children. This relationship, which is discussed in Chapters 2 and 8, is a common theme in South African children's books. In the period up to the 1960s, a number of South African authors wrote books with a single black child as protagonist, usually a boy who lives in a rural or semi-urban area. Stories about the San formed an important subset, the subject of Chapter 7. Although black writers were writing in English at the time, none wrote for children. These books about black children were intended for white children, as the frequent inclusion of ethnographic information and glossaries indicates. They are usually simple accounts of the children's daily lives and domestic events, whether they be modern children who go to school or San members of hunter-gatherer clans in former times. They differ from the white domestic stories by being less sentimental, which suggests how serious-minded the authors were in these projects.

A distinct kind of book, which had a fictional narrative thread but included folktales, praise songs and other verse, history, legends, and lessons taught by their elders, was produced about African boys growing up. The white authors are knowledgeable on the subject and appear to have written the books to inform white readers about African culture and history. A certificate in *Ramini of the Bushveld* by Werner Heyns (1963) announces that it is "suitable for reading by pupils in Stds VI, VII and VIII [Grades 8 to 10]," which definitely meant white children (*Ramini*, n.p.). Other examples are *Zulu Boy* by Lola Bower (1960), *The Adventures of Kalipe* by Anne and Peter Cook (1957), and *Tau, the Chieftain's Son* by G.H. Franz (1929).[47] The latter two are discussed further in Chapter 6.

Probably the first picture book about a black child was *Kana and His Dog* by Jessie Hertslet — the pen name of Mrs. Jessie Winifred Baines (Gould) — illustrated by Katrine Harries and published in Cape Town by The African Bookman in 1946.[48] It was printed in brown on buff paper in landscape format and stapled together. This was the first children's book illustrated by Harries, who was to become the country's most distinguished illustrator of children's books, and it is considered so important that the National Library selected the back cover as one of the 22 illustrations it reproduced for its major first-ever exhibition of children's books, held in Cape Town to mark the meeting in the city of the congress of the International Board on Books for Young People in 2004.[49] (See Figure 3)

In his book on award-winning South African children's books, J.A. Kruger rather unfairly remarks, "If it was not for her [Harries's] attractive illustrations, this book of only 15 pages would probably have passed unnoticed."[50] In fact, the narrative has pace, a climax, resolution and comforting closure, and the story itself is of considerable interest to literary and social historians. It portrays a typical rural Zulu family, in which the father is a migrant worker, leaving a mother and grandmother to bring up the children. When news comes that the father is ill, the mother takes the long walk to the bus that will take her to the distant town to visit her husband. "'I will take care of the women,' said Kana," who is a very little boy, wearing only a loin cloth (*Kana*, 4). He braves a storm to fetch maize cobs and then guide his mother home across a flooded stream. The family is poor: they feast that night on

3 Illustration by Katrine Harries from *Kana and His Dog* by Jessie Hertslet.

bread bought as a treat in the village store and hot sugar-water. The last picture, used in the exhibition, depicts the family and dog cosily seated on the floor around a fire in a beehive grass hut. The factual details are given in passing, without sentimentality, condescension or emphasis on their strangeness to white readers, and the visual details are accurate. This book would appeal to children of any background. It is an excellent effort, well ahead of its time, by white writer and illustrator to produce a non-racist book.

Since the 1960s, the proportion of children's stories featuring black children has greatly increased. More books are being written by black writers. *Our Village Bus* (1985), by Maria Mabetoa, illustrated by an artist known only as Mzwakhe,[51] is also a rural story. It is a milestone, described by the National Library in its 2004 exhibition catalog as "one of the first picture books written and illustrated by black South Africans." According to the catalog, it "has been extensively used for literacy programmes" and reprinted several times as well as translated into various African languages (National Library, 18).

The comic text tells how the passengers in the bus have to get out and push when it becomes stuck in the mud, while Koko (grandmother) beats them with her umbrella to urge them on. The passengers are named and described and their business in town is given. They all join the driver in singing as they take off again. The pictures have progressed from the careful, ethnographic-style illustrations that Gerard Bhengu earlier drew for *Xhosa Fireside Tales* by Phyllis Savory,[52] to the robust, naive "township art" by black artists that came into fashion in the 1980s. A clever perspective picture of the interior from the front of the bus shows all the characters, whom the child reader could have fun identifying. But no children appear in the book.

A significant change after the 1950s was that the settings of children's books shifted largely from the country to the city. As the official policy of apartheid strengthened its grip on the country and opposition to it grew, writers for children and young adults turned to the cities for their plots. If they were politically or socially aware, rural areas offered them no potential for exploratory fiction, because in the country social relations were slow to change and opportunities for young people of different races to interact other than in master–servant relationships remained limited. In the cities and big towns, residential segregation was breaking down, black children could be portrayed in modern circumstances rather than fixed in some timeless traditional past, schools were being integrated, social mixing became possible and young people were exposed to political thinking opposed to apartheid; these were the themes that writers wished to explore.

From the 1970s until the end of the 1980s, when the ban on the African National Congress was lifted, Nelson Mandela was released from prison and the end of white National Party rule was in sight, no physical space as easily identifiable as the Karoo or the bushveld replaced them as the spiritual homeland of white English-speakers. This reflected the sense of alienation of many English-speakers under the National Party government. A number of youth novels of the 1980s described how young white men facing conscription were told that it was patriotic to fight on a notional "border" that included Namibia, Angola and compounds occupied by liberation forces in other neighboring countries, and they explored the skepticism and anguish this caused in the boys, their families and girlfriends. But no local youth literature in English could foster a love of a homeland. No wonder young white English-speakers who grew up in that era left South Africa with such equanimity.

It is only since the coming of democracy in 1994 that the cities, which had been the setting for two decades of novels depicting anguished engagement in transformation, have been joyously appropriated by the youthful characters in literature. The final chapter in this book returns to look at these city children.

2

FAMOUS WRITERS AND BOOKS

Over time, a canon of "important" South African books has developed, partly through the declarations of literary critics and historians, partly through the prescription of books for study in schools, and partly through public opinion based on people's reading or vague memories of their parents' conversations about their favorite books. A few authors or books, whether read or not, become a convenient shorthand in the media for what is South African in literature, and they can end up as national symbols. During the rule of the National Party after 1948, the Post Office often featured Afrikaans writers on postage stamps as part of a deliberate project of the government and cultural groups to assert Afrikaans culture. In reaction to this, a public outcry in 1984 led by the English Academy of Southern Africa shamed the authorities into issuing a special series on English writers. Those chosen were Thomas Pringle, Olive Schreiner, Percy FitzPatrick and Pauline Smith, whom the President of the English Academy, Prof. Ernest Pereira, recommended as the pioneering, defining, English South African writers up to the 1930s.

These four were primarily writers for adults, but each of them also wrote something that featured child characters or is considered by some to be a children's classic. A few other writers for adults who were famous in South Africa and, in some cases, internationally, also wrote child-related works, the most prominent being Sima Eliovson (for nonfiction), Jack Bennett, Laurens van der Post, Roy Campbell, Daphne Rooke, Victor Pohl, Hjalmar Thesen, Stuart Cloete, Ezekiel Mphahlele and Njabulo Ndebele. Their status bestows a particular cachet on their child-related works, which are discussed in this chapter. While several famous Afrikaans poets also wrote poetry for children, the same is not true of their English counterparts. Only Arthur Vine Hall, who cannot be described as famous or important, wrote for both audiences — the *Companion to South African English Literature* remarks, "Unjustly neglected today, he is by no means a writer for juvenile readers only."[1] This chapter brings these works together and considers their place in South African English children's literature.

Thomas Pringle, a Scottish settler who was the first English-language poet resident South African poet, wrote "The Honey-Bird and the Woodpecker," published in 1834, in the form of a children's ballad, making it the first English-language children's poem in the country.[2] Because it is a satirical attack on the British government of the Cape and the Cape Dutch for massacring Xhosas, it was probably not intended for children. After clashing with the Cape government over freedom of the press and the plight of slaves and settlers, Pringle returned to Britain in 1826, where he became Secretary to the Anti-Slavery Society.

The Story of an African Farm by Olive Schreiner (1883), the first English South African adult novel of note, is set firmly in the middle of the Karoo.[3] The first half of the novel gives prominence to the lives of three children among the characters who live on the farm. It has twice been made into a film, once for television and the second time in 2004, when the director, David Lister, unequivocally and grotesquely turned the first part into a children's comedy, which is how it was marketed in the U.S. The verdict of the literary historians A.J. Coetzee, Tim Couzens and Stephen Gray, that the novel "nurtures its own brand of first-generation colonial-born youngsters, striving for roots in the beginnings of a modern world,"[4] points to its significance, which I discuss further in Chapter 7.

Percy FitzPatrick, author of fiction and serious political nonfiction, is best known for his autobiographical *Jock of the Bushveld* (1907), which he claimed he wrote for children and which is considered the first South African children's book of note, though it is perhaps more admired by adults.[5] The premier prize for South African children's literature in English, established by the South African Institute for Librarianship and Information Science in 1974, is named the Percy FitzPatrick Prize after him.[6]

In the previous chapter, I remarked that, unlike Afrikaans stories, English ones seldom featured small country towns or bands of children living there. The turn of the century did in fact produce two well known books of this sort, but neither of them is a true children's book. One is the problematic *Platkops Children* (1935) by Pauline Smith,[7] which it is helpful to contextualize by comparing with *The Diary of Iris Vaughan*, which was written by a young girl who lived in Karoo towns during the South African Anglo-Boer War (1899–1902).[8]

The diary was not published until 1958, and literary scholars argue about the degree of editing that it underwent. It has become a much-loved South African classic. The precocious young author, one of four children of a magistrate, provides a hilarious romp through village life, subversively viewing adult life from a fresh, frank point of view:

> A great thing happened in Cradock. It was the laying of a foundash-ion stone.....It was near our house we saw it all. It is in the veld. They sang and took lovely silver plates round for money, and a great flag was flying, and old people making long talks. Then they all went away. In the afternoon a great dust storm came. Everyone shut the houses, becos it blew everything away. But Pop and Charles and I ran to the stone becos the flag was blowing in the veld and all the silver plates flying in the air. We caught the silver plates and the flag and carried them home and Mom said This is a dredful deed, Cecil. It is steeling. And Pop said Nonsense woman it is a gift from the elemense. I said who is elemense. Pop said the wind. Mom used the silver plates to bake tarts in. She said they only tin. We will have tart tins for many years. The elemens gave us 24.
>
> (*Diary*, 4)

Platkops Children is one of only three books by Pauline Smith, an author greatly admired by scholars. It consists of a series of loosely related stories narrated by a young girl, the daughter of a medical doctor, who lives in a village in the Little Karoo, a hot and sparsely populated region south of the main Karoo. Two prominent scholars have described it as a children's book, but this is disputable. Michael Chapman's literary history calls it a book of "children's stories,"[9] while Margaret Lenta remarks, "The low esteem in which the work has been held is partly because it has been seen only as a work intended for children, a view supported by the use of illustrations in the text, and, more damagingly, by the idiosyncratic discourse of the narrator."[10]

The book has parallels with *The Diary of Iris Vaughan* in that the narrator is the child of a professional man whose life brings her into contact with many different people, and the language in which it is written purports to be that of a child. Incontrovertibly, Smith based the stories on her own childhood, and gives a superb portrayal of a Karoo childhood, the sense of place enhanced by illustrations such as a vignette of a wagon heading across the Karoo veld toward a radiating sunburst, the motif symbolizing the essence of South Africanness that was used in the Juta title page frame. With the mellowness of adulthood, the pace is slower than *The Diary of Iris Vaughan*, the humor gentler, and some of the stories are suffused with adult nostalgia. In place of the artless writing of Iris, Smith created an art form of child language in which "the Paoli one" narrates the stories in the third person:

> An' once the Bishop came to Platkops dorp an' asked Nickum's mother How many of Us there were?
> An' Nickum's mother, who used always to laugh when she saw us an' Tycho,
> laughed again and said Three,
> my Lord. But one's a dog.
> An' when the Bishop met us after that he stopped still in the middle of the road an' said Hullo! And which of you is the dog?
> An' Six was so serprised at anybody askin' sich a silly question as that that he jes' said out loud in a rage: Goodness grayshus! What a bishop!
> An Paoli insplained that Tycho was the dog, an' asked the Bishop please not to tell Six's mother Six had said Goodness grayshus out loud. It was jes' a mistake.
> An' the Bishop promised, an' gave each of us a tikkie, and Tycho as well. But Six still says what an instrornery man he must have been not to know a dog when he saw it.

> (*Platkops*, 150)

Smith started writing the stories at the turn of the century and in 1913/14 submitted them to Maskew Miller in Cape Town, which rejected them. During this time, other children's books by South African authors were beginning to appear, often bringing together stories and articles that had first been published in newspapers and magazines. By the time Smith's book was published in England in 1935, South African publishers were regularly publishing children's books, with both Maskew Miller and its local rival, Juta, prominent in the field. One would have expected any of them to jump at the chance of another local children's book; it seems likely that Maskew Miller was not interested because Smith's book was seen as an adult book.

Platkops Children finds only a small, uneasy place in the meager body of criticism of South African children's literature. Three bibliographies place it as "psychologically convincing and suitable for "over-fourteens,"[11] "for older children,"[12] and as "young adult" (i.e. "ages fifteen years and over"),[13] so they do not consider it suitable for readers of the age of the protagonists. Jay Heale is equivocal, observing that the language "makes it hard for a modern young reader to sort out," and concluding, "Today, it seems condescending; in its time, it was probably good read-aloud material."[14] Some surveys of South African children's literature mention it,[15] but another does not;[16] while the *Companion to South African English Literature* strangely contradicts everyone else by including it in the genre apparently because it is written "in a style accessible to children as well as adults" (*Companion*, 51).

Evidence of a book's reception may help categorize it, because readers may not follow the expectations of authors and publishers. Anna Louw, historian of South African children's literature, cites another historian, Hilda Halliday, who wrote that "the book was a favourite with the children who had it read to them before it disappeared," but says that she herself "still has to find someone who knew the book as a child."[17] A contemporary review in the *Cape Times* praised its nostalgic flavor and authentic local touches, but never suggested it was a children's book. The same conclusion was reached by Sheila Scholten, editor of the new edition in 1981, even though she cited a letter by Pauline Smith indicating that she had had child readers in mind as well as adults.[18] The conclusion must be that *Platkops Children* has never been received in South Africa as plainly a children's book.

Another guide to the readership of a book is to compare it with other books of the period, in this case, even if Pauline Smith did not know them. Among South African children's books of the nineteenth and first half of the twentieth centuries nothing else is written in child-language. Baby-talk appears occasionally, but only in the dialogue of cute tiny tots, as in Sir Henry Juta's *Tales I Told the Children* (1921): "'Doodness dacious, where is I? We is wake up in our nursery. What is you doin' in my 'ittle bed?'"[19] Smith's idea of writing in child-language was probably a unique notion on her part. She may have thought at the time that the stories would be read by or to children, but she did not know that no other children's books were being written like that (her early reading being the Bible, *The Vicar of Wakefield* and "The Ancient Mariner" (Scholten [139]).

Contemporary works of fiction that most resemble *Platkops Children* in that they were written by women about a group of South African children are *An Africander Trio: A Story of Adventure for Boys and Girls* by Jane Spettigue (1898),[20] *The Cape Cousins* by Edith Green (1902),[21] and *The Chronicles of Peach Grove Farm: A Story for S. African Children* (1910) by Nellie Fincher.[22] *An Africander Trio* and *The Chronicles of Peach Grove Farm* are typical of children's books of the period in that they announce, somewhere in the peritextual material, that they are "for children"–an announcement *Platkops Children* notably lacks. Confirmation that *The Cape Cousins* was also intended for child readers came with its subsequent publication in the children's magazine *Everyday, With Which is Incorporated "Sunday,"* which ran from 1917–1925.

Of the three, *The Chronicles of Peach Grove Farm* provides the most fruitful comparison, because it is the only one published in South Africa, and the only one by a novelist for adults that is avowedly for children. In her day, Nellie Fincher (the pen name of Mrs. William Wells-Wyld) was well known, particularly for her first novel, *The Heir of Brendiford* (1909). *The Chronicles of Peach Grove Farm*, which was published in her home town of Pietermaritzburg, is one of the best works of fiction about farm children published in South Africa in the first half of the twentieth century and deserves to be much better known, but unfortunately, it is almost forgotten: copies are extremely rare, and it is usually left out of bibliographies of Nelly Fincher's writing, including the entry in the *Companion to South African English Literature*.

What makes it particularly comparable to *Platkops Children* is that it consists of a series of stories about the activities of a group of sisters, which purport to have been written severally by them for their family magazine. The author has avoided the anomaly that Lenta identifies in *Platkops Children* (Lenta, 34), that, if a child were writing the book, she would not reproduce her spoken language. The girls write the chapters for *Peach Grove Farm* in their usual written language, which is completely intelligible standard English that a modern child could understand as easily as a child of 1910. It has a few deliberate spelling errors and idiosyncrasies of style, but they are foregrounded by the metanarrative, in which the girls tease each other about the way they write. In other words, the author draws attention to the language as part of the entertainment of the book. Clearly, it does not have the sophisticated distancing function of the child-language of *Platkops Children*, which Lenta likens to that of *Huckleberry Finn*.

The only way *Peach Grove Farm* could be suspected of being for adults is that the author has a few sly jokes of the "out of the mouths of babes" variety, when the girls write things in innocence that an adult reader can construe differently. For example, writing about the small human figures they make to inhabit their miniature farm, one of them comments, "Jim, our herd boy, was not altogether a success; but I believe, by what I hear my father and my uncle say, that herd boys sometimes are not" (*Peach Grove*, 4).

Unconscious humor like this, which probably only an adult would appreciate, also features in some other children's books of the period, including *The Cape Cousins*. It is a puzzling convention, best explained as self-indulgence by the author. On the other hand, it provides a major part of the appeal of books genuinely written by children such as *The Young Visiters* by Daisy Ashford (1919) and *The Diary of Iris Vaughan*.

Compared with the comedy of manners of *Peach Grove Farm* and *The Diary of Iris Vaughan*, *Platkops Children* often hints at darker matters such as death; in requiring the reader to go beyond the child's naivety to appreciate what Lenta calls the "implied insights of the adult" into colonial relations (Lenta, 35), it is subtler and more serious.

Two books by Smith's British contemporary Kenneth Grahame give a direct indication of the readership of such books at the time. *The Golden Age* (1895) and *Dream Days* (1898) are similar to *Platkops Children*, being volumes of stories about a group of children that are based on his own childhood, but they are written in standard English. Like *Platkops Children*, they are admired by adults for their nostalgic recreation of a lost, idyllic world. Reference books usually concur with the conclusion of the *Oxford Companion to Children's Literature* that with them, "Grahame thus became established as a writer about childhood, though not as a writer for children,"[23] and the same verdict applies to *Platkops Children*. The distinction between books for adults and children is never rigid: Lenta is probably right in judging that *Platkops Children* works at two levels — one of entertainment, which can be enjoyed by both adults and children (if they are able to get past the language barrier), and a more profound level of social commentary.

The next children's book by a famous woman author for adults appeared in the 1950s, when Sima Eliovson tried her hand at a children's picture book, *Little Umfaan*, which she published herself.[24] She was beginning her career as a prolific writer and illustrator of books about wildflowers and garden design. White South Africans have always been great lovers of nonfiction about their country, and Eliovson not only catered to this with her beautiful books, but met the needs of country lovers who lived in towns by writing on how to grow indigenous flowers in urban gardens.

Little Umfaan: The Story of a Road (probably published in 1952) resembled the pioneering *Kana and his Dog* (1946), by Jessie Hertslet and Katrine Harries, in being printed in sepia in landscape format. The conceit for the book is entirely original. Here, for once, was a writer who created her own story without any reference to the tired overseas models that local children's writers relied on. A footpath is personified as a black boy ("umfaan"), winding past the archetypal Cape Dutch homestead. Tom is a little white boy who, after playing on the path, always says, "Thank you for the ride, Little Umfaan" (*Umfaan*, n.p.).

He promises to turn the path into a tarred road that cars can go on, and returns as an adult to do that. A picture shows a giraffe, springbok and insects admiring the road. Big cars take happy families over it on holiday. Tom promises to take Little Umfaan on holiday, and extends the road through an idealized landscape past a traditional African village and country town to the beach. This story was written before roads became places of danger that destroy the environment: it ends with a car standing on the beach, which in the twenty-first century would be illegal. It is a celebration from a less complicated era in which Eliovson could share with children her love of all things South African.

Jamie, by Jack Bennett(1963), stands out as an exception to the mediocre South African juvenile works of fiction that were published in the 60 years spanning the middle of the twentieth century, between *Jock of the Bushveld* in 1907 and the politically conscious young adult novels that emerged in the 1970s.[25] Not only was *Jamie* better written than most, but it was one of a handful that were internationally admired. Yet today, it is almost forgotten; and Bennett, who became better known as an Australian writer after he had emigrated to that country, is largely forgotten in the country of his birth.

Jack Bennett was a South African-born author who acquired an international reputation. Many of his fourteen books were also published in translation. *The Voyage of the Lucky Dragon* (1981), for instance, about Vietnamese refugees who flee to Australia, was also published in Norwegian and Japanese and ran into ten editions in Spain, where it was made recommended reading in schools.[26]

Jamie was his first novel. It is about a young white boy who lives on an impoverished farm in the Eastern Cape; when his father is killed by a rogue buffalo, he vows to take his revenge, confronting his deepest fears. He succeeds in shooting it while narrowly escaping death.

The book was published in English in Britain and, in the same year, in the U.S. Twenty-seven years after its first appearance, it was finally published in South Africa. It was also published in Dutch, Swedish and Afrikaans. The American edition had quotations on the cover from the *Times Literary Supplement* describing it as "a moving, refreshing and distinguished first novel" and by a critic who extravagantly compared it to an American classic: "It has taken twenty-five years, but here at last is a novel to take its place beside *The Yearling*" (*Jamie*, cover). The cover of Bennett's next book quoted more enthusiastic reviews for *Jamie*, such as, "Magnificent.… In its own right a Book of the Year" from the *Catholic Herald*.[27]

Bennett may not have written *Jamie* for juvenile readers; aspects of the contents and the focalization (which vacillates, as in so many South

African children's books, through a lack of authorial skill rather than for deliberate structural reasons) suggest otherwise. For example, after 10-year-old Jamie has shot his first antelope, the chapter ends, "It had been a good day, one of the days a man remembers to the end of his life, better even than his first having of a woman, because it was a complete, well-ended event, with no hangover of regret, or any feeling that it might have been better" (*Jamie*, 28). However, the comparison with *The Yearling* indicates that at least one critic saw it as a young adult work, and the American Library Association placed it on its 1963 list of significant books for young adults. When it was eventually published in South Africa in 1990, it was unequivocally packaged as a young adult novel.

Jamie went on to receive the ultimate accolade in international popular publishing, being selected as a *Reader's Digest* Condensed Book in 1965, when it was included in a volume with novels by John Masefield and Arthur Hailey. The film rights were bought and repurchased several times, but it was never filmed, whereas Bennett's Australian bestseller *Gallipoli* was turned into a successful film featuring Mel Gibson.

Bennett was one of several internationally admired South African-born writers of the mid-twentieth century who wrote a work like this. Two of them came from members of a famous trio, Laurens van der Post and Roy Campbell, who, together with William Plomer, founded the controversial literary journal *Voorslag* (1926), which is regarded as a landmark in South African literary history. All three left South Africa and went on to achieve international fame: Sir Laurens van der Post as one of the great spiritual gurus of the age, counselor to Prince Charles, godfather of Prince William and confidential adviser to Margaret Thatcher; Campbell as a firebrand poet and essayist; Plomer as a distinguished English man of letters and librettist for some of Benjamin Britten's operas.

Laurens van der Post wrote three novels featuring teenage boys, *The Hunter and the Whale* (1967), *A Story Like the Wind* (1972) and its sequel *A Far-off Place* (1974). None of these is considered a book for children or young adults; but *The Hunter and the Whale*, a complex book dealing with political and metaphysical themes but partly about a boy who spends his holidays as a hand on a whaler sailing out of Durban, has to be included in any account of South African literature dealing with adolescent rites of passage.[28] The other two are vehicles for van der Post's theories about the San and his political ideas about the threat of communism in southern Africa. His self-appointed and dubious role as an authority on the San is discussed in Chapter 7.

Roy Campbell, South Africa's leading English-language poet of the 1920s and 30s, wrote a children's story, *The Mamba's Precipice* (1953), in which a family of three boys and a girl have a holiday adventure in Natal that is nothing more than a macho fantasy.[29] The older brother shoots a leopard, but without danger or any feelings. In a comic scene, his younger brother shoots its mate at night with a shotgun, thinking it a ghost. After pausing to watch a fugitive murderer die of strychnine put out for the leopard, one boy rushes off to hunt a mamba. Spanish and Portuguese political exiles demonstrate bull fighting with Afrikander bulls at the cattle dip — Campbell loved Spain and was not going to leave that out. The lurid cover is in keeping with the contents: not only does it repeat the zebra and sensational deadly serpent that feature in the Juta title page framework, but it has a striped Asian tiger stalking the zebra. It is hard to say what possessed Campbell to tackle a children's book: he clearly had very limited knowledge of the genre. The book is clichéd, bombastic, factually inaccurate, improbable in plot and deservedly forgotten by the public today.

Equally as disappointing as Campbell's venture into a children's story is one written by Daphne Rooke, *The South African Twins*, published in the same year. She was a South African novelist of international renown, respected both for her style and the seriousness of her novels, which dealt with South African society, multiculturalism, social prejudice and miscegenation. A reviewer in *The Times Literary Supplement* concluded, "She is an outstandingly accomplished writer of English prose"; and a review of *The Greyling* (1962) in *The Guardian* declared, "Gordimer, Lessing, Rooke, and the greatest of these is Rooke."[30] While these inflated opinions would not be repeated today, she is still held in high regard by serious critics.

Rooke's first children's book was *The South African Twins* (published in the U.K. in 1953), subsequently published in the U.S. as *Twins in South Africa* (1955).[31] She apparently did not have South African readers in mind when she wrote it: the dedication reads, "This book is for Rosemary and for all girls and boys who like to read stories about strange places" (*Twins*, n.p.). She also wrote two further books in the international "Twins" series, *The Australian Twins* (1955) and *The New Zealand Twins* (1957).

Like Campbell, she grew up in Natal; like Bennett, she emigrated to Australia, and like Campbell, she wrote her South African children's book after leaving. Her settings and characters are based closely on her childhood experiences, but the result is just as unsatisfactory as *Mamba's Precipice*. Her idea of what constitutes a children's book consists of clichés — her only intertextual reference is to *Peter Pan*. The country suffers from drought, which is followed by rain that symbolically falls at the end of the story, solving problems. Typical of farm stories, the plot involves crooks and lost treasure. The white boy has a black playmate, who is comically greedy and admires his white playmate for being tanned and fit and good with a rifle. Like a nineteenth-century book, it has no focalizer; adults are forever explaining things to the children in old-fashioned, patronizing language, such as when a game ranger launches into an excursus on tsetse flies (a popular trope of the previous century as well). Like Campbell, Rooke trivializes the archaic literary set-piece of shooting a dangerous beast. The white boy shoots a lion, and it is all over in half a page. His sister's reaction is to think what a story it will make for the writing competition she wants to enter.

Another internationally known South African author of books about boys and wild animals in this mid-century period was Victor Pohl. His books were addressed to both adult and young readers, published abroad in translation, and recommended for school reading in South Africa and New Zealand. Most of them were clumsily written nonfiction about wildlife, his ancestors and his adventures, but they include *Savage Hinterland* (1956), a children's novel featuring a pair of San and white boys struggling for survival, which was translated into Afrikaans, French, Dutch and German, and his major novel on the San, *Farewell the Little People* (1968).[32] His popularity, which was very high until the early 1970s, has not lasted.

Hjalmar Thesen, though not as well known abroad as Bennett, also wrote a novel about a young person facing a marauding predator, which was also selected as a *Reader's Digest* Condensed Book. *A Deadly Presence* (1983) features a young man rather than a boy as the protagonist, but is similar to *Jamie* in elements of plot and theme and in being addressed apparently to both young and adult readers.[33] It is recorded as a young adult novel in Jay Heale's authoritative bibliography, *Young Africa Booklist*.[34]

Closest in plot and theme to *Jamie* is the short story "The Claws of the Cat" by Stuart Cloete (in *The Soldiers' Peaches*, 1959), in which a boy, left alone on his bitterly poor family's farm to protect their small flock of sheep, shoots a "lynx" (strictly speaking, a caracal) that nearly kills him.[35] Cloete was a best-selling novelist throughout the world, author of tales of lust and adventure set in South Africa, often in historical times, such as *Turning Wheels* (1937) and *Hill of Doves* (1942), which was made into a successful film. He was a short story writer, especially popular in the U.S., where his stories were published in *Saturday Evening Post*, *Esquire*, *Cosmopolitan*, *Argosy* and *Colliers*. "The Claws of the Cat" was also acclaimed in South Africa and was made into a short feature film for South African television. Though written for adults, it became an accepted part of the canon of reading for high school students, evidenced by its inclusion in two anthologies of stories for South African schools published in 1969 and 1979.[36]

What enabled Jack Bennett to rise above the nondescript attempts at children's books by his predecessors was that he broke out of the limited range of literary models that South African children's writers had depended upon since they first started writing in the late nineteenth century. They had a poor knowledge of developments in children's literature in other countries, and produced inferior pastiches of what they thought was being published abroad. But now South Africans, after participating in the Second World War, were less insular.

Bennett and Cloete were like their contemporaries Geoffrey Jenkins and Wilbur Smith, South African writers of popular thrillers that sold worldwide, who knew world literature and the world markets and wrote accordingly. The assurance and sophistication of the writing in *Jamie* and "The Claws of the Cat" demonstrate their familiarity with American literary models. Almost certainly it was because they both actually wrote these works for adult readers that they could break free from the banal and silly models for children's books that had kept South African children's writers in thrall and were the downfall of Campbell's and Rooke's efforts.

The influence of American writing on South African children's writers was not new. In the nineteenth century, the novels of the American James Fenimore Cooper were widely read in South Africa, and as local writers emerged, they drew for their models on Cooper and the British boys' stories that were modeled on his work but set in South Africa. One of the British authors was Thomas Mayne Reid, who portrayed South African society and nature in terms of the republican principles he had absorbed during a long sojourn in the U.S.

After the era of boys' adventure stories was over, American literary influence was confined to adult writing. Deneys Reitz, a Boer fighter who authored (in English) one of the most highly rated memoirs of the South African Anglo-Boer War, *Commando* (1929), was influenced by American writers such as Owen Wister, author of *The Virginian: A Horseman of the Plains* (1902). Classic stories of the American West continued to be respected for their literary value in South Africa until the 1950s, evidenced by the prescription for study in high schools of *The Virginian* and *The Oregon Trail: Sketches of Prairie and Rocky Mountain Life* by Frances Parkman (1849).

South African girls in the nineteenth century read American novels such as *Queechy* and *Wide Wide World* by Elizabeth Wetherell and *The Lamplighter* by Maria Cummins, but there is no evidence that local writers imitated them. Olive Schreiner was deeply influenced by the

American Ralph Waldo Emerson. (The boy in *The Story of an African Farm* is even called Waldo.) But Emerson's influence was not passed on, secondhand, through Schreiner. In the first half of the twentieth century, American influence on South African children's literature was limited to imitations of Joel Chandler Harris's *Uncle Remus* stories (1880) for young children, which are discussed in Chapter 6.

Another strand of American writing had an impact on South African literature when Herman Charles Bosman, South Africa's greatest short-story writer, successfully adopted American humorists and short-story writers such as Mark Twain and Edgar Allan Poe as his models when he started writing in the 1930s, but his style never reached local children's literature. The next wave of American influence to be seen was when the slick black writers of the "*Drum* era" (a popular magazine of the 1950s) took over the style of Langston Hughes, the Harlem Renaissance and Damon Runyon; but again, none of them wrote for youthful readers.

Bennett and Cloete naturalized Ernest Hemingway and John Steinbeck in South Africa, revolutionizing the prose style of South African children's literature. Bennett later acknowledged in an interview, "There was a time when I went through the 'Ernest Hemingway fan' phase."[37] In his introduction to *The Soldiers' Peaches*, Cloete describes how he learned to adapt his writing to the requirements of American magazines, arguing, "If such stories are not art they are certainly craft" (*Peaches*, 11). He need not have been modest; they remain among the best South African short stories.

Here is Bennett in monosyllables, concentrating on physical details to convey the stark, unsentimental life of Jamie and his Xhosa companion on the farm:

> Kiewiet was waiting for him in the kitchen, kneeling down before the fire with his hands over the coals. Jamie poured out two cups of coffee in big tin mugs, added milk and sugar and handed the African boy one. They sat in silence. Kiewiet leaned back against the wood-box, his mug beside him. After a while Jamie stood up and took the empty mugs over to the wash-basin. He washed them and dried them and hung them up on the sideboard.
>
> (*Jamie*, 45)

Jamie is introduced by his stern father to the masculine, adult world of guns:

> How often he had sat on the bottom stairs and fingered the cool steel of their barrels and the velvet-smooth oiled stocks, imagining himself cuddling them to his cheek, sighting down the long avenue

of the barrel, notching the bead into the vee, between the eyes of a charging lion...boom! He knew them all — the heavy single 12 bore, the long-barrelled double 20 bore with its big hammers, the light point four-ten, the long lean Mauser 9 millimetre, the heavy army Lee-Enfield, the short, wicked little Walther twenty-two, and the long, heavy BSA air-rifle with its lever loading action and long butt with the pistol grip.

(*Jamie*, 11)

To capture the simplicity and ruggedness of South African country people, Cloete married the style of the American authors with that used by Pauline Smith in her classic adult masterpieces, *The Little Karoo* (1925) and *The Beadle* (1926), creating a Biblical, Afrikaans-sounding dialect that was also used by Alan Paton in his famous novel *Cry, the Beloved Country* (1948) and by Herman Charles Bosman. A common technique was to change the word order: "Like a big black-bearded baby was this bold husband of hers" ("Claws," 155). Dialogue is pedantic and echoes the Authorised Version of the Bible:

"Do not fear for me," his father said. "I cannot die. I can only be killed. It is not reasonable to think that I shall be the first of my race to die in bed like a woman. Fear nothing," he said, "and do what your heart prompts you, for through it courses the wild blood of your people."
"I shall fear nothing," the boy said.

("*Claws*," 156)

Bennett also adopted a structural technique from Steinbeck's *The Grapes of Wrath* (1938) of inserting interludes, or "inter-chapters," that feature characters who have little to do with the plot except in enhancing the generic effect of drought and poverty. He was not the first South African writer to do this; Paton had done the same in *Cry, the Beloved Country*.

One scene in *Jamie* could have come straight out of *The Grapes of Wrath*. As the drought worsens, the first to leave their farm are a poor family with "seven scrawny children":

Wally, a tall, thin man with a deep tan, raised his hat. ... His blue striped shirt, worn without a collar, was frayed and dirty, and his braces were grubby loops of cord, clipped onto the tops of patched khaki trousers. He smiled vaguely and gestured towards the high-piled truck. "We're moving," he said. ... "The old people are coming too." He nodded towards old Dom and his wife, standing, looking curiously lost, amid the household debris beside the truck. Old Dom gave Edward his usual vacant grin. Mrs Lemmer, a drab, work-wearied woman in her sixties, showed the ghost of a smile.

(Jamie, 75)

The North American influence brought an unheard-of maturity to writing about South African children. It extended beyond style to plots and themes. Bennett and Cloete depict the rite of passage of a boy to manhood that entails the killing of a wild animal when it charges and wounds him. The plot and mood of *Jamie*, about a boy growing up on a struggling farm, learning hard lessons about life, are reminiscent of Steinbeck's *The Red Pony* tetralogy (1937). It is not surprising that *Jamie* was compared on the American dustjacket with *The Yearling* by Marjorie Rawlings (1938), because the latter has a similar theme drawn from the mythology of the American frontier.

Bennett's second young-adult novel, *Mister Fisherman* (1964), was about a boy and an old fisherman. Very likely he was inspired by Hemingway's *The Old Man and the Sea* (1952), in which the old fisherman is cared for by a young boy who is his faithful acolyte. Hemingway's short novel was well known in South Africa, where it was prescribed for study in schools in the 1960s and even translated into Afrikaans in 1964. Comparisons can be not only retrospective but prospective: the South African critic Jay Heale has compared *Mister Fisherman* to another celebrated American children's story, *The Cay* by Theodore Taylor, which followed it in 1969 (Heale, 37). Both feature a white boy who is thrown together with an old black fisherman from whom he learns to mature and overcome prejudice.

The similarities between *Jamie* and other books and films extend beyond the U.S. to the two Commonwealth countries whose youth literature often resembles South African equivalents, Australia and Canada. Although Bennett had not yet moved to Australia when he wrote *Jamie*, a critic has remarked that *Jamie* is "modelled on the lines of the *Smiley* films, which were made in Australia during the time Jack wrote it."[38] In Canada, *Starbuck Valley Winter* by Roderick Haig-Brown (1944) introduced a run of novels over the next twenty years about boys who learn to become men from their encounters with nature.[39] At the climax of *Starbuck Valley Winter*, the young hero slaughters an entire pack of marauding wolves that attack him. *Jamie* is the closest in powerful writing that South African youth literature of the period comes to this classic Canadian story.

Jamie and "The Claws of the Cat" resemble the North American books in another way that marks a new development in boys' adventure stories both overseas and in South Africa: unlike the yarns of the previous century in which the characters were given no interiority, or the trivial adventures of Enid Blyton-type children in the first half of the twentieth century, of which Campbell's *The Mamba's Precipice* and Rooke's *The South African Twins* were still part, they explore the protagonists' inner thoughts and conflicts as they mature.

Jamie has to face his new responsibility for the drought-ridden farm now that his father is dead:

> He whispered urgently on his knees by the window, Please God let it rain before it is too late. He felt suddenly and enormously the loss of his father; a frightening wave of insecurity washed over him, leaving him sobbing, lost and terrified. In the new realisation of his helplessness, the realisation of how much he had depended on that stern, quiet man, he felt an almost overwhelming need to rush downstairs and clamber into his mother's bed, clutch her to him in a paroxysm of atavistic terror.
>
> (*Jamie*, 105)

The publisher's announcement at the front of *Jamie* says that it has two themes, of which the first is Jamie's determination to avenge his father's death. The blurb continues:

> The novel's other theme deals with the boy's friendship — an unquestioning, undemanding friendship — for Kiewiet, a small black picannin of his own age. The Africa shown here is one that gets very little publicity these days. The problems are not of race, creeds or politics, but of such things as rain, drought and erosion. The picture is of a hard, silent land and of a silent people of simple virtues.
>
> (*Jamie*, n.p.)

In adopting the theme of the friendship between white and black boys, Bennett, whether he was aware of it or not, was simply continuing a trope that had been pervasive in children's books throughout the transitional colonial period of the first half of the twentieth century and would continue for decades more. In the form of the relationship between an adult white man and his loyal retainer, it goes back to the earliest boys' adventure yarns set in South Africa. Bennett actually resurrects one of the great set-pieces of these books, when the loyal retainer rescues his master from a charging wild animal. However, things are not so simple in the mid-twentieth century; the shooting is messy, because Jamie initially only wounds it because of his borrowed rifle's bad sights, and the buffalo breaks Jamie's leg before Kiewiet manages to distract it so that Jamie can finish it off.

Accounting for the popularity of the theme of white and black playmates in the children's literature of a racially divided country is a complex matter. Both Afrikaans- and English-speaking whites on farms sanctioned friendship between their children and the children of their black employees. They often formally allocated a black child to be the white child's companion for safety reasons, so that the children could then roam the farm, because the black child was often wiser in the ways of the bush and could therefore protect the white child and find the way home. Such friendships continue to this day. A firsthand account of one was given by a 14-year-old Zulu boy, Mboma Dladla, in his life story, transcribed by Kathy Bond in 1979 and published as a book for children: "So I worked and learned on the farm and played a lot with the white man's children, GG and Khonya. We are very good friends."[40]

These friendships were also tolerated in towns, where white children played with the children of domestic workers. Children's writers who used this theme were reflecting what actually happened, but they made an effort to show the black children in a favorable light. They would have seen themselves as offering readers an enlightened liberal view. Yet their stories often showed the white child going away to school, leaving the black child to a future as an uneducated laborer, which was nothing more than the reality of the time.

The 1920s story *"Snow," The Brave Little Kaffir Boy*, by G.M. Rogers (192-), was something of an exception, because Snow, who lives in a hut in the garden of a house near Johannesburg, and who saves his white charge from a snake, goes to school at the same age as the white boy.[41] Rogers feels constrained to explain this: "… because, although he was a little Kaffir boy, his mother wanted him to learn to read and write" (*"Snow,"* 4).

Until the 1970s, authors concentrated on the sentimental aspects of the relationship, implying that this showed the black and white children devoid of cultural difference, sharing a common humanity: in the film *e'Lollipop* (distributed overseas as *Forever Young, Forever Free*), written and produced by André Pieterse in 1975, the boys stop in unison and companionably urinate side by side. The use of nudity in this film and a number of books to make the same point is discussed in Chapter 8. Pieterse has recalled that it was a challenge to make a film featuring this friendship in the 1970s, and it risked being banned. (It was not screened in Bloemfontein.)[42] In 2004, the film was relaunched at the Cannes Film Festival and put on circuit again, when the publicity stressed the interracial friendship.

But these liminal transgressive moments were restricted safely to childhood, for South African whites were always uncomfortably aware that boundaries of culture and race are easily permeable. Prevailing Christian morality taught that people were the children of God, but this did not mean that in adulthood they should mix equally. In *e'Lollipop*, for example, the black boy dies saving his friend at the end. To be fair, Pieterse says that he based the story on an incident in his own childhood, when a black boy was killed saving him from a runaway horse.

The sentimentality with which South African whites and their authors treated these friendships betrays the ultimate hypocrisy of white society at the time. The wording of the blurb for *Jamie*, "the boy's friendship *for*," rather than *with*, hints at the power relations in the friendship. Bennett portrays the boys conversing in *fanakalo*, "the bastardised English-Afrikaans-Xhosa mixture called kitchen-kaffir" (*Jamie*, 33), which Jamie is said to have learned in the kitchen and which was traditionally used in a master–servant relationship; Jamie refers to Kiewiet as a "picannin," and Kiewiet always addresses Jamie as "*Baas* Jamie" ("Master Jamie").

In both respects, Bennett is probably factually inaccurate; it is more likely that the boys would have spoken fluent Xhosa together, and Kiewiet's use of "*baas*" while they are still young does not ring true. Nevertheless, this is the way Bennett chose to depict their relationship, and it affirms that Jamie and Kiewiet are never equals, but only companions, whether Bennett intended it or not. The sentimental portrayal of equality between black and white children by Bennett's predecessors was showing cracks when he wrote this at the height of the apartheid era. Peter Davis's observation, in his study of black and white buddies in films about South Africa, applies equally to *Jamie*: the blacks are "throwbacks to the Faithful Servant persona whose function is to inflate the central white hero rather than...characters with an independent existence."[43]

Bennett's liberal enlightenment is patchy. He makes no attempt to explore Kiewiet's personality; the boy is a one-dimensional character, his single trait being that he is comically superstitious — another longstanding literary stereotype. Significantly, in the revised edition published by a Cape Town publisher in South Africa in 1990, when apartheid had almost disappeared, the references to "kitchen-kaffir," "picannin," "baas" and comic superstition were removed. Nothing could illustrate better how a novelist's portrayal of race relations is more dependent upon the time in which he is writing than the time of the fictional events.

Bennett makes one gesture toward political critique, when a neighbour refers to Xhosas as "kaffirs," which is an extremely offensive appellation:

"I wish he wouldn't say kaffirs, thought Jamie, father never did, not in front of them, anyway" (*Jamie*, 121). When the man calls Kiewiet a "little kaffir," "he spoke kindly, meaning no harm, but Jamie saw the flicker in the boy's eyes, before they became flat, opaque, servant's eyes again, and the white teeth flashed in the cheerful way expected of an African with whom a white man has condescended to joke" (*Jamie*, 122).

Four years later, Laurens van der Post made a white boy's moral indignation at the way white men treat Africans a theme in *The Hunter and the Whale*, but it would be another 20 years before authors for young adults regularly showed up adult racism through the eyes of young people.

As for the playmates theme, as found in *The South African Twins* and *Jamie*, it met its reversal in later years. In *Waiting for the Rain*, Sheila Gordon (1987) satirized the earlier acceptance of the status quo: young Frikkie asks his pal Tengo, "Will you be my boss-boy when this is my farm?" and they end up as enemies in the fight for liberation.[44] The white narrator of *Khetho* by Dennis Bailey (1994) returns from overseas to find himself in the same express academic school class as his childhood friend, the garden boy, Khethukutha, now a "township radical," who takes him under his wing and shows him the ropes at school. Their relationship develops into friendship between equals.[45] It is a typical story of the transitional period, showing teenagers struggling to adapt to social change.

The author of *Sharp Sharp, Zulu Dog* (2003), Anton Ferreira, was probably not aware that he was updating the playmates theme, because he appears to have been unaware of the literary tradition in which he was writing.[46] An awkwardly told and unconvincing story, it has the typical weaknesses (such as uncertainty over the focalizer) and employs many of the clichés of South African children's books, including the rain that comes at the end to break the drought and symbolize the resolution of the tensions in the story.

The action is in the present, and concerns childhood friends — a Zulu boy and the daughter of a white farmer whose property adjoins the tribal area where the boy lives. This is a reversal of the same-sex friendships of tradition. Not only do they persist in their friendship against the wishes of adults until, at last, after the boy saves her life, they win over their elders, but the white girl refuses to go away to a smart girls' school in Johannesburg and wins the battle to be allowed to stay on and attend the local mixed-race high school with her friend. Jubilantly, she publicly hugs him: "The embrace was so heartfelt, so natural, so…right!" (*Sharp Sharp*, 136). However, as Donnarae MacCann has pointed out, the paternalist plot resolution sees the white farmer offering the black family a life of dependency on his farm. Bailey's novel was still in thrall to the ideology of an earlier era.[47]

A long gap followed *Jamie*, during which well known writers for adults did not produce anything for younger readers. Then the distinguished South African man of letters Es'kia Mphahlele wrote a children's or young-adult novel, *Father Come Home* (1984),[48] and later a children's short story, "The Dream of Our Time" (1991).[49] Mphahlele, who spent many years in exile, including a spell as an academic in the U.S., returned to South Africa in his retirement, where he was honored as the doyen of the literary scene. Among his many works of fiction and nonfiction, some of them autobiographical, his account of his childhood, *Down Second Avenue* (1962), is internationally admired.[50] It is still in print and often prescribed for reading in schools.

Father Come Home is similar in style to another young adult novel written by an African academic, *The Silent People* by K.S. Bongela, published the year before (1983).[51] The illustrator of *The Silent People* was Ronnie Ndzombane, and the National Library's 2004 exhibition catalogue records it as "one of the first youth novels both written and illustrated by black South Africans."[52] It is overtly didactic, although billed on the cover as an "Exciting modern adventure for the young adults of Southern Africa." The story covers the life span of two Xhosa brothers from infancy to middle age, and teaches the lesson (spelled out in the preface) of what happens if people consider themselves too modern to respect their ancestors and participate in the prescribed rituals of thanks in times of prosperity.

Father Come Home has a similar tone of earnest purpose and also covers a long time span in an episodic narrative structure. It is heavily didactic and told at a deliberate pace, with dialogue in an archaic diction: "The ancestors are wise, son of my brother. Let him be the miser he wants to be, but I will not let him vomit his temper on my brother's son. The ancestors know, he has a good wife, he is more fortunate than he deserves, hear me tell you" (*Father*, 11). It is curious that Mphahlele was content to use this technique for conveying African speech that had been introduced by the earliest British colonial writers and that is still used by white writers such as Cicely van Straten (see Chapter 8).

An old man tells the story of his life, with a great deal of recounting and explanation of the historical and political events that shaped the lives of black people from 1913 onward, as well as digressions on ancient tribal history and traditions. The narrative argues that teachers should not adhere to what is in the text books (which were written by whites) but teach children African culture and mores. He gives, for example, technical details about praise names and reproduces the texts of praise songs. While not endorsing pre-Christian beliefs and practices such as prophecy and respect for ancestors, as Bongela had done, he argues that Christians should respect them. The lesson of the novel is that strong ties of kinship and friendship were what had helped black people survive their harrowing exploitation in the twentieth century.

Seen from the perspective of the twenty-first century, the book was a product of despair and paradox. Mphahlele had loved Western learning and literature since he was a young boy, and he had been helped in his career by prominent white mentors. But, in the early 1980s, there seemed no hope for his people and his country, which the civilization he had absorbed was betraying.

The book did not appeal to white readers and was not a success. Writing in 1996, the distinguished literary scholar Michael Chapman came to the defense of this kind of writing:

> What we need to be vigilant about from the outset is a still widespread tendency in literary study to dismiss as "not fully achieved" those stories and novels that do not comply with the formal realist criteria.... We might recognise, instead, that an oral "residue" could manifest itself to effect in strong story lines, episodic plots, recurrence, copious repetitions, aggregative, additive thought, and closeness to the "life world" that preserves several traditional values.... The [oral] style should feature, certainly, in the articulation of an aesthetic that hopes to understand literature as having the stamp of "African experience."
>
> (*Chapman,* 48)

The mood of the country, and Mphahlele himself, had changed by the time he wrote "The Dream of Our Time" in 1991, and the tone of his writing is accordingly incisive. The adult narrator describes an experience he had as a boy. The dialogue is modern and amusing: "You'll go home with a bruise and she'll come at you with a stinging tongue because you tried to break your neck — and didn't.... She'll chase after you to do it for you! ("Dream," 86, original ellipsis). He wryly admits he was a "country bumpkin," which shows a different view of country roots to that of the earlier book. He recounts that he had a vision as a child of "the beauty of the land but also its ugliness — an ugliness that sours our lives as well as that of the people who go out of their way to hurt us" ("Dream," 90). His vision gave him the power to believe in himself and envisage a new hope for the country, a power that all his people needed.

Mphahlele's mantle fell on a younger professor of English, Njabulo Ndebele, who also returned from exile, but in time to build a distinguished career culminating in appointment as Vice-Chancellor of the University of Cape Town. Both of them have been awarded the Gold Medal of the English Academy of Southern Africa. Ndebele's important works include a volume of essays, *Rediscovery of the Ordinary: Essays on South African Literature and Culture* (1991), and *Fools and Other Stories* (1983), which won the Noma Award for Publishing in Africa. *Bonolo and the Peach Tree* (1992) is an intriguing and original book-length fable for children about a boy who lives in a village in Lesotho.[53] He spends his childhood dreaming, almost in a trance, never actually doing anything, but telling people what he has seen in descriptions of great beauty. He sits under a peach tree, but eventually the tree almost dies because he has never tended it, and he falls into a fever. Recovering, he realizes that he must actually be productive; "that the dreams in his head would never add anything if they did not tell his hands to make the world beautiful, and more beautiful, and more beautiful" (*Bonolo*, 79). He cares for his tree, but, with the encouragement of the people of the village, he never stops telling stories, urging them "to ever know and create, to make life beautiful" (*Bonolo*, 82). The National Library's 2004 exhibition catalog described *Bonolo and the Peach Tree* as a book about the "power of the story," and that, in fact, is the title that the Library gave to the exhibition: *Amandla eBali: The Power of the Story.*

3

ECOLOGY

The natural environment and wildlife have provided the backdrop to most South African children's literature and have often been its focus. Traditional oral literature in the indigenous languages is rich in this subject matter; as for written literature, the very first children's poem set in South Africa was a protest, by the English writer Reverend Isaac Taylor, at the hunting of ostriches.[1] The interest continues unabated.

English-language authors' attitudes toward nature, and their didactic motives in writing about it, have varied. Much of what they have produced — which presumably was acceptable to the public at the time of publication — is repugnant to the modern reader. Studies in ecological literary criticism and environmental history contextualize this writing, suggesting how it can be understood, appreciated and evaluated.

Defining "ecologically-oriented criticism," Dan Wylie explains that it "pursues some satisfactory triangulation of the dynamics of: a) observed social, scientific, and environmental contexts; b) a stylistically or aesthetically based criticism of literary works being produced within those contexts; and c) an ethical standpoint which is neither narrowly sectarian and masking of the complexities of the works themselves, nor disengaged from the real-world effects of the works."[2]

This model is an appropriate guide to criticism of children's literature featuring the environment. The first of Wylie's points covers the work of historians, necessary for placing children's books in their social context. Second, children's literature should be subjected to stylistic and aesthetic criticism like any other literature. Third, criticism of children's literature must take an ethical standpoint because the literature is intended for young unformed readers, and it has, at least in part, a didactic intention, which is marked in the case of books about the environment.

In nineteenth-century children's books set in South Africa, both fiction and nonfiction, hunting featured prominently. Historical studies such as those of John MacKenzie,[3] and environmental criticism, for example by Stephen Gray,[4] have given considerable attention to hunting and the construction of "nature" that it reflects. The early adventure stories embodied colonial and imperialistic assumptions of power and the right to strip colonized lands of their natural assets. They made much of wild animals, which they showed being hunted for sport, trophies, scientific collections, food or the commercial value of their tusks, hides and feathers. Initially, writers such as Thomas Mayne Reid portrayed hunters killing predators for trophies or the thrill of the chase and the danger involved; but as the twentieth century advanced, writers such as Percy FitzPatrick and Victor Pohl put more emphasis on other motives. For example, they suggested that visiting hunters killed predators to protect local residents, or because the predators were depleting the supply of antelope that the hunters wanted to shoot for the pot.

Writers admired, feared or despised animals, and projected their conception of human society onto them by giving them human qualities. Predators, for example, were stamped as evil and ruthless. This kind of anthropomorphism continued well into the twentieth century in the books of Victor Pohl, and in fact, is still common today in nonfiction children's books on dinosaurs, which sort them into goodies and baddies.[5]

Hunting featured progressively less in children's books in the twentieth century, except in historical novels and a few anachronistic books such as Pohl's. Hunting for commercial gain now featured in the form of whale hunting and the slaughter of seal cubs to protect fishing resources. In *The Hunter and the Whale* (1967), Laurens van der Post used whaling allegorically and as a test of character for boys, but never questioned its ethics.[6] From his novel there was a leap of only 21 years to *When Whales Go Free* by Dianne Hofmeyr[7] and *Song of the Surf* by Dale Kenmuir,[8] both published in 1988, which feature angst-ridden boys who reject their fathers' role in these traditional harvestings. This rejection is central to their strained relations with their fathers, while the readers are swayed to disapprove of the slaughter because the boys are portrayed sympathetically. Nowadays, although hunting for sport and trophies continues to be a popular pastime for the white hunting fraternity and wealthy overseas hunters, publicly it is hardly mentioned — the media carry only hostile coverage of scandals such as "canned" lion hunting — and it does not feature in children's books. No author or publisher for children would want to appear so politically incorrect as to endorse it.

In nineteenth-century children's fiction some of the boys and men engage in collecting specimens in the name of science, which was indeed a common reason for early travelers to penetrate the interior. Much of the time their activities could not be distinguished from hunting, because collecting entailed wholesale shooting of wild creatures as well as the more effete picking of plants. Novelists also included scientific information on natural history in the course of their narratives, giving their fiction some didactic respectability. Whether their young readers accepted these digressions, which added to the length of the already long books, or whether they just skipped them, is impossible to tell; but twentieth-century readers had to be treated differently, and such longueurs disappeared except in the occasional anachronistic book such as Campbell's *The Mamba's Precipice.*[9]

A typical writer who was a traveler, hunter and collector of information about geography, animals and people was W.H. Bryden, who came to South Africa in 1876 and was still writing for children in the next century. A prolific author of travel books, history and fiction, he produced a handsome reference book for children, *Animals of Africa* (1900), which was the first of its kind, and later an adventure story, *The Gold Kloof* (1907).[10] Bryden was deeply involved in the imperial enterprise, assisting the British authorities in mapping and planning administration, and participating in drafting legislation on the control of hunting and the creation of game reserves in the colonies.

After Bryden, South African writers continued to publish books on natural history for children, such as *Elementary Lessons in Systematic Botany, Based on Familiar Species of South African Fauna,* by Harriet Bolus (1919),[11] *A Bird-book for South African Children*, with notes by Dorothy Norman and verses by J.Y. Gibson (191-),[12] and *The Monkeyfolk of South Africa*, by Frederick Fitzsimons (2nd edition, 1924).[13]

Books for little children that taught lessons about natural history often enlisted fantasy and verse. In the most ambitious, *The Strange Adventures of John Harmer* (1928), sometimes published in three separate volumes, Dr. S.H. Skaife reduces a boy to the size of the insects, birds and fish with which he has salutary encounters, teaching him respect for nature.[14] Dr. James MacKay, in *Some South African Insects, Described in Rhyme with Nature Notes from a Southern Clime* (1915),[15] covered an extraordinary variety of creatures, many very small, such as "psychids and caddis worms," which is a change from the limited range of creatures in contemporary talking-animal fantasies, though the resemblance otherwise is strong. In this readable and entertaining book, the creatures speak in comic verse, and this is the style of his notes: "Fancy not having a mouth! Just think how you would feel if you had only two little slits on both sides of your jaws, instead of a proper mouth. I can imagine you being rather cross at not being able to take a nice bit of chocolate, or a tasty helping of pudding at dinner, and chew it like our brothers and sisters" (*Insects*, 22). Many years later, Cecil Shirley (1943) told stories in which he anthropomorphized the "wee people" of the veld such as porcupines, "weasels" (he apparently used incorrect terminology) and butterflies.[16] Like MacKay, he supported the stories with notes.

A didactic novel about natural history for older children, *Umhlanga, A Story of the Coastal Bush of Natal* by Dorothy Wager, published in Durban in 1946, shows how anachronistic South African writers could be and why their books were so soon forgotten.[17] The hoary nineteenth-century animal favorites recur: a picture of a secretary bird on the title page, a whole chapter headed "A Master of Camouflage" about a trap-door spider, and a picture of a dung beetle, which provided intertextual reference to *Jock of the Bushveld*, the first edition of which famously showed the beetle pushing a ball of dung with its forelegs instead of its hindlegs. In a hackneyed device, twins from America dutifully ask questions that the scientist answers in tedious detail or by referring them to reference books: "'The mechanism,' his father admitted, 'is most ingenious. Nature has evolved an intricate process...microscopic bladder....' 'Here, you take Leonard Gill's book. His is easier for beginners because there aren't as many illustrations in it as in Austin Roberts'" (*Umhlanga*, 28, 95). Contrasted with the pedantic father, the children's dialogue has all the exclamation marks and jolly slang of other books of the period. It ends, "'Oh Tod,' he called excitedly, 'come and see what I've spotted!'" (*Umhlanga*, 148).

By the time South African children's writers emerged at the end of the nineteenth century, the heyday of imperialist writing about adventures in wildest Africa was over and the country had been domesticated, divided up into farms. Literary historians such as Egoff and Saltman and Niall have remarked on how Canadian and Australian children's literature has depicted nature as something apart from human society: in Canada, wildest nature was a nurturer of the few humans who ventured there, while in Australia, untamed nature was regarded as terrifyingly dangerous. South Africa, on the other hand, has contributed a large corpus of children's literature in which farms and nature reserves form liminal zones in which, or by means of which, humans interact with nature.

In *The Chronicles of Peach Tree Farm*, by Nellie Fincher, one of the girls describes how their father conducts "the spruit [stream] that I call a Dutch ditch" into a pipe, from where it is run into furrows in the garden: "The spruit became English when it entered our farm."[18] The girls play out colonization in miniature when they build and play with their little Peach Tree Farm, while their own lives on the farm that is their home also show how the wilderness is tamed.

Three dramatic stories of the mid-twentieth century played on the liminality of farms as the borderline between civilization and the last traces of the old untamed wilderness, which is symbolized by wild animals that irrupt into farms. These are the stories, described in Chapter 2, that received international recognition: *Jamie,* by Jack Bennett,[19] in which Jamie shoots a buffalo that has crossed into their farm from a nature reserve and killed his father, "The Claws of the Cat" by Stuart Cloete,[20] in which Japie shoots a lynx that is killing their livestock, and *A Deadly Presence* by Hjalmar Thesen,[21] in which a young conservation scientist, Cliff Turner, traps a leopard that has invaded farmlands from mountainous state land where it would have been protected.

The buffalo and the lynx provide the boys with desperate tests of character and initiation into manhood, of a degree almost never encountered in urban life; while the black leopard, which is terrorizing Afrikaans farmers and their labourers, forces Cliff to confront both his fear of a black wild creature and his arrogant colonial inheritance as a member of the English-speaking former ruling class that assumes he has a right to decide that the leopard should not die.

Bennett, Cloete and Thesen modernized colonial stories in two respects. First, the characters are no longer Britishers, out to plunder the land before returning home, but South Africans — all three writers stress the characters' centuries-old settler ancestry. Bennett's and Cloete's boys are fighting to protect their patrimony; Thesen's scientist has reached the stage when he has to interrogate his.

Second, the action takes place on farms. Ostensibly, the whole country, except for game reserves, had by now been tamed by settlement and agriculture; the average children's story was set on a farm of marked domesticity. The wild animals that intrude upon the farms are all the more of a horror than in the days when they roamed everywhere, because they are unexpected and out of place.

Many postcolonial critics (for example, Patrick Brantlinger) have pointed out how whites feared Africa as a place of darkness.[22] This is easy to demonstrate from nineteenth-century boys' adventure stories, but the traces of the English-speakers' half-fearful fascination with the mysterious lingered until the mid-twentieth century. The eminent novelist and intellectual Sarah Gertrude Millin wrote in her study *The South Africans* (1926): "And then, underneath all this fierce brightness, also its darkness, the menace and mystery of the land...." [23] Hints of the mysterious and supernatural were fundamental to the immensely popular books about the country by Lawrence Green, T.V. Bulpin, Lyall Watson and Credo Mutwa. Jan Juta wrote in his collection of sketches and children's stories, *Look Out for the Ostriches* (1949), about "the mystery of Africa, the black, ancient mystery that has so far baffled man's search," and even remarked that the Kruger National Park "has a remote, mysterious quality about it."[24] The stories by Bennett, Cloete and Thesen suggest that, for white people, atavistic fears of darkest Africa were still uncomfortably close to the surface. But they represented the last gasp of this colonial theme; later children's writers no longer entertained it because no more menacing wild animals remained lurking on the fringes of cultivation.

These three writers pursue, as Malvern van Wyk Smith has said of Laurens van der Post's novels, quoting from A *Story Like the Wind*, "quests for origins and authenticity in the African wilds as a cure for the *malaise* of an over-intellectualized and exploitive western civilization: 'the magic which life in primitive Africa...possessed before we arrived from Europe to spoil it.'" This, he observes, "has proven a popular recipe with a vicarious readership both in South Africa and abroad, exploited by writers from Stuart Cloete...to Wilbur Smith."[25] Jamie and Japie find manhood, and Cliff finds absolution, through a primal struggle that is unknown to city boys.

Now that the African wilds had been tamed, farming could provide the rural integrity missing in towns and cities. Young white readers could be sent back in literature to their putative roots to learn simple values. Cliff, in *A Deadly Presence*, meditates,

> The mountains looming blue in the background and the forest beneath were nothing more than a scenic backdrop to the beach life and the tinkling of ice in glasses and the swaying of dancers. The gregariousness of human occupation and its pursuit of comfort did not permit much interest in the land or the life of the land, especially if it were in any way uncomfortable: and the forest was uncomfortable; so were the mountains except as scenery and so basically were the poorer whites on their smallholdings and the even poorer Coloured people."
>
> (*Deadly Presence*, 7)

Children's literature until the 1950s showed none of the insecurity that crept into adult fiction and nonfiction about farming — what Gray has called "the uneasy feeling of the white man's failure to belong to the land" (Gray, 158). Leonard Flemming's panegyrics to the veld such as *The Call of the Veld* were immensely popular, but they did merge into rueful humour about his incompetence as a farmer in *A Fool on the Veld* and *More Veld Foolery*. The cover of *Fool on the Veld*, published in Cape Town, visually represents the meeting of eurocentred culture and the veld: a medieval court jester is seated above a panel containing a picture of the radiating sun that is almost identical in size and shape to its exact contemporary, the vignette of the sunburst at the bottom of the Juta's Juvenile Library title page frame.[26] Flemming's mild satire struck a chord with English-speakers: he launched a minor South African genre of wry memoirs by rookie farmers such as *Two Innocents on a Natal Farm* by Walter Hewetson (1928), *How We Went Farming* by Helen M. Collins (1931), *Bushveld, Bananas and Bounty* by Kay Cowin (1954), and *Futility Farm* by Elizabeth Jonsson (1957).

The popular magazine for adult readers in those days was *The Outspan*, which, in spite of its rustic antiquated title, was enjoyed by not a few town dwellers. Until the 1960s, the methods of modern scientific agriculture were of widespread interest in white society, and children were expected to learn about them. Soil conservation featured in school syllabuses and Boy Scout tests, and a youth organization, the Land Service Movement, was devoted to it. In *Children of Mount Imperani* by Baffie Coetzee (1987), members of a school Land Service Club work to protect a nest of black eagles.[27]

In the *South African Boys Twenty-story Annual* of 1945 (published by Knox, on its wartime paper), among all the exciting stories of Scouts, footballers, cricketers, sinister Chinamen, wartime air aces and a science fiction flying machine, appeared a stern article headed "Save our Soil," berating the "heedless farmer," the consumer, "Mrs Townswoman" and the government for selfishness and neglect. "Are we going to determine to grow up in the service of our country, to put back into life more than we take from it and teach our children to do likewise?" Norman Herd demanded.[28]

Another book of the period, showing the same concern for the future of the country after the war and the part that children had to play, was *The Veld and the Future: A Book on Soil Erosion for South Africans* by Edward Roux (1946), which announced in the Preface, "This little book...has been written for the use of school children, farmers and townsmen."[29] The following year saw the publication of *South African Bilingual Verse* (1947) by B. Schwartz, which has poems called "The Burn," about sugar cane farming, and "Soil Erosion," which opens,

I really cannot stand
This leprosy of my lovely land![30]

Stories and poems dwelt on the ravages of droughts and veld fires, and farm stories often incidentally carried information on soil conservation and sound farming methods, following the cycle of the seasons. A typical one is *From Beacon to Beacon* by William Herbst (1959), in which, among chapters devoted to the young protagonist's various little adventures such as a gymkhana, there is one called "The Living Earth," which opens with background information on the cultivation of lucerne and rye.[31]

Like *Umhlanga* by Dorothy Wager, a full-length story by George Klerck, *At the Foot of the Koppie* (1929), is filled with boring socratic dialogue, this time between a brother and sister who live on a farm and their tutor, a scientific expert.[32] They are extraordinarily ignorant, but very obedient, and make good listeners as he expounds on an enormous range of agricultural topics such as the harm caused by burning veld, how to fight drought through planting drought-resistant plants, and the life-cycle of the sheep scab. One would think their father and neighbors had never given a thought to their farming, considering how he has to teach them as well why prickly pear is a pest and how to fight locusts, stalk borer and anthrax. He demonstrates that the father was wrong in punishing the boy for boring holes in the trunks of fig trees, because the culprit is a actually a beetle. One can only say, the author did warn readers in his foreword, "To show both old and young the rewards of good farming is the purpose of this book." His glossary of Afrikaans words at the end (*donga, klompies, sloot, riems,* and so on) shows that in 1929 it was quite possible to write Afrikaans correctly, which is an indictment of the cavalier approach of English children's writers to the language for so many years.

Klerck explicitly makes good farming a patriotic virtue. Invoking the children's Voortrekker ancestors who established the farm, he declares that should they learn their lessons about farming, "they gave promise of being worthy descendants of those hardy people who saw the dawn of a white race in their new southern country" (*Koppie,* 7). He regards their father as "a true patriot" (*Koppie,* 91) because he is a wise farmer. Farming, in all these twentieth-century books, is still a moral allegory for bringing order to the African landscape and making it fruitful — a theme that had run through the literature of the imperial era from *Hardy and Hunter* by Harriet Ward (1859) to *Prester John* by John Buchan (1910).

Contrary to the farming concerns of her contemporaries, Fay King wrote *Friends of the Bushveld* (1954), a story about a quixotic white family who turn their farm near the Kruger National Park into a nature reserve.[33] When they started, the black people, except for wise old Sezulu, thought they were mad to conserve wild animals; and "in the eyes of their [white] neighbours the le Rouxs were not only mad, but dangerous" (*Friends*, 17). The attempt fails, as they cannot make a living out of it, but to give the story a happy ending, they are saved from ruin by the discovery of gold treasure in a cave.

As the last suitable land for farming was allocated to whites in the early twentieth century and the prospect of the extinction of wildlife loomed, various campaigns were launched to create nature reserves. Jane Carruthers, historian of South African nature reserves, has shown how they were first mooted by wealthy English-speaking whites for the preservation of game for hunting purposes.[34]

In *Jamie*, the escape of the buffalo from a neighboring nature reserve fills the chief ranger of the reserve with mixed feelings of regret and determination to continue with conservation. This is of such concern to Bennett that he awkwardly switches from Jamie to the ranger as the focalizer for a while.

Similarly, Thesen makes the dilemma of his conservator protagonist a central concern of *A Deadly Presence*. As a scientist, Cliff wants the leopard to survive, although it has become a man-eater that threatens farmers' lives and livelihood — by 1982, the sensibilities of the environmental lobby would not tolerate seeing it killed. But he must face the guilt that the farmers instill in him for this perverse morality and for being a descendant of the white elite who created nature reserves for their own pleasure, regardless of the interests of neighboring people. As a "fourth-generation English-speaking South African,...he was acutely aware that he was a member of the minority of a white minority, the now-impotent English speakers whose forefathers had engineered much of the wealth of the country and who once had lorded it over all their fellow countrymen, including the Afrikaans-speaking whites" (*Deadly Presence*, 21).

In an act of abjection, he places himself as the living bait in a trap. Abjection, says Julia Kristeva, is caused by a loathsome act that "disturbs identity, system, order."[35] Only by performing this unnatural act can Cliff rectify the abnormality that has developed in human beings' relations with nature. Luckily for him, he survives when the leopard is captured.

These novels reflect the awkward shift that was taking place to modern concepts of conservation; government authorities could no longer create and manage "game reserves" exclusively for wealthy whites, but had to move to the wider *conservation* of certain mammals (initially excluding predators). This was extended in the 1960s to the conservation of entire ecological zones. Later still, parks authorities realized that they had to accept social responsibility toward surrounding communities as well. To begin with, they took only white communities into account; consideration for black communities would take another half century (Carruthers, 1995). The preservation of animals for hunting shifted into private hands, and in the twenty-first century is big business for game farmers, while conservation has become the prevailing public ethic. Children's literature has followed this chronology.

After the Kruger National Park was established in 1926, game reserves became places that could keep alive for whites the ancestral memories of Africa as a place teeming with game. Children's stories set in the Park followed, featuring either animals (usually anthropomorphized in the usual way), or visiting children. By 1985, when K. Argyle wrote a set of aetiological stories about animals, the title had to be *Stories from the Game Reserve*, because where else did wild animals live?[36]

In analyzing the history of the establishment of South African game reserves, South African scholars have come to the same conclusion as the environmental historian John MacKenzie, that "constructions of nature inevitably have a national or racial component" (MacKenzie 1997, 226). Carruthers argues that the circumstances leading to the establishment of the Kruger National Park in 1926 included "the nascent rise of Afrikaner nationalism, the consolidation of a Voortrekker mythology and the search for a unified white South African national identity. The new national park reinvigorated the exclusion of Africans.... [It was] a symbol of cultural unity concentrated around a particular South African asset: wildlife" (Carruthers 1993, 6, 8).

Eco-philosophy is inextricably linked to eco-politics. Game reserves developed another significant function in the 1920s and 1930s, according to David Bunn.[37] In this era, when the Kruger National Park was developed, "the idea of compensatory enclaved and conserved natural domains played a key role in the discourse of modernity." He demonstrates "the emergence of such notions of enclaved, 'primitive' space — the space of the "Reserve" as an imaginary repository of value forms lost in the process of modernization" (Bunn, 38). Reserves were artificial spaces where white people could go to escape temporarily from urban life and, incidentally, ignore the system of labor reserves and migratory labor, which is what the rest of the rural countryside was used for and on which the economy was based.

According to Bunn, this use of the bushveld found its fullest expression after the Second World War in the development of private reserves such as one adjacent to the Kruger National Park that was owned by a Natal sugar magnate, where the owners maintained the notion of parks as spaces reserved for the privileged few, though no longer hunting preserves. The pristine bush provided an escape from the devastated Natal landscape of the canelands. He describes how, in the peculiar lifestyle of these isolated reserves, blacks were restored to the older role of "picturesque labour," and the white men and their senior black staff enjoyed a familiar relationship typical of officers and their sirdars under the British raj.

A paternalist hierarchy of this sort was the unremarked backdrop to most farm stories until the 1960s. The trope of the loyal black retainer who plays a fatherly role toward the young white protagonist goes right back to the earliest boys' adventure stories set in Africa in the nineteenth century, such as *Hunting the Lions* by R.M. Ballantyne (1873) and *Hendricks the Hunter* by W.H.G. Kingston (1884).

Nevertheless, while most South African children's books until the 1960s simply reflected the prejudices of their time, it is possible to find one or two authors at any time who have taken a principled opposite stand. *David Goes to Zululand* by K. Marshall (1935) typically features a Zulu man, Fagazi Boutelezi, who serves as mentor to the white boy David.[38] David behaves respectfully toward his senior, for example by addressing him correctly. In fact, Marshall's peritext makes a point of correct naming: "'Fagazi Boutelezi' is as much the real name of my hunter friend as 'Begamuze' is the name of the river on whose banks he lives like a lord" (*David*, ix). The book condemns the way white hunters treat Boutelezi. "You, white child, have a full understanding, and at once feel at peace with a black man when you speak to him," he tells David, as a preface to asking David not to shame him by paying any attention when he has to play the obsequious servant to the hunters (*David*, 157).

Laurens van der Post's *The Hunter and the Whale* parallels Marshall's novel in this regard, and is a fictional illustration of Bunn's account of the English elite of Natal. Van der Post makes much of a 14-year-old white boy's bond with Zulus and his ability to speak their language. Like David, he respectfully addresses them by their own names, despising the custom of whites who give them European names. A wealthy Natal businessman objects to his consorting with "servants" in their quarters. The narrator (the boy once he has grown up) remarks how the magnate dresses his butler in an elaborate uniform while insisting that he should remain barefoot — a typical practice of white employers, he says, which is intended to symbolize their servants' black savagery and enforce their humility in the presence of whites.

Notwithstanding these instances of dissent, the social hierarchy of game reserves has continued to feature in children's books. Dale

Kenmuir, in his game ranger stories published in the 1980s and 1990s, still portrayed black retainers steeped in tradition as to how they are expected to behave toward their employers and their employers' children. In *The Catch* (1993) (narrated by the son of a man who runs a fishing camp at Lake Kariba), he conveys through the gradations in the way the elderly man Hlube Zulu addresses his employer's teenage son the subtleties of degrees of familiarity in their relationship:

"This do, Umfaan [boy]?" he asked.
"Don't 'Umfaan' me," I groused. "I'm a Madoda [man] now."
"Maybe, maybe," the old cook grunted as he carried on with the dinner preparations. "We will see."[39]

Later, the tone changes from affectionate teasing to seriousness: "The old man scratched his grizzled beard and shook his head sadly. 'Nkosana [young sir],' he said, and I knew he was in a serious mood, otherwise he'd have called me Paul" (*Catch*, 34).

The dilemma for a literary critic, or an adult discussing the book with children, is how to deal with such a text, because Kenmuir's writing is delicate and sensitive but the relationship it portrays is obnoxious to postcolonial sensibilities. It is easier to take a principled stand over a case cited by Julia Martin.[40] She has pointed out that in *Tikki's Wildlife Adventure* by David Phiri, published as recently as 1995 and endorsed by the Wildlife Society,[41] the fact that a black child, the son of a game scout, who grows up in a game reserve, does not go to school is unmarked, as though it is a matter of course. This silence, she argues, "naturalizes the hierarchic, authoritarian (racist?) relations between white warden and black game scout and family" (Martin, 12).

The silent assumption in Phiri's book that black rural children do not go to school is refuted in *Thoko* by Brenda Munitich, also published in 1995, in which the author writes convincingly and authentically about the Zulu people whom she knows well.[42] A girl from a poor rural family works on a sugarcane farm in the seasonal labor system of KwaZulu-Natal that continues to this day. Her whole focus, and that of the novel, is on how she can raise the money to get to school. This fictional account is corroborated by the Zulu boy Mboma Dladla in his autobiography, *The Story of Mboma*.[43] Set in the same remote region, it tells of the Zulu people who live on white farms where they provide seasonal labor, of the bloody "faction fights" between rival Zulu clans and of his chronic malnutrition, through all of which he struggles to obtain an education.

Julia Martin identified a cluster of outmoded values in South African children's literature and drama featuring modern nature conservation.[44] She agrees with writers on eco-philosophy since the 1960s who have demonstrated "the role of mainstream Judaeo-Christianity in promoting ways of seeing 'God', 'man' and 'nature' that have been used to justify environmental abuse...with a simultaneous complicity in the abuses of colonialism, imperialism and phallocentricism." She found traces of this in some plays and books, and shows how such values are perpetuated through simple binarisms. She does concede, however, that "in other works the Judaeo-Christian certainties are explicitly questioned" (Martin, 17).

Martin observes that the old image of game rangers as macho paramilitary fighters is perpetuated in the stories of Dale Kenmuir, of which *Sing of Black Gold* (1991) is an example.[45] Her criticism is near the bone. Peter Slingsby, a prominent environmentalist and children's book author, observed in the South African children's literature magazine *Bookchat* in 1991 that "environmental education is, thankfully, trying to shrug off its macho short-pants-and-green-epaulettes-in-the-bush image."[46] Kenmuir, a qualified and experienced nature conservator, responded, "I was in the game department in Rhodesia/Zimbabwe for years, and never came across anyone fitting the image Peter Slingsby paints. In fact, these types were scorned in National Parks."[47] The solution to this debate is not to generalize. His heroes, such as Tom of *The Tusks and the Talisman* (1987), do perform manly deeds, but they are in certain respects sensitive people.[48]

While early conservation protected game for the hunting or recreational viewing of whites, modern environmentalism, on the other hand, is bound up with social justice. As Martin points out, nature conservators are attempting to identify and acknowledge the African roots of conservation, and they work with displaced and neighbouring African communities. She singles out for praise fiction such as Marguerite Poland's *Shadow of the Wild Hare* (1986),[49] Mazisi Kunene's poetry (1982),[50] the African storytelling of Zanendaba Storytellers, and theater such as that of Nicholas Ellenbogen's Theatre for Africa, which draw on traditional beliefs to expound a philosophy of harmony between humans and nature.

Donnarae MacCann and Yulisa Amadu Maddy, in *Apartheid and Racism in South African Children's Literature, 1985-1995* (2001),[51] take the opposite point of view, attacking white authors for presuming to interpret African beliefs. Referring to "the strong element of romanticism that appeals to conservation-minded white readers and to children," they claim, "The black population knows that such works are often a biased white project and that 'ecstatic communion' with the animal world can be a seductive cover-up for white supremacist sermons" (MacCann and Maddy, 96). They argue that in *Witch Woman on* the Hogsback by Carolyn Parker (1987)[52] and *Shadow of the Wild Hare* by Marguerite Poland, "Africans are seen to need Westerners to show them the conservation path": this is "storytelling that posits the white child as the 'Great White Environmentalist' (supplanting the earlier 'Great White Hunter')" (MacCann and Maddy 2001, 94, 95).

MacCann and Maddy would have been justified in making this assertion about Fay King's *Friends of the Bushveld*, in which the local African people, with the exception of one, regard the le Rouxs as mad for trying to conserve wild animals. King's books are steeped in the patronizing racial attitudes of whites in the 1950s. However, a close reading of Parker and Poland would show how far white writers had come since then. For them, white children have to learn the true meaning of conservation from black people. As with so much of the criticism of MacCann and Maddy, it is difficult to recognize the books in their critique of them.[53]

In *Jamie,* by Jack Bennett, a surprising turn occurs in Jamie's attitude toward nature after his father has been killed by the buffalo. In the agonizing wait alone next to his father's body, he has to come to terms with the relationship between humans and the creatures of the bush, and it is not the science of the conservation officer from the neighboring nature reserve that comforts him, but the indigenous knowledge of his friend Kiewiet and the other Xhosa people he knows:

> He decided to keep his mind occupied by repeating the Xhosa he had learned with Kiewiet. The little bat there is *Uluwane,* and those big moths with markings like a skull on their backs are *Ivivingana,* the death's head moth. And the baboons barking there in the krantz are *Imfene,* and their little brothers the monkeys are known as *Inkowu.* ...He rolled the soft melodious Xhosa names off his tongue and felt, for the very first time, an affinity with the bush. No longer the affinity he had felt as a boy with an air-gun, but the real affinity, something which brought tears to his eyes, and made his throat go tight. And the swift-jumping duiker is *Impunzi,* and the bushbuck is *Inyati* and then it all came back to him with the name, and he whispered *Inyati* over and over again and the dam burst within him so that the hare bounded away in sudden fright.
>
> (*Jamie,* 85)

Patricia Pinnock drew on African tradition in another way to produce an outstanding modern book with an environmental message. *The King who Loved Birds* (1992) is a picture book in landscape format told in the style of an African folktale, illustrated by Keith van Winkel.[54] (See Figure 4.) His colorful dramatic pictures accurately portray

4 Illustration by Keith van Winkel from *The King who Loved Birds* by Patricia Schonstein Pinnock

various wild birds. An eyecatching feature is the modern appearance of the characters — the handsome young King in denim shorts, hiking boots, a Xhosa top and Xhosa jewelry, and the Wise Woman, a young woman who combines traditional Xhosa dress with modern, eco-friendly accoutrements. Each of the birds the King watches has its call: the fish eagles call, "Wee-ah, hyo, hyo, hyo." When drought hits his country, he cages all the birds to feed them, but they stop singing, the animals and people fall silent, and the land dies. He sends for the Wise Woman, who tells him to free them, and the earth is revived. In this book, there is no split between ancient African wisdom and the work of modern environmentalists. Four reference books are listed at the end and a glossary gives some chatty explanations: "Do you know what a euphorbia tree is? It belongs to a huge family of 'milky' plants...." Pinnock published it through her own press. The note that she places at the front is justified: "African Sun Press was established to teach children literacy through ecology. Its books encourage children of all cultures in Africa to care for the earth and each other" (*King*, n.p.)

Since the 1960s, many books for children and young teenagers have made modern ecological concerns the focus of the plots. The long tradition, in both indigenous folktales and stories by white writers, of anthropomorphizing flowers, birds, insects and animals (especially small creatures) has ensured that in modern children's books the emphasis is not so much on the "flagship animals" — the "Big Five" and other large mammals, which, except for the monkey and snake, were the only ones to feature in the 1920s Juta title page frame — as on the worth of all fauna and flora. Stories of children versus crooks have them battling white, not black, poachers, who poach for money — their target more likely nowadays to be crayfish (*Who's Afraid of Spiders?* by Helen Brain, 1997)[55] than elephants (*The Tusks and the Talisman* by Dale Kenmuir) — and who steal protected plants (*The Secret of Big Toe Mountain* by Klaus Kühne, 1987;[56] *The Poacher of Hidden Valley* by Alexander Prettejohn, 1986).[57] Children tackle officialdom that threatens areas of natural importance (*Kobie and the Military Road* by Peter Younghusband, 1987;[58] *Remember the Whales* by Lawrence Bransby, 1991)[59] and corporations that dump toxic waste (*Cassandra's Quest* by K.H. Briner, 2000).[60] Fantasy stories such as *Warrior of Wilderness* by Elana Bregin (1989)[61] have children fighting forces of evil that threaten the environment. The potential that conflict offers for a good plot about conservation is too good to miss; but other approaches can also be found. Pieter Pieterse is a sensitive writer who shows in *The Misty Mountain* (1985) that ecological integrity may be too complicated to break down into a simple polarity of protection as good and killing as bad.[62]

The insistence, in folktales and their imitations, on harmony in nature and between humans and nature, has led to stories pointing simple lessons about littering (*The Earth Must Be Free* by Pieter Grobbelaar, 1984),[63] chopping down trees (*The Boy and the Tree* by Vivienne Brown, 1989)[64] and similar behavior. Stories featuring the disappearance of the San and the Khoi people (*The Old Man of the Mountain* by Ursula McAdorey 1992;[65] *The Joining*, 1996, and *Jedro's Bane*, 2002, by Peter Slingsby)[66] not only portray them as natural environmentalists but draw lessons about genocide.

Wylie's model for ecologically oriented criticism has proved to be helpful in providing an approach to children's books that deal with nature and the environment. First, we can see them in historical and social context; they are the product of, and reflect, trends in attitudes to the environment and in the relationship between South Africans and nature. If by chance a young reader should come across old books today, they should provide that reader with an insight into how far South African society has come since they were written.

Second, conceptions of the environment provide a focus for analysis and appreciation of the books. Identifying the environment as a theme has enabled critics to single out and fruitfully compare certain stories, poems, plays and picture books.

Third, in evaluating the ethics of these works, readers can usefully follow Wylie's endorsement of Wayne Booth's stand in his classic work, *The Company We Keep* (1988).[67] Booth explores the moral dilemma faced by the reader of literature of a previous era that embodies values different from those of the present. He rejects the "plea for historical relativism" (Booth, 410), maintaining that readers cannot absolve themselves from taking an ethical stance on the content of old fiction: "I have a positive *obligation* to an implied author, whose creator is long since dead" (Booth, 165). To argue that modern readers must tolerate something because it was "widely accepted" at the time of writing is to argue that if it were widely accepted today they should necessarily assent to it (Booth, 412); to argue that because something was written long ago they need not engage with it is simply to let the writer off the hook (Booth, 410).

Stories that uncritically portrayed whites as exercising a self-proclaimed exclusive right to slaughter animals for fun or to claim land for reserves, or connived at maintaining the racial and political status quo regarding the use of natural resources, deservedly invite our disapproval today. In the same way, contemporary authors should be judged on their treatment of sensitive social issues such as the role that black people and their beliefs might play in modern approaches to ecology and conservation, and the light in which the books portray black people.

4

FAIRIES, TALKING ANIMALS
AND PATRIOTISM

The vignettes in the four corners of the frame for the title pages of books in Juta's Juvenile Library fix the parameters of many stories for young children for the first half of the twentieth century. They have their roots outside Africa, in European settlement, fairytale and myth or the stories brought to the country by enslaved people from the East. Even the hearth with its fire before which the children are seated, though not improbable for this country, is not typical — as the sunburst motif and recurrent references in the stories to sun, clear skies, heat and drought remind the reader.

The marrying of foreign and indigenous elements in South African English children's stories in the first half of the twentieth century is the story of colonial transition: intimate and revealing documentation of white people learning to become African. English-speaking people from the British Isles had been arriving in South Africa in increasing numbers throughout the nineteenth century, in immigration schemes of the 1820s and 1840s and later in pursuit of wealth following the discovery of diamonds, followed by gold. Suddenly, after the Union of South Africa was formed in 1910, they were on their own, their direct political ties with Great Britain severed.

But a great Afrikaner leader, General Jan Smuts, who had fought against the British in the South African Anglo-Boer War, kept close ties with Britain. He served in the British War Cabinet in the First World War and, as South African Prime Minister, was an honored ally of Britain until the end of the Second World War. According to literary historian J.P. Wade, "Smuts defined the white-English-South Africans' own identity for them. He linked them with their presumed Englishness while embodying their white-South Africanness."[1] The literary history by Coetzee, Couzens and Gray records, "To the white English writers, the post-[First World] war years offered the relative security of what might be called the Smuts period, dominated by its links with Britain and upholding a firmly emulative attitude towards the cultural supremacy of English literature, education, and moral values."[2]

The Second World War had a crucial effect on English speakers. Guy Butler, writer and academic, has written of how it brought the South African troops fighting with the allies into personal contact with European culture for the first time, making them feel alien and aware that their roots were now in Africa.[3] After the war, Afrikaners moved to the cities in greater numbers, making more English-speakers aware of them and their language. English-speakers also continued their process of urbanization and mixing, out of which emerged a reliance on South African-born, rather than expatriate, teachers and clergy as cultural models, and a common South African spoken form of the English language. The war created a fervor of patriotism that was primarily South African and only secondarily "British." The period of transition came to an end in 1948, when the National Party came to power, determined to impose Afrikaans culture and hegemony.

For nearly 50 years, from the first decade of the twentieth century until the turning point at the end of the 1940s, English-speaking South African writers for little children churned out mawkish, whimsical stories about fairies, animate toys and talking animals, usually of the small variety, modeled on English and American books but set in South Africa. At the same time, older children were served with the farm stories described in previous chapters. These genres marked a complete break with the adventure stories set in southern Africa by British children's writers up until the end of the nineteenth century, which featured epic journeys through untamed wilderness, battles with the indigenous people, and endless bloody hunts of big game. When left to themselves after Union, South Africans switched to portraying their country as domesticated and miniaturized.

The extraordinary hybrid genre of South African fairy and talking-animal stories ran in parallel with stories about European fairies produced both in Canada and Australia. Elizabeth Waterston has described how in Canada, Peter Pan created a craze for "gauzy fairies" and "flimsy fairytales" and writers turned to the "whimsical world" and "pretty pastel shades" of Milne and Barrie.[4] Australian books of this kind first appeared in 1891, and included stories by Atha Westbury, who set the tone for the future; Ida Rentoul Outhwaite and Hume Cook.

Most of the South African writers were typical obscure English-speaking South Africans — housewives, teachers, Guide and Brownie commissioners, and a few semiprofessional writers. Sometimes they illustrated their books themselves or enlisted relatives to do it, regardless of artistic skill. At least 70 books were published, most of them containing a collection of stories — *A Book of Children's Stories* by Ellen van der Spuy (1931)[5] has 40 — while others were collections of verse, and there was at least one play. Two full-length talking-animal stories were also published: *Skiddle*, by Dorothea Fairbridge (1926), which was serialized first in the *Cape Times*,[6] and *Papa Baboon* by F.A. Donnolly (1933).[7] This adds up to hundreds of stories and verses. Their publishers, significantly, were also South African — a situation that was to change later in the century, when important writers such as Jenny Seed had to turn to England to have their work published. The naturalization of foreign genres was a local project.

Typifying how seriously it was taken, the male authors were often manly types, such as F. Dawson, a pioneer railway builder, who was, in fact, the first in the field. In 1909, he included in *Fact and Fancy from the Veld*, amidst anecdotes of adventurous trips to the remote interior, a story about little David, an invalid who dies on his cot in the garden while talking to My Lady Barberton Daisy.[8] Dawson was, perhaps, a little self-conscious about venturing into this field, as he wrote under the pen name F.D., but his successors had no such reservations. They included one who styled himself "Major E.G. Ridley, M.C.," who was the author of *Tales of the Veld Folk for the Kiddies* (193-);[9] Cecil J. Shirley, author and illustrator of *Little Veld Folk* (1943), an armless and legless pioneer from Ireland who had shot leopards, shown in the frontispiece photograph dressed in khaki and pith helmet, seated at his easel in the veld;[10] Sir Henry Juta, speaker of the old Cape Legislative Assembly (1896–1898) and later Judge President of the Cape and an Appeal Court Judge, author of stories such as "The Water Baby" and "Cloud Babies" (1921);[11] and Herbert Leviseur, who wrote the stories such as "Queen of the Fairies" collected in *Desert Magic* (1945) "for my daughter Shirley Ann" while he was a soldier in the Libyan desert, and dedicated them "To my brother officers, who used to read them before they were posted."[12]

In considering what lay behind the widespread adoption of the fairy and talking-animals genres in the colonies, one can speculate that there is some truth in Graeme Harper's observation, "The cultural links between white Australia and the one-time 'home-country', Great Britain, could be said to have relied considerably on fantasizing away the distance between the two countries. Certainly the hermetic maintenance of a 'European' identity in a fundamentally Asia-Pacific region was for a long time an act of active imagination."[13] However, in the case of South Africa, the bulk of the effort did not go into denying an African identity but in marrying the old with the new. The curiously bipolar titles and names of characters suggest the tension of the project: *Fairy Tales from the Sunny South*, *The Pixies of the South*, *Picaninnies: South African Fairy Tales*, "Betty and the Mealie Goblins," "The Banana Elf," "Protea Pixies," "The Cloud Fairies, the North Wind and the Bakbakiri," "The Vijgie Fairies," "The Rain Forest Elves." An illustration that epitomizes this hybridity accompanies the story "The Ox with the Red Star" in *Glimpses of Fairyland* by Sadie Merber.[14] It depicts an African herdboy, an Afrikander ox (a local breed), and a gnome who looks like an English garden ornament.

Here were writers seeking to reconcile their own childhood, symbolically rooted in Europe, with their adult identities as South Africans. Their informal education in their families, their formal education, which was deeply Eurocentred, including a settler version of South African history that is symbolized in the Juta title frame by the picture of a Cape Dutch farm, their knowledge of a smattering of "Dutch" or Afrikaans and pidgin African languages, and their reading of current English children's books gave them the references and framework for creating books for the new generation of children, who were obviously *very* South African.

In the years immediately after the South African Anglo-Boer War, which ended in 1902, the status of British immigrants, and indeed all English-speaking residents, in South Africa remained a delicate question. The interim British administration under Lord Milner applied a deeply resented policy of Anglicizing the Afrikaners through imposing English-medium education. In the debates that led up to the establishment of the Union of South Africa in 1910, much attention was given to the union of the two "races," Afrikaner and English-speaker. It was not forgotten that one of the main points of contention leading to the war had been the status of foreigners — "uitlanders" — in the Transvaal Republic, where President Paul Kruger had refused to give them the vote. After Union, subsequent legislation further weakened South Africa's constitutional links with Great Britain, and in the 1920s Afrikaans became an official language and the country adopted a new flag incorporating the symbolism of unification.

In this context, Dorothy Fairbridge, author of novels and historical studies, wrote *Skiddle*. She was a member of an old distinguished Cape English family, and cousin of the writer Kingsley Fairbridge, whose work was much admired by English-speakers in South Africa and

Southern Rhodesia as encapsulating the essence of their regional culture. The central characters of *Skiddle* are a family of grey squirrels, a European species that had been introduced to South Africa. A dassie — the hyrax, an archetypal South African creature — calls Skiddle an "uitlander" and "foreign adventurer," but the father squirrel tells his children, "You are of this land, though your mother and I were brought across the seas from another country. But you are of South Africa, bone of its bone, blood of its blood, and all feather and fur of its forests are your brother" (*Skiddle*, 10, 8). Skiddle takes his words to heart and befriends all the creatures of the Cape Peninsula.

The opening of a story by G.M. Rogers shows how desperately English-language writers tried to marry Europe and Africa: "Gnomes and fairies, elves and pixies and all kinds of strange, quaint creatures dwelt in Oupa's wide mealie-patch."[15] (See the illustration on the title page reproduced in Figure 1.) Fairies were perversely foisted on the rugged Drakensberg Mountains (the Khahlamba Mountains, to which Europeans had already given this fantasy name, meaning "Dragon Mountains"); a children's novel by Nendick Paul, *A Child in the Midst* (1909) opens with a little girl looking at them and exclaiming, "'Mother, it looks like Fairyland!' She was lost in thought, picturing the fairies and elves who lived in the nooks and crannies of those rocky heights."[16] As late as 1968, Victor Pohl, a rugged Afrikaner who as a boy had been taken prisoner of war by the British and who wrote stories of animal and hunting adventures, still searching for appropriate language for a children's novel about the San (who were small of stature), wrote that when contemplating a peak in the Drakensberg to which settlers had given another fantasy name, Giant's Castle, "One forgets the giants and castles and is reminded instead of Lilliputians, fairies, gnomes and elflike creatures."[17]

European traditional literature provided models and characters: Snow White, Mother Goose ("She might indeed have stepped out of Mother Goose's Nursery Rhymes"),[18] Mother Hubbard, Aesop's fables (which, ironically, might have been originally African), Greek myths, Norse legends, Till Eulenspiegel, Merlin; and so did great literature: the Bible, Shakespeare (Titania and Puck appear), and Blake's verse.

The North, signifying Europe, resonated with authority. In "The Birthday Ostrich" by Edith Ablett, the ostrich flies to the North to fetch presents for the Brown Babies, the Children of the South, who live in "the land of the Golden South where the sun always shines and the sun is always hot — that was why the Brown Babies wore no clothes" (*Fairy Tales*, 13). She brings them "picture books about the children in the great lands in the north" (*Fairy Tales*, 17). In return for these gifts, an angel arrives in a ship with a white sail (recalling white traders and colonizers from the North) and asks them for warmth for the Children of the North. They happily comply, but then turn cold and have to be kept in the ostrich's nest until the sun comes out again the next morning. Thus, even in fantasy, European culture is exchanged for African commodities.

Inevitably, the only South African intertextual reference is the name of a dog called Jock in A.E. Bailie's *The Pixies of the South* (1944),[19] obviously intended to capitalize on the popularity of FitzPatrick's *Jock of the Bushveld*. The Queen of Sheba makes several appearances, presumably because of the conviction of whites in those days that the remains of early cultures in southern Africa such as rock paintings and stone-walled cities must have been made by the people of Sheba and the Phoenicians.

Only occasionally is an intertextual reference actually named, as when a boy dreams about a fairy battle after reading Robert Louis Stevenson at bedtime, in *The Locust Bird* by Ella Mackenzie,[20] and when children of *The Candle on the Windowsill* by Norah Perkins (1926), after reading *Peter Pan*, call their black nanny Tinkerbell because her name is Annabelle.[21] In a comic story in Sampie de Wet's collection, *The Monkey's Wedding* (1939), a book that a young lion with literary ambitions steals from a car in the Kruger National Park turns out to be the *A.A. Handbook*.[22] A touch of irony like this is welcome among all the unreflective derivative stories.

Very often the stories, verses and illustrations are blatant imitations of English, French, Swiss and American children's fantasy by writers and illustrators from Charles Kingsley up to the immediate contemporaries of the South Africans. Henry Juta's series of "babies" stories ("Jam Babies," "Cloud Babies" and so on) may have been inspired by Kingsley's *The Water Babies*, but, on the other hand, he may have known of a more appropriate gritty colonial model — the well known Australian *Snugglepot and Cuddlepie*, first of the Gumnut Babies series by May Gibbs, published three years earlier.

From the nineteenth century, George MacDonald's *At the Back of the North Wind* (1871) suggested a short story in *The Little Fir Tree and Other Stories* by Gladie McKay, in which the north wind is linked with the "bakbakiri" (a variant spelling of *bokmakierie*, a kind of bird).[23] The classic fantasy, *Alice in Wonderland* (1865), seems to have been too difficult a book for most South Africans to imitate, except for Yvonne Jooste, who has a little girl fall down a hole into Cotton Wool Land,[24] and E.G. Ridley, who plunders it frequently; he has a springhare who exclaims, "Oh dear, Oh dear" and recites:

Now here's a thing I'd like to ask,
In fact, a ticklish question;
Supposing we the Sausage ate,
Should we get indigestion?

(Veld Folk, n.p.)

There is hardly a writer of children's fantasy who is not imitated or copied: Kenneth Grahame, Beatrix Potter, Alison Uttley, J.M. Barrie, A.A. Milne, Walter de la Mare, P.L. Travers (*Mary Poppins*), Juliana Ewing (*The Brownies and Other Tales*, later popularized by Baden Powell as the founding myth of his girls' movement) and Rudyard Kipling from England, Jean de Brunhoff (*Babar*), Felix Salten and Père Castor from the European continent, and Joel Harris *(Uncle Remus)*, Hugh Lofting *(Dr Dolittle)*, and, by the 1950s, Walt Disney from the U.S. Other, more ephemeral, models were obviously influential, particularly the craze for flower fairies.

Just how unnecessary it was to turn to foreign models is illustrated by the writers' heavy reliance on Joel Harris's *Uncle Remus*. The stories he tells are African tales brought to the U.S. by African slaves, and many of their equivalents are to be found to this day in the mother continent. Yet, when English children's writer Jane Shaw spent the 1950s and 1960s resident in Johannesburg, she chose to write a retelling of *Uncle Remus*.[25]

The range of fairies that fill the stories was astonishingly eclectic, including flower, wind, mist and snow fairies, gnomes, goblins, pixies, elves, sprites, imps, brownies, mermaids, ogres, giants and dragons, to which may be added all the talking animals. Characters were given names straight from the sources: Rikki, a mongoose (from Kipling), Mother Carey, who cares for sea-fairies in Cape Town (from Kingsley), a rabbit (which is not a South African animal) called Cottontail (from Potter); Brer Rabbit for the trickster in the retelling of a traditional African folktale by Minnie Martin in *Tales from the African Wilds*.[26]

The resemblance was sometimes close. In *Wideawake Rhymes for Little People* by Margot le Strange (1942), the sentimental drawings of children by an unidentified artist are imitations of E.H. Shepard's illustrations for A.A. Milne, and the verses follow suit: "I went to a party all dressed up/I wore my best hat too," and,

I like to dip my arms in deep
And feel about below,
For in the froth the queerest things
Hob-goblins, Pixies, Gnomes and things,
Go swimming to and fro.[27]

As can be expected, the effete concoctions of these derivative books are filled with sentimentality, hypocorisms and twee expressions. Adults can still hear elves whisper, little sister is called Fairy, mother is called The Adorable, Spring spreads her mantle, and Dame Nature presides over a land filled with rainbows. Ellen van der Spuy's *A Book of Children's Stories* is a prime example. Dedicated to "Dear little Children of the World," it repeats the long-outmoded maudlin deathbed of a child:

> On a little bed a maiden lay dying.... 'Mamma darling, do not cry. I am not *really* going away from you!'... But who knows? Maybe there is a heaven for 'chicky-wicks', dearest little children.

> (*Children's Stories* 2)

Annette Joelson describes an exotic fairy feast that is served up in the "Fairy Queen's Palace of Proteas," a blend of clichés of Englishness and the Orient: "Wonderful things to eat. Honey served on violet petals, cakes, made from the scent of roses and honeysuckle, lay on butterfly wings and in acorn cups there was red wine, as sweet and delicious as lemonade, made from the flowers of the pomegranate tree."[28]

Along with the favorite words "peep" and "wee," diminutives abound: chicky-wicks, kiddies, hidey-hole, bunny, froggy. Since Afrikaans can turn any noun into a diminutive by the addition of the suffix *tjie* or *ie*, it is brought into service: characters are called Catotjie, Jantjie and Sannie, and special mention is made of flowers called suring blommetjies, moederkappies, pypies, vijgies, bobbejantjies and kalkoentjies. According to Andreé-Jeanne Tötemeyer, "Afrikaans children's literature between 1920 and 1950 also produced some fantasy literature presenting a prettified universe inhabited by *lente-babetjies* [little spring babies], *blom-kindertjies* [flower kiddies], *sterrekindertjies* [star kiddies], *prinsessies in die veld* [little princesses in the veld], and *veldkindertjies* [veld kiddies]."[29]

Just when one would have expected this style to be coming to an end, somewhere around 1945 Simba Toys published *The Story of the Little Moo Cow* by Madeleine Masson.[30] It was a first in two ways: it imitated Disney — Jay Heale has pointed out that the pictures resemble Disney's Clarabelle — and it is, according to Heale, probably the first children's book printed and published in South Africa in full color.[31] But this is how it is written: "So little Moo-Cow ran to the tearoom, and she was hungry and thirsty, and she did sit down and say, 'Bring me a glass of milk and a big bun.' And they did bring it to her and she did eat and eat her bun to the last crumb" (*Moo Cow*, n.p.).

While all this saccharine whimsy seems incongruous in a South African setting, many of the authors tried hard to incorporate local elements in order to naturalize their stories and verse. The settings are very South African — drought-stricken veld, veld fires, windmills and locusts are standard. Unlike Margot le Strange's little girl, who expects to find "hob-goblins, pixies, gnomes and things" in the washtub, Sally Starke's child wonders,

What lives back of the prickly pears?
Lizards or meerkats or little spring-hares?[32]

When Mr Uilspiel (Annette Joelson's spelling for Eulenspiegel or Uilenspiegel), who appears in the shape of a goblin, "clapped his tiny weeny hands together…a pretty little gabled house, with ever such a lovely thatched roof and green shutters, appeared among the trees" — the archetypal Cape Dutch house, straight out of the Juta title frame.[33] In *Mummy, I'm Listening*, about Rainbow Valley, where naughty fairies shoot the rainbow with arrows and squeeze the flowers, Yvonne Jooste drew an illustration for her story that shows the surrounding mountains looking exactly like those in the paintings of Pierneef, the famous Afrikaans artist who was regarded as the supreme interpreter of the South African landscape and Afrikaans culture.

Phyllis Juby wrote a book called *Picaninny: South African Versions of Popular Nursery Rhymes*.[34] The idea had potential:

Wee Picaninny runs through the kraal,
Here, there, and everywhere south of the Vaal;
Tapping at the window, beating at the wall,
"Are all the children fast asleep, or Tikolosh will call."

(*Picaninny* n.p.)

She succeeded only too well in transposing the rhymes, as they are riddled with racist terminology and attitudes: "Tanzi was a Hottentot, Tanzi was a thief…." (*Picaninny* n.p.)

South African animals, birds, insects, flowers, trees, fruit and vegetables fill the stories and verses. The cover of *Nunku the Porcupine and Other Stories* by Esme Lewis (1939) emblematically features three cobs of maize (corn) lying on the ground, a maize plant and a pumpkin.[35] Maize (mealies) and pumpkins were particularly popular, which is ironic, because neither is endemic to the country. Mealie pap (porridge) has to be eaten as a rather unpleasant duty — Edith King's "Morning Song" includes the line, "Eat your plate of mealie pap"[36] — or is reserved for naughty children and the Man in the Moon.

In *The Locust Bird* by Ella MacKenzie, illustrated by Cythna Letty, "The Pumpkin House" tells how the Beetle family took up residence (see Figure 5), and the illustration for "Betty and the Mealie Goblins" shows pumpkins among the mealies (*Locust Bird*, 16, 63). A black fairy dresses in a pumpkin leaf in Juliet Konig's "Black Fairies" (*The Little Elephant Hunter*, 1944);[37] "pumpkin goblins" appear in *Picaninnies: South*

5 Illustration by Cythna Letty from *The Locust Bird* by Ella MacKenzie

African Fairy Tales by Kathleen Wilkinson (1943);[38] Minnie Martin wrote a story called "The Dassie and the Pumpkins" (*Wilds*); and in "The Smiling Pumpkin" by Ellen van der Spuy (*Children's Stories*), a prince jumps out of a pumpkin and tells John he has broken the spell of the Wicked Witch. In another of her stories, "The Family Goes for a Holiday at the Seaside" (*Children's Stories*), a black servant has the name Pampoen, meaning "pumpkin," an insult in Afrikaans, but which she no doubt intended to be facetious.

In keeping with the prevailing emphasis on the diminutive in this genre, inherited from Grahame and Potter, most of the animal characters are small. This puts them on a level with the fairies that they interact with, creating the mixture of indigenous and alien that is typical. To take just one example, in *The Pixies of the South* by A.E. Bailie, when pixies pinch a teacher's foot, she exclaims, "Oh! Oh! Something has pricked my foot. I hope it's not a scorpion," (*Pixies*, 15) and the pixies chant,

> To their reeds the finches hurry,
> To their holes the meercats scurry;
> Under leaves the insects hide —
> All humans are inside.

> (*Pixies*, 18)

Meercats (mongooses) and dassies (hyraxes), typical small mammals with their familiar Afrikaans names, were favorites. This focus on the diminutive resulted in a perspective on South African wildlife different from that presented in the majority of animal stories later in the century, which generally feature the larger mammals to be found in the bushveld. Intriguingly, it creates a tension between the prevalent cosy stories set in the Karoo and the contemporary Juta title frame, which features large animals and snakes, suggesting the sensational.

The stories give a good idea of the life of white families on farms, celebrating Christmas and birthdays and enjoying the domestic round. Some writers used animal stories for social comment. Two unusual books portrayed the comedy of manners of adults living on farms, with illustrations showing animals strongly resembling adult humans. They hold tennis parties and gossip: "All their clothes come from Johannesburg, I am told," remarks a character in *Minnie Moo Cow and Her Friends on the Veld* by Jac and Mac.[39] A couple of characters resemble Toad of Toad Hall: "Peter Pig glanced at himself in a puddle and arranged his speckled bow tie, before starting off in his Ford car" (*Minnie*, 7), while another crashes a motorboat and has other rash adventures.

Field Mouse Stories by Annette Joelson (1926) contains harsher social comment: "Mrs Field Mouse was a shy little thing, very much afraid of her loud-voiced, fierce-whiskered husband and always ready to agree with everything he said, which was exactly as he wanted it to be.... Oh yes, they were the happiest couple in the whole of the Great Open Veld for he was very proud to be the Voice of the Family, while she was merely a very weak and very shrill Echo."[40]

Writers enjoyed applying the ancient formula of the aetiological (or *pourquois*) story to the country's novel fauna. For example, Ridley wrote "How the Dassies Came to Have No Tails" (*Veld Folk*). Usually the plots are inventive and the results successful.

A few writers obviously took care to study the behavior of the animals they anthropomorphize, so that they achieved a charming blend of realism and fantasy. Esme Lewis was good at this: "In his rage, Grys-veer [Grey-feather, the secretary bird] ran swiftly over the ground and even rose into the air and flew a short distance. After his flight he felt calmer and, coming down to earth, he continued his stately walk" (*Nunku*, 45). The secretary bird is one of those creatures, like the trapdoor spider and the honey-guide, that were favorites of children's authors, cropping up repeatedly from the earliest colonial stories of the nineteenth century right through the later talking-animal stories, in which their appearance and behavior is discussed. Although this repetition is hard to explain, it does indicate that writers regarded certain creatures as representing the essence of the country.

On the other hand, writers also had alien creatures mix with endemic animals in the same stories. Minnie Martin, for example, includes a wolf, a fox and Brer Rabbit in her stories (*Wilds*); in a story by E.G. Ridley, a tom tit joins an ostrich, a springbok and an elephant at a picnic (*Veld Folk*).

A few writers invented African fantasy creatures. Minnie Martin created "a nasty gogo," which she glosses as "a small devil" (*Wilds*, 1). Her source for this is not clear, since *gogo* is a variant spelling of *gogga*, an Afrikaans word of Khoi origin meaning "insect." Annette Joelson writes about "the great, dark, gloomy cave of Mamba, the fierce veld Dragon" (*Ostrich*, 7) — a fantasy that neatly corresponds with the illustration of the fantasy serpent in the bottom right hand corner of the Juta frame. But the fantasy creatures of African mythology — the milk bird and the lightning bird, the many-headed snake and the great water-snake — are absent. They were beyond the knowledge of these white writers.

Vegetation, which often plays an important part in the stories, tells us something about the authors. Time and time again the trees are bluegums, wattles, pepper trees and bottle-brush from Australia, jacarandas from South America, and European pines, firs, willows and oaks, imported and now typically found around human habitation almost anywhere. In a poem called "Veld Trees" by Edith King, none of them is endemic: "The willow, the gum, the wattle tree,/The yellow-fruited peach" (*Veld Rhymes*, 24). Most of the flowers that flower fairies paint are imported garden species. And even if the text referred to South African trees, the illustrators were prone to draw wooded landscapes that look like scenes in the northern hemisphere. Only too obviously, the stories, poems and illustrations are the work of urban people.

Sometimes factual errors suggest sheer ignorance, such as when Kathleen Wilkinson puts a banyan tree in the Drakensberg Mountains (*Fairy Tales*, 47). Mistakes like this are unforgivable. Stephen Jay Gould has pointed out that the novelist Vladimir Nabokov, who worked as a professional lepidopterist, "frequently asserted … that literature and science meet in mutual respect for detailed factuality, with the highest virtue of accuracy residing in the evident beauty of such material truth."[41] It is an indictment of the neo-colonialism of white South African writers for children that they imposed so many inaccuracies about their native country on their readers. Absentee British authors of the nineteenth century filled their books with nonsensical mistakes, but twentieth-century South Africans should have known better.[42] According to the literary historian Henry Saxby, Australian children's literature of the first half of the twentieth century was similarly riddled with errors, which he deplores, declaring that there is "no excuse" for the "falsification," "distorting" of "even the basic facts," and "ludicrous" mistakes.[43]

Language is a giveaway about the writers and their intentions. They tried to give their stories an authentic South African flavor by using Afrikaans, African-language and South African-English names and phrases, but in doing so, many of them betrayed their insular English-speaking urban backgrounds, for just as they were ignorant of local birds, animals and plants, they made egregious linguistic errors.

Local words could be very effective. One technique was to use the generic African or Afrikaans word as the proper name for an animal character, such as Nunku (Zulu *nungu*) the porcupine, or Podder (Afrikaans *padda*) the frog, though writers also used them as common nouns to give a local flavor; when Dorothy Gard'ner introduces "a perfectly true story of a verkleurmannetjie" [chameleon] she is simply showing off, especially since she gets the spelling right.[44]

Some writers took over the Afrikaans usage of calling a hyena a "wolf" *(wolf)* and a leopard a "tiger" *(tier)*; whether they did this out of ignorance is hard to say. But E.G. Ridley showed signs of being uncomfortable about applying these alien names; one of his stories, in which a jackal objects to being called "wolf" by another animal, takes the form of a debate on the subject (*Veld Folk*).

As part of the local flavor, English-speaking children are given Afrikaans names such as Klara and Jan. The writers were often inventive in naming. A.E. Bailie (*Pixies*), for example, names a pixy Tiki, after the Zulu word *tiki* for the threepenny coin, thus naturalizing the pixy.

But even allowing for the confusion of spelling caused by the transition from Dutch to Afrikaans after it was made an official language in the 1920s, many English-speaking writers, with honorable exceptions such as Mabel Waugh, who wrote *Verses for Tiny South Africans* (1923),[45] clearly knew little Afrikaans. They had a small repertoire of words and phrases that crop up repeatedly. The lexicographer William Branford says that the linguistic stereotype of English culture that he encountered in the 1970s was typified by a small range of words that constituted what he called the English of Van der Merwe stories (jokes about a stupid, country-bumpkin Afrikaner, like the Paddy stories about an Irishman). When he invited readers of *Personality* magazine to send him typical South African English words, he found that they could only generate sentences such as "Eina [ouch] Marie, there's a gogga [insect] in my veldskoen [rough hide shoe]."[46] Sure enough, Maude Bidwell's play *Breath of the Veld* (1923) has the line, "Eina!... There is a duiweltjie [thorn] sticking into the heel of my foot!"[47] Nevertheless, Bidwell does include completely idiomatic and correctly spelled Afrikaans dialogue in her play, which is very rare.

When writers attempted to use expressions from black African languages, they revealed only too obviously the social situation, because most of them relied on *fanakalo*, the pidgin Zulu used by whites to speak to servants and laborers. Those who apparently heard pure African languages spoken relied on their own transcriptions for the spelling, as whites did not have an opportunity to learn them formally.

Under the influence of Uncle Remus, the writers reverted to the practice of expatriate adventure writers of the nineteenth century who put in the mouths of Africans a literary version of African-American speech, with all its degrading connotations of the comic negro: "Yes, Baas, I'll cut dem from de tick part ob de tree" (*Fir Tree*, 21). When Dorothy Gard'ner uses the word "croon" for African singing, she has taken an American word that must have been suggested to her by its association with African Americans (*Verses*, 33).

Normal South African English is mixed with un-South African language, like other alien elements. From England come "wood," "woodland," "jungle" and "folk." It is difficult to understand why South African writers should have fancied the word "jungle," since there is little vegetation in the country that could be thus described. To call the lion the "monarch of the jungle" as Annette Joelson does (*Ostrich*, 27) is a complete misnomer. When "jungle" crops up alongside "aasvogels" (vultures) and "kopje" (a little hill rising from the open plains of the interior), it is clearly a product of the imagination. Possibly its prevalence, especially in the popular collocation "jungle lore," is due to the influence of Kipling's *The Jungle Books* (1894, 1895). "Folk" is typically found in the collocations "jungle folk," "little folk" and "veld folk," which may have been used because it has a twee English connotation, but also because it is cognate with the Afrikaans word *volk*; the word *veldvolk* is used to describe small creatures in Afrikaans stories about talking animals.

The frequent collocation of "mealie" with "patch" and "plantation" suggests American models such as Brer Rabbit's briar-patch: South African English would have "mealie field" or "mealie lands" (borrowed from the Afrikaans *mielielande*). "Patch" does not sound South African in the term "prickly pear patch" used by Minnie Martin (*Wilds*, 5).

Mention has already been made of how the Second World War paradoxically made South Africans more aware of foreign cultures while bringing English- and Afrikaans-speaking whites together in a common South African culture. *Desert Magic* by Herbert Leviseur, which gained sentimental celebrity in South Africa, illustrates this well. It is precisely placed by an announcement at the front of the book: "These stories were written at Mersa Matruh in the latter part of 1941 for my daughter SHIRLEY ANN." This typified the situation of most South African servicemen and women, who were separated from their families for years while serving with the Allies in the North African desert and Italian campaigns.

Each story is usually given a specific setting and context; in a couple of the stories Leviseur describes the topography — an oasis and a "waddy" — and in another he explains Ramadan, which is important for what follows. The illustrator, Ernest Ullmann, adds the war touch by putting South African soldiers' helmets on some of the animals.

Leviseur does not give personal names to his characters, but names them as they were most likely named by the soldiers: the Barrani spider, the Bengasi beetle, the datebird. Typically of expatriates, he resorts to analogies from home as he tries to explain to his daughter what the new creatures are like — desert anteaters have "scales as big as tickeys."

A couple are given Afrikaans names: *baklymakaar* (lizard) and *waaistert gykie* (gecko). That they are spelled incorrectly suggests that Leviseur learned them from Afrikaans-speaking fellow soldiers and that, like so many other English speakers, his school Afrikaans did not add up to much. Thinking of his little girl back home, trying to use imagery that she would understand, and using the terms that his fellow soldiers had for the strange creatures they encountered in the desert intensified his South Africanness.

Leviseur's stories all feature talking creatures (the insects, lizards and camels of the desert) who, after desert-induced vicissitudes, change into princes and princesses, marry and live happily ever after in palaces that miraculously materialize. A mouse turns back into a fairy and is reunited with her mother, Queen of the Fairies. In some stories, the creatures' clothing, servants and possessions are more obviously eastern, and Ullman illustrates them in the style of the Arabian Nights.

These two men, it can be assumed, were autodidacts in the writing of fairy stories for children. To create and visualise the *Desert Magic* stories Leviseur must have drawn on the Arabian Nights because memories of those stories were all that he had to make sense of the Arabian world he found himself in; and Ullman (who was a German immigrant) must also have drawn on the literature of his own childhood. Ironically, an Afrikaans scholar, I.D. du Plessis, had for years been researching the culture of the descendants of the formerly enslaved people of the Cape, known then as the Cape Malays, and published an English translation of his collection, *Tales from the Malay Quarter*, in Cape Town in 1945.[48] In his preface, du Plessis says that the stories come from "the *Thousand-and-one-Nights*, entangled with the fairy tales and fables of Europe and Africa" (*Malay*, n.p.). Eastern literary motifs had already been part of South African culture for hundreds of years.

No matter how South Africans had tried to give fairy stories a local flavor, by the Second World War the project was doomed. Maureen Walsh, with hindsight, could say the same of Australian fairy stories, seeing the writing on the wall as far back as 1918, when *Snugglepot and Cuddlepie* by May Gibbs was published:

Then [at the end of the nineteenth century] Australian fairy books began to appear, native animals of the gentler sort were seen to mingle with the familiar rabbits, and the prettiest wildflowers clustered with the daisies in dim woods and on grassy hills. Elegant, well-dressed European fairies settled into their adopted home. But the grey-green bush, with its ragged scribbly-bark gums and small, dry flowers, its brown creeks and rough bush tracks, continued to hold its own secrets.[49]

At least one early Australian writer had seen this genre for what it was and distanced herself from it. Mrs Æneas Gunn opens her story *The Little Black Princess of the Never-Never* (1905): "She didn't sit — like fairy-book princesses — waving golden sceptres over devoted subjects, for she was just a little bush nigger girl or "lubra," about eight years old. She had, however, a very wonderful palace — the great lonely Australian bush."[50]

In South Africa, even before the fairy genre had reached its peak, some writers evinced hints of unease at importing overseas elements. Mabel Waugh wrote in 1923:

> **Are there fairies...?**
> A little girl from England
> Came to visit us today;
> She doesn't *like* this country,
> And hopes to go away.
> She thinks there are no fairies
> And no witches and no elves
> Because there are no foxgloves
> Where they may hide themselves....
>
> But in the great proteas,
> In the silver-trees and pypies,
> In the disas and the ixias,
> The gousblom and the vygies,
> The loveliest little fairies
> Flit to and fro all day.
> I'll show her where to find them
> Then I'm sure she'll want to stay.

> (*Verses*, 15)

Waugh has deliberately chosen non-English flower names of the Cape Peninsula to emphasize their unique South Africanness. The peritext to the poem adds to its message about national identity, since the title of the book from which it comes is *Verses for Tiny South Africans*.

Four years later, G.M. Rogers produced a classic sendup of a fairy story called *Peggy's Frog Prince* (1927).[51] It opens, "Ever since the beautiful picture book had come from England, little Peggy Barton had always had a great love for the delightful fairy story called 'The Frog Prince'" (*Prince*, 8). While she is sitting by a sluit (water-furrow) reading her favourite story, a bull-frog appears, knocks the book into the water and sits on it.

> Peggy did not know that these big bull-frogs that live in the swamps and streams of Africa are nasty, spiteful fellows. They sometimes bite and are often poisonous. There he sat and looked at Peggy showing all his teeth.
> "He's the Frog Prince!" cried the little girl suddenly. "I'm sure he is the 'Frog Prince'. If I wait here I am sure he will turn into a real Prince. He is sitting on his book because he knows his story is in it and he knows I love him so!… Let me see if I can think of a magic word that will change you into a Prince."
>
> (*Prince*, 12)

He jumps at her, and she falls over and squashes him dead, whereupon Aunt Fanny remarks, "Ha! That's the end of him. As for the story-book — we must get a new one" (*Prince*, 15).

An ominous note was sounded in 1943, when Margaret Herd recorded this encounter:

> "Are you a Tokoloshe then?" Mary asked.
> "No, I'm not. I'm an elf. You can see me because you are a white child, but only black children can see the Tokolosh."
> "But why?" Mary asked. She was very sorry because her nanny, Selina, had told her many stories about the Tokoloshe and she wanted so much to see him.
> "I don't know," answered the elf crossly. "But you are very lucky because if you were a grown-up you would not be able to see anything. As it is, you can see all the people of the white fairy world."[52]

It is clear where Mary's allegiance lies.

Then came Juliet Konig (Marais Louw), who made things even worse with *The Little Elephant Hunter*. One of her stories ends, "Phyllis never saw the Pixies because they have a rooted objection against being seen by little girls" (*Hunter*, 67). Maudlin hypocorism had no place in her stories:

> Only Elaine could see the fairies because she was thirteen months old. She sat in her play-pen and the father-fairy, wrapped in a pumpkin leaf which he was using as a blanket, perched on the edge and blinked the whites of his little eyes. "There!" said Elaine, holding out a squashy banana for which she had no further use.
>
> (*Hunter*, 92)

Konig took the fairies-in-Africa notion to its logical conclusion. The fairy that Elaine sees is African, and Konig states emphatically, "African fairies are black" (*Hunter*, 92). To acknowledge this openly was inconceivable in a country on the brink of formalized apartheid, and the death knell of the fairy story had sounded. The National Party, which was to implement formal apartheid, came to power four years later.

A literary critic, Emily Zinn, has commented, "Neither fairy tales nor feminism received much attention in apartheid-era South African literature and criticism....Fairy tales and the realm of fantasy... were traditionally rejected by South African writers under apartheid, particularly by white authors."[53] While she is right in saying that no one wrote fairy tales anymore, her observation is unhelpful in that she ignores the substantial body of indigenous folktales and fantasy that was written for children and the published critical discussion of them.[54] But she does point out, intriguingly, that the country's two winners of the Nobel Prize for Literature did consider the place of fantasy in South Africa in the 1980s, and took opposing viewpoints.

Nadine Gordimer wrote a mock fairy story, "Once upon a Time," in which a white family barricade themselves ever more securely in their affluent suburban house, placing coils of razor wire along the garden wall, but, after their little boy is given a book of fairy tales, "he pretended to be the Prince who braves the terrible thicket of thorns to enter the palace and kiss the Sleeping Beauty back to life," and he crawls into the tunnel of coils and is torn to shreds.[55] She also took a cynical view of the place of fairy tales in South Africa at the end of her novel *July's People*, in which a white family are ironically rescued from a black uprising by their black domestic worker and sheltered in his rural village, where they live in fear: "The real fantasies of the bush delude more inventively than the romantic forests of Grimm and Disney."[56]

Gordimer's relentlessly cutting, satirical view of life under apartheid is echoed less brutally in a young-adult novel, *Freefalling*, by Shelley Davidow, published in 1991.[57] The narrator, a young woman, recalls her thoughts in her final year at school when the dreadful decade of violence preceding political transition was drawing to a close. All her childhood she had made up stories about being a fairy princess, but now,

> This was South Africa. How could you change into a fairytale princess in the harsh violent climate that surrounded you? Was there a way? Could I with my brown-gold hair and my European skin turn into something good and beautiful under the hot African sun? I was not the Snow White of all children's dreams.... And I wasn't the princess with golden locks.... I was some *inbetween*

element, in South Africa of all places, and it was painful. I was filled with images of *Grimm's Fairytales*, of *More British Fairytales*, but my daily life had nothing to do with them. The morals of those stories were not the morals of my environment.

(*Freefalling*, 81)

On the other hand, Nobel laureate J.M. Coetzee, in his Jerusalem Prize Acceptance Speech delivered in 1987, regretted that South African writers were too overwhelmed by truth to emulate Cervantes' Don Quixote, who "leaves behind hot, dusty tedious La Mancha and enters the realm of faery by what amounts to a willed act of the imagination."[58]

In 1949, B. Swemmer prefaced his talking-animal stories by remarking, "I had always thought that fairy tales made the strongest appeal to children, but I discovered long ago that most children — as well as many adults — prefer jungle stories."[59] He was right in observing that "jungle" — talking animal — stories would outlive fairy stories. Whereas fairy stories were usually flights of inconsequential fantasy, animal stories offered endless interest in nature, and could always be turned in some didactic or allegorical way to greater ends.

The most serious social purpose came with the Second World War, when animals, the Kruger National Park and the war came together to give explicit utterance to the national aspirations of the country in the series of four *Cock-Olly* books by May Henderson — *The Cock-Olly Book* (1941), *Looma, Teller of Tales* (1942), *Tortoo the Tortoise* (1943), and *Mrs Mouse of Kruger Park* (1944)[60] — and the book of verse *We're Telling You* by C.S. Stokes (1943).[61]

Proof that they struck a patriotic chord is that all of them became hugely popular best-sellers. In 1943, the cover of *Tortoo* reported that 12,000 copies of the Cock-Olly books had already been sold, so the note on the dust jacket of *Mrs Mouse of Kruger Park* was probably not exaggerating when it claimed, "The animals in the Cock-Olly books are probably the best-known and best-loved animals in South African children's literature" (*Mrs Mouse*, cover). By May 1944, *Cock-Olly* and *Looma* were in their "fourth large printing" (*Mrs Mouse*, cover). *We're Telling You* went into several editions, running at least from 1942 to 1950, when a revised edition containing some new material and illustrations was published by a different publisher. These are astonishing figures for South African children's books, figures that make nonsense of the brief history of South African children's books in English by Eve Jammy, who listed only five books published before 1949, but did not include those by Henderson and Stokes, and went on to state, "There were a few other books published but none very successfully."[62]

The name "cock-olly bird," usually written "cockyolly bird," meaning a dear little bird, is obscure. In England, it crops up in comic stage shows and books. It is not listed in the *Dictionary of South African English on Historical Principles*, but Percy FitzPatrick mentions a "cockyolly bird" in one of his stories, where it appears to mean any common bird of the bushveld.[63] Because the South African Light Horse were known as the "Cockiolly birds," Henderson may have chosen it for its military associations.[64]

The war provided the context in which the *Cock-Olly* books were published and made its presence known within the stories. It is likely that the publisher, Knox of Durban, flourished during the war because it was impossible to import children's books from England at that time. It published other books identical in appearance to *Cock-Olly* on the same poor-quality paper, described in a note in *The Cock-Olly Book as* "War-time Paper Manufactured in England."

Henderson could, on occasion, satirize the army, following a tradition found in children's story, poetry and picture books during the South African Anglo–Boer War. Major Ridley had continued in this vein in a story called "A General Engagement" (in *Veld Folk*), in which a general (who resembles Lord Roberts in the illustration) is looking for a recruit to be a private, as everyone is a general. The private, once appointed, scares him by popping a paper bag. Henderson introduces similar bumbling pompous officers, one with a monocle and a walrus moustache, in a story about a locust army: "It's the General's moustache — it has got mixed up with his ribbons and has to be unravelled" (*Cock-Olly*, 31).

But she could also be more serious. In another story, she satirizes world politics. Says Cock-Olly, "If you take a penny from Lindi the elephant when he isn't looking — that's stealing. But if you take a country from a people, even if they are looking — that's annex- annex- — oh dear! I don't remember the word, but it means that you just take it for your own country, and of course, that's not stealing" (*Mrs Mouse*, 20). When an army of rhinos has been persuaded by Mangy the jackal to invade the Kruger Park, a white bird who attends the council of war of the animals in the Park convinces them not to fight back. When the animals of the park provide a friendly welcome, the rhinos cannot understand, and their king asks,

> "Why are you treating us as friends, instead of enemies? Tell me that."
> "Why should we treat you as enemies?" asked Tortoo, "when you have never done us any harm?"

> (*Cock-Olly*, 65)

Most of the plots are about animals wrongly seizing power and the duty of citizens in a democracy to ensure that the state functions effectively and justly. *Mrs Mouse* ends, "The Imp of Mischief had been banished, and all was peace and joy" (*Mrs Mouse*, 74). The illustration shows that this imp is a foreigner — tall ears, a cloak and tights ending in curly toes. So much for foreign fairies.

The animals are very patriotic, which the author is determined to illustrate. She does this by having a column of real soldiers march into the Park to a loyal welcome from the animals.

To begin with, the war in Europe was remote from South Africa. The back cover of the first volume proclaims, "The royalties from their sales are to be given to the Air Raid Heroes Fund and to help those whose homes have been destroyed by enemy action in Britain" (*Cock-Olly*, cover). By the time the second volume, *Looma*, came out in 1942, the war was closer to home; many South African servicemen and women were involved in fighting on the African continent, and war charities were directed to them. The cover announced that it was published "in aid of the Gifts and Comforts Fund for SA soldiers" — though the cover of *Tortoo* (1943) still said that the royalties went to what was now called the "Air Raid Victims' Fund." *Looma* included a "foreword by Mrs Smuts (Ouma)." Mrs. Smuts, the wife of the South African Prime Minister, was affectionately known as "Ouma" ("Granny"), and was an icon of patriotism in the war years, renowned for her support of the war effort.

Peritextual material in the four books makes the claim that their purpose is to encourage national pride in the animals of the Kruger Park and give information about them. Willis Mackeurtan, president of the Victoria League, a jingoistic organization keeping alive English culture in South Africa, proclaims in his foreword to *Cock-Olly*, "In this fair land of ours whose vast spaces are teeming with animal life it is only right that stories for our children should be woven around the birds and beasts that inhabit it, and so in this book May Henderson has taken us to the Kruger Park, that National Sanctuary which has attracted so many visitors to our country.... [T]hese stories delightfully portray veld life in this country" (*Cock-Olly*, n.p.).

A note on the front inside flap takes this further: "Apart from their value as first-rate fiction they will help to make young South Africans more appreciative of the wonders of their own land, and these wonders, the real glories of South Africa, they will help to introduce to any of our little child-visitors from overseas who are fortunate to read them (*Cock-Olly*, cover). The "child-visitors" probably refers to evacuees.

Mrs. Smuts, in her foreword to *Looma*, stresses the importance of being authentically South African. She distinguishes Henderson's realistic animals from the fantasy elements of European fairy stories, using South African words that emphasize the local flavor: "They are wonderful little people. They are as at home on our veld, among our krantzes and kloofs as the Snow Queen was in her Ice Palace in the middle of the Arctic wastes. They know the spirit of the land as only true South Africans can. They are *true* South Africans" (*Looma*, n.p.).

The question can be asked why there was this insistence on the educational and patriotic nature of the stories. Possibly, for the person who wrote the blurbs and for Mrs. Smuts, who obviously had not read the stories, the Kruger Park just had to be a patriotic symbol, and their emphasis on education assuaged reservations about the frivolous nature of fantasy — especially because there was a war on.

The language of the blurb of *Looma* gives away the true state of affairs as regards the instructional value of the stories: "This book is a helping hand, and who would rejoice more to know this than our own little Jungle friends on whom the curtain now rises." Nobody who knows the Kruger Park could describe it as "jungle," but the jargon slipped easily off the pen. The truth is that, in spite of these avowals, there is little in the books that is recognizably Kruger Park. Although Henderson had hundreds of wonderful bushveld birds to choose from, Cock-Olly himself is no recognizable kind of bird, and the stories feature, along with South African creatures, a domestic dog, an Indian mynah (a bird regarded as an invasive pest) whose name is Monty, and, of all things, a peacock. Continuing the tradition of the previous thirty years of concentrating on small animals, she made some of her main characters a small bird, a tortoise, a mouse, a lizard, an antbear and white ants; when an elephant does appear in an illustration, he is their size.

Children reading her books must have found this strange, as most people would associate the park with large mammals. By contrast, *The Monkeys' Wedding*, Sampie de Wet's book set in the park, features baboons, monkeys, impalas and a full-size elephant, illustrated by Hilda Stevenson-Hamilton, the wife of the famous first warden of the park, who also makes an appearance in one of the stories. Her stories abound in references to the melodious place names of the park such as Punda Maria, Letaba, Satara, Skuzuza and Malelane.

Henderson, on the other hand, invents unidentifiable animals called "Tiger-Wolf" and "Cheetah the Leopard," and confusingly calls one "Bulbul the Frog" (whereas a bulbul is actually a kind of bird). The animals eat exotic food: oranges, bananas, nuts and dates; and there are uncritical references to bottlebrush trees and blue gums, which are actually invasive Australian plants that are almost absent from the park. No sense of place is created: for example, the animals assemble for debates in the English-sounding "Village Square."

Many aspects of the *Cock-Olly* stories follow European models closely. In the traditional style of European folk tales, the animals are typecast, and include the very European "Wise Owl, Judge of Kruger Park." They hold "Midsummer revels" (unheard of in the southern hemisphere), celebrate Guy Fawkes Night, and take "tea" at six (which is not a South African custom). When Horace the Hippo dons a pink policeman's uniform, the illustration shows that it is a British bobby's uniform. The language contains British colloquialisms such as "'She is in a paddy this morning,' thought Buzz Fuzz the Bee" (*Mrs Mouse*, 10).

However, Henderson also incorporates South African expressions and references: "The indaba is over"; "She'll stop our Saturday tickeys"; the "lock-up kraal"; "pumpkin fritters and biltong pie" (an impossibility, since biltong is dried meat); and the park animals' battle cry is "'Oo-soo-tu!'" (a misspelled version of the nineteenth-century Zulu war cry, "Usuthu"). She refers to "veldschoens" (homemade country shoes), but uses the long-obsolete Dutch spelling instead of Afrikaans.

Her mixture of British and South African idiom epitomizes the linguistic process taking place at the time, which the linguist Len Lanham described as "a great dilution of urban, nineteenth century British English by the main stream of rural, local South African English";[65] and it confirms J.M. Coetzee's observation: "It is no over-simplification to say that landscape art and landscape writing in South Africa from the beginning of the nineteenth century to the middle of the twentieth revolve around the question of finding a language to fit Africa, a language that will be authentically African."[66]

May Henderson appears to have known precious little about the Kruger Park or Afrikaans, but she did attempt, from what appears to have been a narrow English-speaking base, to give her stories an African flavor. They fit what the *Companion to South African English Literature* has characterized as being typical of local children's books of the first half of the twentieth century — "'English' in spirit and 'colonial' in tone and idiom."[67]

We're Telling You by C.S. Stokes is a collection of verse in which the animals of Kruger National Park speak out about who they are and celebrate their sanctuary from hunters, while Miss Rhino and Miss Hippo comically exchange insults regarding their girth. Unlike May Henderson, Stokes had the credentials to write knowledgeably about the animals of the Kruger Park — he also wrote a very well known book about the park, *Sanctuary* (1942). The illustrations parallel the combination

Fairies, Talking Animals and Patriotism • 85

of fact and comic fantasy: some are stately animal portraits by Alice Stokes and renowned big-game artist C.T. Astley Maberly, while others are comic sketches.

The early editions of *We're Telling You* also carried a foreword by Mrs. Smuts in which she repeats the claim of the *Cock-Olly* books that this fantasy is of educational value: "I hope, with the author, that these pages will lead us all to know our wild creatures better, and will spur us on to join the ranks of those who are fighting for the preservation of our magnificent fauna" (*Telling*, p.4).

A very wide range of animals is covered — and here there is no concentration on the diminutive. They tell us facts about themselves, sometimes quoted from named authorities:

> In a book by William Drummond you'll find it's told to you
> That my horns have taken human life, and claimed a
> leopard's, too.
>
> (*Telling*, 44)

Traditional South African human background is brought in, for example by the crocodile, who says, "And Basuto and Bakwena tribes obeisance have for me" (*Telling*, 22).

Stokes makes all sorts of learned allusions: to classical mythology, Nimrod the Hunter, Epstein, Kipling, Omar Khayyam and so on, but elements of modern international popular culture such as Pop-Eye and *Ripley's Believe It or Not* also feature.

Of all the outside references, the war is intrusive. The keynote is patriotism. Mrs. Smuts, the key figure selected to write the foreword, is introduced as "Wife of Field-Marshall J.C. Smuts, P.C., C.H., K.C., D.T.D., Prime Minister, Minister of Defence and of External Affairs, and Commander-in-Chief, Union of South Africa." An Author's Note in early editions announced that the book was "earning something for war funds" (*Telling*, n.p.). In one poem, the Springbok alludes to his name being used as the popular name for South African national sports teams and the armed forces:

> As sons of Southern Africa fight in the teeth of war,
> Be it in the British Commonwealth
>   or on some foreign shore,
> They're lauded as the Springboks....
>
> (*Telling*, 5)

This fits in well with the constant note of national pride in the country's achievement in creating its national parks.

In *We're Telling You,* the war imagery is also pervasive as a meta-phorical way of seeing things. There are mentions of rations, "railway engines that blitz the night's repose," "metallic birds" (of "no ill intent"), the animal chorus crashing "like a ton or two of bombs, against the lowveld ground," searchlights, "a cannon in the orchestra of war," and even Old Bill (head of the MOTHs, an ex-servicemen's organization). Describing the park and its denizens in terms of this alien imagery was unprecedented, and shows how South Africans were looking at even their most precious possessions in a new light.

The talking-animal genre, unlike the fairy stories, found new significance in the war. The pressure of patriotism obliged writers to make it ever more identifiably South African. Leviseur's North African creatures, before their magical transformations, were grittily real but alien until they were given Afrikaans names and the odd South African touch. Henderson's animals were learning to speak South African English, reminded by the war that they should be patriots. Stokes's animals were exuberantly real and at home, safe in their sanctuary and safe also from the distant sounds of war. By providing sanctuary for their wildlife heritage, South Africans were keeping the soul of their country alive.

5

FOLKTALES

While the early stories and poems that placed European fairies in South Africa were being published, an equally strong publishing tradition affirmed that the country had its own indigenous stories of fantasy and the supernatural. An obvious way to introduce them to children would be to convert to an African setting the traditional European image, pictured in the Juta frame, of the old woman telling stories to children at her knee in front of the hearth. Instead of "Auntie Loo" telling a story about the witches they can see in the embers (as in *The Locust Bird* by Ella MacKenzie),[1] they could have a black nurse telling tales from her own culture to her white charges. Yet this could be a tall order for a white writer who had only the faintest notion that the indigenous people and the descendants of the previously enslaved people from the East possessed their own oral literature.

Some stories that are framed by a black narrator betray the author's ignorance. For example, Corinne Rey provides a strange mixture of history and African and European elements in one of her *Tales of the Veld* (1926), called "The Flitting."[2] A white mother tells her children a story that she heard from "Nanny, the old kaffir nurse," of how during the South African Anglo-Boer War the "Little Folk" got Nanny to assist them in escaping on an ox wagon from the fighting of the white people.

Annette Joelson made crass attempts to frame her stories with African narrators. In *How the Ostrich Got His Name* (1926), "Her dearest companion was a fat, jolly old kaffir-maid, with a big merry face, all kindness and wrinkles. Each night...Aya Sara would take Little Lady Blue Sun-Bonnet on her lap, and tell her the most delightful stories of fairies, elves, animals, and strange beings that lived thousands of years ago that one could wish to hear."[3] When, in one of her stories, two children meet Uilspiel (Eulenspiegel — a traditional Germanic trickster) — the author remarks, "Of course like all South African children, Klara and Jan had heard a great many strange stories about the elusive Uilspiel from the native servants" (*Ostrich*, 19). In spite of the indigenes' miraculous knowledge of European fairies, the publishers (Juta) included a Note with the usual stress on the South Africanness of the stories: "The manuscript submitted by the author contained a considerable number of further stories....Should the sales warrant it, and South African children prove that they enjoy reading stories of their own country, then further volumes will be published from time to time" (*Ostrich*, n.p.).

Carrie Rothkugel was equally confused in her patriotic book *The Gift Book of the Fatherless Children of the South African Soldiers and Sailors* (1917), in which the Black Picanniny says, "You know the black children have their own fairy tales, and this is the one they love best: it's all about the Bogey Man, and as Queen Titania notices that the white children are all afraid of our favourite, the Bogey Man, so here am I to tell you all about him."[4] It transpires that the Bogey Man, who is unheard of in African folktales, lives up a chimney (an architectural feature not to be found in African homes) and is a friend of Father Christmas.

Possibly the Bogey Man is Rothkugel's version of the tokolosh, which generations of white writers latched onto as the one feature of African beliefs they knew about. The tokolosh was a mischievous spirit creature of Nguni folklore that took the form of a small, hairy, priapic man reaching as high as an adult's knee. He was known for his lascivious propensities, but that is not mentioned in the children's books.

The tokolosh gave his name to the title of a short story by Kathleen Wilkinson, published as late as 1943: "Long ago, when South Africa was a wild sort of place with only black men living there, and lions and tigers used to prowl about the forests at night, high up among the snows of Table Mountain there lived a naughty little imp known as the Tokolosh."[5] The Tokolosh, shown in the illustration as a European imp, is restrained by the Snow Fairies. They have a party attended by "bunnies," which, like tigers, have never lived there. Seeing that Nguni people never reached the Cape Peninsula in pre-European times, and it seldom snows on Table Mountain, Wilkinson's mélange is a particularly extreme example of simply looting folklore for a story.

"Tokolosh" can be contrasted with a tale told in Afrikaans by an indigenous narrator in *Ou M'Kai Vertel* (Old M'Kai Tells) by Pieter Grobbelaar (1964), which is far more appropriate to the Cape Peninsula, because he sets it among the San hunter-gathers who were its first inhabitants.[6] A boy appeals to their deity Kaggen to save Table Mountain from a fire (which is a frequent natural occurrence on its slopes), and he responds by sending the mist rolling down to extinguish it.

In Margaret Herd's *Tok-Tok: Stories for Very Young South Africans* (1943), little Mary, the girl who is told that she cannot see the tokolosh because she is white, persuades a little black girl to tell her about him.[7] Herd invents a taboo that prevents Mary calling him by his name, so she calls him "Tok-Tok."

In real life, white children of country and town had African nannies and could mingle with African farm laborers and have black playmates. Here, then, was the opportunity; if one really listened to black people, one might hear authentic stories of Africa. Dorothea Bleek first heard the stories of the San as a child in 1878 from men of the /Xam group who had been imprisoned for crimes such as sheep stealing when white farmers occupied their hunting grounds. Her father, Dr. Wilhelm Bleek, a distinguished German linguist living in Cape Town, took them to stay at his home, where he and his sister-in-law, Lucy Lloyd, transcribed some 12,000 pages of their lore. The publications by the Bleek family, such as *Specimens of Bushman Folklore* by Bleek and Lloyd and the classic *The Mantis and his Friends* by Dorothea Bleek, provided the material, and even style of language, for many subsequent retellings.[8] An authority on the Bleeks, David Lewis-Williams, describes Dorothea's childhood experience:

> /Han=kasso was gentle and kindly. The colonial children gave him much pleasure, and he played with them and made them birthday presents, such as a set of diminutive bows and arrows or a *!goin!goin*, a bullroarer that /Xam people used as an instrument to make the bees swarm. The children loved to hear him tell his stories. They could not understand the /Xam language, so a member of the Bleek family gave them an outline before the performance began. Then, enthralled, they watched his "eloquent gestures," feeling rather than knowing what was happening.[9]

Elizabeth Helfman is one children's author who was inspired by the words of the San recorded by the Bleeks, as she acknowledges in "A note on the source of the stories," which prefaces her excellent book *The Bushmen and their Stories*, published in New York in 1971.[10] She describes their slaughter and enslavement and movingly tells of their religious beliefs, stories and longings while imprisoned, quoting the words of //Xhabbo, which also inspired Pieter Grobbelaar to write a story about the San (discussed in the next chapter).

Since the beginning of the twentieth century there had been children's writers who knew perfectly well that the indigenous people had their own folktales, and, what is more, that some useful collections had already been published that could be reworked for child readers. Their robust narrative frames, with a strong South African flavor, introduced the real thing. Indigenous tales were more appropriate to an audience of sunburned, barefooted youngsters of the veld than were northern fantasies about gossamer fairies. These were not English moppets, and their sense of humor was not, perhaps, very subtle. In Juliet Konig's down-to-earth stories in *The Little Elephant and Other Stories* (1944), local children were more likely to offer a fairy a squashed banana than have it sip dew from bluebells.[11]

The first two collections for children were stories of the Khoi people, pastoralists who had occupied the country after the San but before the arrival of black people from the north. By the twentieth century their descendants for the most part spoke Afrikaans. *Old Hendrik's Tales* by Captain A.O. Vaughan (1904), opens:

> The day was hot, and the koppies simmered blue and brown along the Vaal River. Noon had come, dinner was done. "Allah Mattie!" said the grey old kitchen boy to himself, as he stretched to sleep in the shade of the mimosa behind the house.... But round the corner of the house came the three children, the eldest a ten-year-old, the youngest six. With a whoop and a dash the eldest flung himself astride the old Hottentot's back, the youngest rode the legs behind, while the girl, the eight-year-old with the yellow hair and the blue eyes, darted to the old man's head and caught him fast with both hands. "Ou' Ta! Ou' Ta!" she cried. "Now you're Ou' Jackalse and we're Ou' Wolf, and we've got you this time at last."[12]

In the next children's book of Khoi stories, *Outa Karel's Stories* (1914), Sanni Metelerkamp[13] takes 11 pages to build up the atmosphere and introduce the narrator around whom the children gather in front of the fire in their home in the Great Karroo, "when the short wintry day had ended, and, in the interval between the coming of darkness and the evening meal, their dear Outa Karel was allowed to tell them stories.... His lower limbs were clothed in nondescript garments fashioned from wildcat and dassie skins; a faded brown coat, which from its size had evidently once belonged to his master, hung near his knees; while, when he removed his shapeless felt hat, a red kopdoek [bandanna] was seen to be wound tightly round his head" (*Outa*, 9). After a "gurgling cough" reminds the master to lubricate his throat with a ritual *soopje* (tot), he commences (*Outa*, 9, 10).

The tradition continued in the brisk *Jantjie's Aunt and Other Stories* by G. Daniell (1930), where a Zulu story is framed: "This is what Old Mieta told Blossom the day she fell out of the pepper tree, and took most of the skin off her hands and knees. Of course they healed afterwards, but there were scars on her knees for a long time."[14]

In the first book of Xhosa folktales for children, published in 1908, Dudley Kidd frames them as stories told to a Xhosa child.[15] *The Bull of the Kraal and the Heavenly Maidens* is a panegyric to African children in which he purports to relate a week that he spent visiting a Xhosa settlement, observing the lifestyle of the people and the daily activities of the little boy Mahleka (Laughter), who is the "Bull" — the heir to the chief. He describes the children's games, their bird traps (with diagrams), health charms and customs surrounding a new baby, and gives the words of songs with accompanying music. This information, which is based on "the experiences gathered during 15 or 16 years of desultory study,"[16] provides the context for the folktales that Mahleka's grandmother tells each night. The implied reader is apparently an English child, with whom Kidd shares the information that he gives with more technical detail in his ethnographic work *Savage Childhood*.

As the century advanced, an increasing number of white writers published versions of indigenous folktales in translation for children, and this interest has never abated. By 1950, about 50 volumes for children had been published in English, most of them by overseas publishers. Compared with the 70-odd books of fairy and European-style talking-animal stories published in the same period, this is a significant number. It also far exceeds the number of Canadian and Australian children's collections of indigenous folktales published in the same period. By the beginning of the twenty-first century, the total had reached more than 150 in English. Many others have been published in Afrikaans, and a few in African languages.

To begin with, writers and publishers could not escape the prevailing sentimental, whimsical view of childhood that lingered until the 1940s not only in South Africa but in other parts of the world. A keyword in this culture of childhood was "fairy," which was loosely and perversely attached to indigenous tales when they were translated into English. The classic example is the series of color "Fairy Books" published in England by Andrew Lang between 1889 and 1910, which contained folktales from all over the world, including Rhodesian ones contributed by the South African Kingsley Fairbridge to *The Orange Fairy Book* (1906).[17] They were written in a "high" style of language and illustrated with elaborate drawings by H.J. Ford in preRaphaelite style.

Continuing this use of "fairy," South Africa had *Fairy Tales from South Africa, Collected from Original Native Sources* by E.J. Bourhill and J. Drake (1908), *Tales of the Fairies* by L. Marsh (19-), *Native Fairy Tales of South Africa* by Ethel McPherson (1919) and *Fairy Tales Told by Nontsomi* by M. Waters (1927).[18] In Australia, Frank Dalby Davison prefaced his retelling of an Australian aboriginal folktale, *Children of the Dark People* (1936), with a verse by Henry Lawson:

Oh, tell them a tale of the fairies bright —
That only the bushmen know.[19]

It was difficult for South African writers to wrench themselves away from the magic word. In *Two Little Strangers Meet* by Helena Hersman and H. Lily Guinsberg (193-), when a little girl, M'sonda, who "thought that because she was black every other child was black," encounters a white girl, her reaction is, "She must be a fairy," and the white girl's reaction is, "She must be an elf."[20] As recently as 1994, in a reworking of many traditional African tales into a single adventure story called *The Kingdom Above the Earth*, Vicki Forrester uses the term "fairy" for a supernatural woman who comes from the Kingdom Above the Earth.[21]

The stubborn retention of the word "fairy" and romanticized portrayals of African culture can be interpreted as an attempt to validate the project of recording and publishing the folktales of colonized peoples by reference to Europe. This European romanticism can be seen in the style of illustration for some early books, such as those for Fairbridge's stories in *The Orange Fairy Book*, and the way the stories are told.

In Ethel McPherson's *Native Fairy Tales of South Africa*, for example, she has excluded the formulae for opening and closing stories as well as all songs, chants or repetition, dismissing them in her author's note as "wearisome iteration," and instead follows European models (*Native Fairy Tales*, 10). "The Queen of the Pigeons" opens, "Once upon a time there lived a maiden who was as fair as a star. She was the delight of the village and her mother loved her above all else in the world" (*Native Fairy Tales*, 44).

To the critics Samantha Naidu,[22] Donnarae MacCann and Yulisa Maddy,[23] the motives of white writers who write about indigenous beliefs can never be innocent, but are always intended to impose Euro-centred subordination and control. While their views are extreme, the phenomenon of folktales in translation does demand investigation. The question of why they should constitute one of the major genres of South African children's literature has been a subject of study and debate in recent years.[24] In broad terms, it is generally agreed by modern critics that whites have always seen folktales as the most *national* form of children's literature. This notion can, in turn, be broken down.

Chief among the characteristics of a national literature is that it must be authentic, and folktales have always fitted the bill, as Kathrine van Vuuren found in interviews that she conducted with librarians and publishers as part of her research for her M.A. in the last decade of the twentieth century:

> The people who buy children's literature are adults who are in some way involved with children, rather than children themselves, and are concerned with what they consider to be "good" for a child, rather than with what a child might actually want.... Publishers realising who the actual buyers of children's books are produce blurbs that are intended to appeal to adults who are interested in stories that are in some way "universal" in their appeal, as well as "authentic" in their South Africanness. According to booksellers I interviewed, adults buying books expressed concern about what type of books to buy, frequently looking for an external standard or way of assessing the books. In this respect, folktales are perceived by many buyers and readers as being "authentic" examples of South African literature, which makes them the most popular and frequently bought genre of indigenous children's literature in South Africa. Popular amongst local buyers, folktales are also bought as presents to be sent overseas, seen as "cultural artefacts" that reflect some aspect of South African life.

> (van Vuuren, 118)

van Vuuren also points out that after the Percy FitzPatrick Prize for children's literature was instituted, it was not awarded for five years, until it was won by Marguerite Poland in 1979 for her volume of stories in the style of folktales, *The Mantis and the Moon*, and that it was awarded for the second time four years later for another of her volumes in that style, *The Wood-Ash Stars*.[25]

According to Van Vuuren's anecdotal evidence, folktales outsell even children's books about wildlife, the other genre that not only is both essentially South African but also has universal appeal, being attractive to tourists and suitable as gifts for overseas. Some collections, of course, combine both drawing cards by concentrating on folktales about animals. Elsa Joubert's *The Four Friends* (1987), containing only animal stories, features a handsome leopard on the cover;[26] and the collections by Nick Greaves, *When Hippo was Hairy* (1988), *When Lion could Fly* (1993) and *When Elephant was King* (1996),[27] and Dianne Stewart's *The*

Zebra's Stripes (2004)[28] not only comprise exclusively animal stories but provide much ancillary factual information about the animals, enhancing their "authenticity."

In almost every case, publishers and authors of folktales, from the first volume to be published until the present, have apparently felt the need to place them in some kind of substantiating context for white readers. This is provided by peritexts consisting of publishers' blurbs, authors' prefaces, notes and glossaries, and forewords by eminent personages. Yet, even while promoting authenticity, the peritexts betray uncertainty about the exact nature of the enterprise of rendering oral folktales in print in another language, about why authors and publishers should record and publish the lore and who their audience is.

They are vague in their statements as to whether the intended readers are adults or children. For example, the back covers of four modern volumes proclaim that they are intended for "readers of all ages," "young and old alike," "children of all age groups," and "adults as well as children."[29]

Sometimes the editorial apparatus, such as glossaries and notes, is suited only for adults. Geraldine Elliot, author of three collections of African folktales for children, was aware that ethnographic peritexts were mainly there to satisfy adults. In her foreword to *The Hunter's Cave* (1951), she reports that when an adult complained that the Chinyanja names in a previous book were too difficult for white readers, she consulted eleven-year-old Rosemary about what she should do for the next book. The child advised her that a pronunciation table would be "all right if you make it short and put it at the end where nobody need look at it."[30]

Essential to authenticity is the idea of ethnographic accuracy. Ethnographic studies, while constituting the background to the writing of many books of folktales for children, are irrelevant for the child's enjoyment of the stories, yet mediating adults seem to expect authors to supply an ethnographic peritext. An academic, John Murray, for example, praises the famous Australian children's writer Patricia Wrightson for her "commendable scrupulosity" in providing author's notes to her fantasies that incorporate Australian myths.[31]

A good example of how dignitaries can impose their view that a book of folktales retold for children *must* be a product of ethnographic research is the foreword written by Rev. A.P. Bender for *Native Fairy Tales of South Africa* by Ethel McPherson, in which he says, "We persuaded her to allow others…to enjoy the exhilarating atmosphere of her gathered lore" (n. p.). However, she actually says in her author's note, "I can make no claim to original research" (*Fairy Tales*, 9) — she has taken the stories from two earlier collections by missionaries; so the only "gathering" she did was to read a couple of books.

One of the most common reasons for publication given in the peritexts of the early books is that the tales must be "preserved." Early white Australian writers were compelled by the idea that the aborigines' tales should be recorded because they were what K. Langloh Parker in *Australian Legendary Tales* called "a race fast dying out."[32] Mary Grant Bruce actually wrote in *The Stone-Axe of Burkammuk* that it was the duty of "all young Australians" to record tales, as though they were little anthropologists.[33]

In South Africa, the situation was different. Clearly, black people were not in any danger of disappearing, and their stories had not only been collected but were still current in oral tradition; while the descendants of the Khoi lived on and preserved their stories in Afrikaans, from which they were translated by Vaughan and Metelerkamp, and the descendants of the slaves from the East also preserved their stories, which no one thought of recording until I.D. du Plessis collected them in Afrikaans and found that they were versions of the Tales from the Arabian Nights. They were translated into English as *Tales from the Malay Quarter* in 1945,[34] and a shorter children's version by Valerie Stillwell, *Monsters, Heroes and Sultans' Daughters,* followed in 1989.

It was the original occupants of the land, the San, who had disappeared, with more finality than the aborigines of Australia. Without the Bleek family, their folklore would have been lost. Their extinction has aroused complex responses; how these are reflected in children's literature is explored later in this chapter and Chapter 7.

Collecting, translating and retelling indigenous folktales were part of the ethnographic enterprise by which Westerners described and analyzed indigenous societies. Thanks to the work of Edward Said and Foucault, the colonialist discourse of the end of the nineteenth century and the imperialist discourse of the early twentieth century can now be understood to have created knowledge that gave the West the power to define the Other as not only different but also therefore as potentially inferior.[35]

The early interest of South African writers in folktales was part of a wider cultural movement in European societies. In his account of the place of African folktales in French literature, Nyembwe Tshikumambila describes how in the early twentieth century, "A wider public was now being made to accept that non-literate civilizations could exist, endowed with an oral art rich in historical, philosophical and aesthetic traditions" and how the cultures of these civilizations provided inspiration for art, music and dance. What resulted were "just romanticised versions of

African tales, often intended for children, and distorted by the period's taste for cheap exoticism."[36]

There are probably several reasons that white English-speaking South Africans of the first half of the twentieth century published so many more books of indigenous folktales for children than were published in Australia and Canada. Unlike white children in the other two countries, South African white children were vastly outnumbered by black people. Possibly, adults hoped that providing them with knowledge of the other would give them the power to control them; but this is an extreme interpretation. The prevailing political climate among white English-speakers was one of benign paternalism, and adults probably vaguely hoped that reading the stories would make white children feel familiar with black people and help them get on together better.

Many critiques of the nature of ethnography and anthropology have demonstrated how what long purported to be objective science is, in fact, a problematic epistemological act. Post-apartheid South Africa has seen much discussion on the pitfalls of recording and exhibiting indigenous cultures, of which the retelling of indigenous folktales by whites is part. On a much more popular level, people of color have resented white appropriation of the bodies of their ancestors: they equate it with exploitation of indigenous knowledge, such as traditional medicines, without compensation. Objections to the permanent dioramas in the South African Museum displaying life casts of San people have forced their removal.[37] The repatriation from Paris of the body of Saartje Baartman, who had been taken to England and France as an exhibition freak in the nineteenth century, became a national cause in South Africa that the government espoused, obliging the French government to amend legislation in order to allow it.

In the 1990s, the curators of two exhibitions that aimed to expose the abuse of the bodies of indigenes in colonial times ran into severe criticism because they displayed the original offensive material. Various groups claiming to represent Khoisan people objected to the *Miscast* exhibition, which opened in the National Gallery in Cape Town in April 1996, and a similar protest took place in Canada over the controversial *Into the Heart of Africa* exhibition held at the Royal Ontario Museum, November 1989–August 1990.[38]

Further controversy rages over a group of San who were brought to the Western Cape by a white farmer, where they currently live in a so-called traditional way, on display to tourists. Reviewing a book about them by Hylton White, Helize van Vuuren likens these displays to the retelling of folktales:

This study…comes as a timely reminder especially to literary critics and researchers focusing increasingly on the oral tradition(s) of these earliest inhabitants of Southern Africa, of the question of advocacy. We use glib phrases — for example — such as "recovering our lost heritage" or talk of "reconstructing voices from the past" with reference to the extinct /Xam group's oral tradition (which Bleek and Lloyd and later G.R. von Wielligh focused on). It is all too easy to romanticise these "little people" or "harmless people" as symbolising the original South African presence. But are we perhaps merely recolonising exotic material into our defunct white canon with the aim of revitalising it?"[39]

Concern at the appropriation of indigenous culture by unscrupulous people is growing in sophistication. In 2001 the Working Group of Indigenous Minorities in Southern Africa drew up a San Media and Research Contract to "ensure that all San intellectual property (including images, traditional knowledge, music and other heritage components as recorded in any medium) is controlled and protected."[40]

Various critiques of translations of South African folktales for children in recent years (cited above) have shown that producing a written version of an oral tale is a complicated and unreliable process that provides scope for a writer to perpetuate colonialist, racist images of indigenous people. In 1989, as apartheid came to an end, Andreé-Jeanne Tötemeyer argued in a courageous article that the production of translations of folktales for children had indeed served the ideology of apartheid:

> The great admiration for African mythology and the culture of blacks in South African juvenile literature, far greater than in any other country of the west, therefore possibly has ideological foundations…. The belief in the separate cultural identity of each ethnic group…is nothing more than the old British "divide and rule" concept…. By instilling admiration in South African white children for the various black cultures with due emphasis on the differences between them, the apartheid system based on these ethnic differences is perpetuated…. Although this may not be the intention of retellers and collectors of…folk tales, their endeavours can contribute to the reinforcement of the concept of ethnicity upon which the apartheid-ideology is based, depending on the manner in which the stories are told.[41]

Tötemeyer argued that when retellers emphasized how the tales came from a pristine, unspoilt time before the indigenous people met whites, they suggested that the true nature of the culture of indigenous people was "primitive" and "tribal." More recently, as the fate of the last nomadic San of Botswana has become the concern of human rights activists, Duncan Brown has argued that "the myth of the pristine hunter-gatherer is one which has been used, in Namibia and Botswana, to deny Bushman peoples land and political rights — effectively to destroy them."[42]

Until at least the 1980s, the peritexts of volumes of folktales for white South African child readers remarked on how, to whites, they appear exotic. Since then, black writers such as Gcina Mhlophe, Bob Leshoai and Nombulelo Makhuphula have published their own collections of folktales in English, explaining that they heard them from their elders.[43] Here at last are tales retold directly by members of the culture they come from. This is a kind of authenticity that differs from that of the "collector." The note in Dinah Mbanze's books *The Magic Pot* and *The Berry Basket* (1999) gives her own background, which is a common enough life history of a black person, though it may sound strange to white readers who have been sheltered from her marginal, peri-urban world:

> Dinah M. Mbanze taught at a farm school in the district of Bronkhorstspruit in Gauteng until 1998, when, after thirty years, she was retrenched because she lacked formal teaching qualifications. At the suggestion of Jo Bleeker of Tweefontein farm where Dinah lives, she then started to write down the tales she had heard as a child. With the assistance of Jo Bleeker the stories were later prepared and presented for publication.[44]

These writers are sharing their stories with all South African children who understand English, in what may be seen as a deliberate project to promote nationalism. Leshoai acknowledges the political nature of his book in his foreword, when he says, "The choice of these legends, folk-tales and stories has been influenced by the sociological and political life of the people of South Africa" (*Iso le Nkhono*, 2).

In addition to retellings by black authors, a few books are illustrated by black artists. Azaria Mbatha's linocuts for *Tales of the Trickster Boy* by Jack Cope (1990),[45] executed in his idiosyncratic style, which has echoes of traditional art, are very different from the illustrations by white artists that are more common (see Figure 6).

Apart from authenticity, another aspect of the perceived national character of folktales is their universality. Translations have often born the burden of adult hopes that they can bridge the gap between black and white children. This notion is vague and needs scrutinizing, not least to question the profit motive: if folktales are universal, it is

6 Illustration by Azaria Mbatha from *Tales of the Trickster Boy* by Jack Cope

convenient to rework existing collected material with little trouble and be assured of a market for children.

One reason that white people have thought the folktales of indigenous people are universal is that nineteenth-century books by travelers and the novelists who borrowed their material frequently described indigenous adults as "childlike." Comments of this sort could be found in children's books. A character in *Off to the Wilds* by George Manville Fenn (1882), for example, remarks of Matabele warriors, who terrorized large tracts of the subcontinent, "These people seem to me more like children than men" (157).[46] This facile notion was reinforced by the neotenic appearance of the San people, the hunter-gatherers who inhabited the land before the arrival of Khoi and African pastoralists and whites. They were small in stature, with relatively hairless bodies and what Europeans considered to be childlike facial features.

At the beginning of the twentieth century, social Darwinism still governed whites' perception of the indigenous people, identifying them as representing earlier stages in the evolution of human society. These ideas were taken up in the newly developing field of psychology; an individual's development from infancy to adulthood was considered to parallel humankind's passage from savagery to civilization. In 1907, the pioneer American educational psychologist G. Stanley Hall published his influential *Aspects of Child Life and Education* in which he propounded his "recapitulation" theory, that "the child lives again the history of the race."[47] This was such a truism in late nineteenth- and early twentieth-century America that fiction about boys could show them as having the license to be wild. In his study of this literature, Kenneth B. Kidd observes that until the 1920s, "boyhood was presumed rural and preindustrial, such that an urban boyhood seemed a contradiction of terms for a while."[48]

A related belief until the early twentieth century was that indigenous children equaled their white counterparts in intellect and development only until they reached adolescence. It was propounded by clergymen who were influenced by biblical precepts on equality, such as Rev. John Campbell, whose books on his missionary travels in South Africa were considered authoritative. He wrote in 1840: "There is not naturally such a difference between children in civilized and uncivilized countries as we are apt to suppose. The difference becomes more apparent as they advance from childhood to manhood."[49]

To Rev. A.P. Bender, writing the Foreword to Ethel McPherson's *Native Fairy Tales of South Africa* in 1919, this had the implication that folktales have universal significance for children: "We hope that the boys and girls of less sunny climes may be brought to realize that in all parts of the Child-world without distinction there is eloquently evidenced the same natural intuition of kinship with a perennially fresh and fertile imagination fed by the Hand of an inexhaustible love and grace" (*Fairy Tales*, 7).

The notion was given scientific, psychological respectability by Dudley Kidd, who was regarded in Edwardian times as an authority on Africans, in *Savage Childhood*: "As a matter of fact the savage is at his best, intellectually, emotionally, and morally, at the dawn of puberty. When puberty is drawing to a close, a degeneration process seems to set in, and the previous efflorescence of the faculties leads to no adequate fruitage in later life."[50] In another of his books, *The Essential Kaffir*, Kidd did try to qualify this by cautioning, "One of the commonest generalisations made by hasty observers is that the natives are but overgrown children. There is, of course, some truth in the statement — just sufficient to make it very untrue."[51]

The logical conclusion to these theories was that the tales of indigenous people were particularly suited for retelling to children. This is a notion that could still be found in the late twentieth century. In 1985 Hanneke du Preez, the writer of two books of San stories, *Kgalagadi Tales*, announced in "A word to parents and teachers," "Children sense in them a kinship for which there is no rational explanation."[52] Sheila Egoff and Judith Saltman expressed the same opinion in their history of Canadian children's literature: "The legends [of the First Nations]... also have a strong appeal for children because they reveal a world that is in many ways close to that of a child."[53]

That there is a strong belief to this day in the universal appeal of folktales is borne out by the fact that a great many of the collections of South African tales have been published in the UK and U.S. for readers in other countries. By contrast, all the books of stories of South African talking animals and fairies published until the 1950s came from local publishing houses. As the previous chapter showed, their titles and peritexts emphasized that they were patriotic enterprises of South Africans, while the texts belonged to the world of white English speakers.

Finding something common in the South African past that would unite the nation became an imperative after apartheid collapsed at the end of the 1980s, and this need for a knowledge of the past is fused in popular thinking with the hope invested in children. In 1994, Kathrine van Vuuren reported that she had found in her research, "With recent political events moving South Africa towards a more unified state, children's literature is being touted by many of the people who work in children's literature itself as well as by parents and teachers as being a potentially unifying force. This belief ties in with the idea that "children are the 'hope' of the 'new' South Africa" (K. van Vuuren, 13). She identified three genres that were seen as "corrective, trying to make amends for some of the effects of South Africa's apartheid past" (K. van Vuuren, 14). One of them was folktales, the others being historical fiction and teenage social-issue novels.

At a national conference on children's literature held in Cape Town in 1992, Marguerite Poland, one of the country's most distinguished children's authors, explained why, while endorsing the focus on children for the future of the country, she drew her subject matter from the past. She explained her creed, which inspired her to write tales in the style of San and African folktales:

> The real source of my inspiration is and always has been the land…. The people who inhabit it or who once inhabited it, like the San, are also the source of my inspiration. However, I have been questioned as to why I hark back to beliefs and customs dear to the older generation of black South Africans and to people like the San, so long on the fringes of society, when there is an urgent need to attend to current problems and pressures. Is it not anachronistic in this day and age to dwell on the past when there are far more important issues to address? Of course there are important contemporary issues to address. It is vital to do so. Nevertheless I believe — and fiercely — that the old beliefs and traditions of which I speak are a valuable and precious commodity in the desolation of our contemporary world.[54]

She quoted the poet Mazisi Kunene's prayer that children should "sing the songs of their forefathers," and went on, "These old beliefs, rooted in the land and reverend to nature, give another, richer dimension to our way of seeing things" (Poland, 18). It was all the more important to instill this understanding in children, because "It has always been children who are the possessors of hope" (*Poland*, 20).

Folktales have a part to play in contributing to the modern South African nation. In a way, this was foreseen by Frantz Fanon in his famous book *The Wretched of the Earth* (1961), which was banned in South Africa.[55] Reviving precolonial myths, he said, rehabilitates the nation and serves as a justification for the hope of a future national culture. Irish academic Ciara Ní Bhroin argues that this is what happened in Ireland in 1902 when Lady Gregory published her version of the Cuchulain story: "*Cuchulain of Muirthemne* was a seminal book in translating tradition at a key moment in Ireland's decolonisation and in laying the foundations for a national children's literature in English."[56]

The South African situation was studied by Samantha Naidu for her M.A. dissertation.[57] She explains the tensions in the project:

> The main aim of the "new nationalist" discourse is to bridge the cultural gaps of a post-apartheid society. It employs the indigenous folktale as a symbol of unity and patriotic pride and has its roots in anti-colonial and anti-apartheid resistance movements. In the face of domination by transplanted European culture, the decolonising nationalists had to construct a discourse which incorporated and amalgamated the "essences" of local culture, whilst assimilating aspects of the hegemonic foreign cultures. At the centre of this African nationalism is the paradox of utilising local cultures and histories, together with the Western discourses of modernity and nationalism, for purposes of liberation and self-determination.
>
> (*Naidu* 2001b, 17)

She acknowledges that the colonial desire to preserve African culture is worthy, but points out that its result was to essentialize that culture as something stuck in the past and outlandish. On the other hand, the danger of promoting a multicultural new nation is that ethnic identity may be lost in the process: "Common to both discourses is the view that the tale texts are able to bridge gaps and heal rifts in our society. This ameliorating role of folktales texts can be achieved only if both the risk of eliding differences and the challenge of positively rearticulating difference are forcefully tackled" (*Naidu* 2001b, 24).

Her solution is to contextualize the tales by "cross-cultural education" (Naidu 2001b, 23). Rather than drawing attention to parallels with tales from other parts of the world, the peritexts should explain obscure aspects of the tales. Furthermore, she has no hesitation in approving the rewriting of tales in a "hybrid text" appropriate for written literature, citing in support Harold Scheub's introduction to *Tales from Southern Africa* by the Xhosa writer A.C. Jordan.[58]

> Jordan…witnessed many *ntsomi* [folktale] productions in the Transkei as a child. He has now recast them, and if the result is closer to the short story than to the *ntsomi* in structure, elements of the *ntsomi* nevertheless linger. Repetition has been muted, but that is also the case with the great oral artists' works. Jordan has retained many of the core-clichés…. He has also added descriptive details of character and scene…. He sometimes interpolates comments of his own, as would any really good oral performer….

There can be no doubt but that the oral flavour of the performances is gone.

(*Naidu* 2001b, 24)

Thus Naidu, strong critic of colonialist and imperialist treatment of indigenous folktales, ultimately not only accepts that they are inevitably altered in the process of translation and reworking in literary form, but approves the addition of information in the peritext and insertion of explanatory information in the texts.

Any writer, whether black or white, who attempts to set the tales in the past treads a narrow line between exoticizing black people — essentializing them as primitive and strange — and bringing them alive, creating sympathetic portraits that only imaginative literature can provide. One way of recreating the context is to write stories about children that include episodes in which they are told traditional tales. This has been tried a few times in South Africa. The first attempt was by Dudley Kidd in *The Bull of the Kraal and the Heavenly Maidens*, already mentioned. The title indicates the dual nature of the work, as the Bull is the child and the Heavenly Maidens are the subject of one of his grandmother's tales. Kidd's contextual information is accurate, but the book is very outdated in style.

Mary Phillips attempted to do the same thing in two more-recent books, *The Bushman Speaks* (1961) and *The Cave of Uncle Kwa* (1965), in which a San boy is told the lore and myths of his people in the course of what purports to be an account of historical events affecting them in the late seventeenth century.[59] The works fail because the fictional contexts are incredible and the historical details are highly inaccurate.

In 1953, Daphne Rooke made the novel that frames tales multicultural. In *The South African Twins*,[60] various people tell stories of the Zulus and the Voortrekkers. The white girl Tiensie tells her grandmother Zulu tales, and when the old lady refuses to hear "that awful one about the two-headed snake" she softens her up by retelling *Peter Pan* before going on to "Juba and the Death Tree" (*Twins*, 97). Other works of fiction for children that incorporate traditional tales and information on folklore have been described in previous chapters.

A symbolic way in which children's literature has been used in the quest for creating a multicultural nation in which all the tributary cultures of the country have an equal part is to include traditional tales from these various sources in the same book. This was, in fact, done in a few books from the 1920s to the 1940s, after which it was not seen again until the very end of the century.

At the same time that Juta was publishing its Juvenile Library with the iconic frame for the title page, its great publishing rival in Cape Town, Maskew Miller, published a set of school readers with yet another of those patriotic titles that were popular at the time: *Maskew Miller's English Readers for Young South Africans, Standard I* (n.d.).[61] This was another project in nationalism for white children. Where Juta has the sunburst motif at the bottom center of its frame, the Maskew Miller cover has as a vignette a dramatic picture of Cape Town's Table Mountain, with streaming clouds accentuating its grandeur. For centuries, Table Mountain was the classic symbol of South Africa, though its prominence has waned since the end of the twentieth century, when the new government chose new national symbols from farther across the interior, such as Mapungubwe Hill on the Limpopo river, home of an eleventh-century African kingdom.

The contents of the reader follow Juta's frame of references, but go further. Where Juta has the English granny telling stories, Maskew Miller has poems by English writers such as Charles Kingsley, George MacDonald and Juliana Ewing; where Juta has a slave on a Cape Dutch farm, Maskew Miller has stories of the Dutch in the Cape, but also in America, and stories from slaves in America; and where Juta has African animals, the reader has a genuine African folktale.

The South African content is spelled out in a way that equates the folktales of white and black: "We have had two stories already in this book. The first was one that the Dutch people at the Cape used to tell: it was the story of Van Hunks and the smoking match. Then we had a story about the Dutch people in America.... Now we are to have another South African story. This time it will be one of the stories that the Natives like to tell each other" (*Maskew Miller*, 53). The story of Van Hunks is the best known Cape Dutch folktale, providing yet another version of the origin of the clouds on Table Mountain — they come from the pipes of Van Hunks and the Devil when they engage in a smoking match. The origin of the African tale, "The story of the white cow," is not given in the list of acknowledgments, but it appears to be a retelling of one of the tales in the classic nineteenth-century collections.

The reader gives intriguing evidence of the continuing reference to America in South African English culture. A historical section on how "South Africa was not the only part of the world to which the Dutch went at that time" (*Maskew Miller*, 29) introduces the story of Rip van Winkle. Brer Rabbit stories of Uncle Remus, which were being imitated so freely by South African writers at the time, are included, whereas there are no local animal stories; and they are told as the stories of slaves, whereas the stories of the descendants of slaves in the Cape are ignored. To a modern reader, the introduction on American slaves is astonishingly disingenuous: "You may work for anybody you like, or you may work for yourself if you can make things that other people wish to buy. You are free. There was a time when many people were not free…. Long ago coloured people from the East were brought to the Cape and sold as slaves…but after a while people saw that it was not right to have slaves, and they were all made free" (*Maskew Miller*, 86). The treatment of people of color in South Africa since the emancipation of slaves is ignored.

After an interval of 60 years, two spectacular collections of folktales that are emphatically multicultural were published at the beginning of the twenty-first century. In *African Myths and Legends* (2001), Struik Publishers combined two previously published collections, *Daughter of the Moonlight and Other African Tales* by Dianne Stewart (1994) and *South African Myths and Legends* by Jay Heale (1995).[62] The former volume had contained stories labeled San, Khoikhoi (an alternative spelling of Khoi), Swazi, Zulu, Xhosa and Sotho; the latter had contained a few San and African stories together with South African Dutch/Afrikaans ghost stories and legends (such as Van Hunks and the Devil, which had appeared in the Maskew Miller reader) and one historical story, of a brave boy who survived the wreck of the *Grosvenor* in 1782. All the stories are accompanied by modest informative panels well suited to the needs of a young reader. The resulting volume, in large format and brightly illustrated, may deservedly be considered a creation of a transformed South Africa.

A year later, with great fanfare, an expensive volume printed on high quality paper and with magnificent full illustrations by leading illustrators was launched, entitled *Madiba Magic: Nelson Mandela's Favourite Stories* (2002).[63] The new brand of patriotic title contains the magic name of Mandela, patron of children's causes, and the book bears out Kathrine van Vuuren's observation that folktales were becoming one of the media for focusing on children as the hope for the future of the new democracy. Typical of the spirit of the time was another colorful book published in Cape Town in the same year, *Letters to Madiba: Voices of South African Children* (2002), which has a cover photograph of Mandela holding a little girl.[64] "Madiba" is Mandela's clan name, which is used as a mark of both respect and affection. Both names carry so much weight that Mandela's lawyers are constantly at work to protect them from widespread commercial infringement.

The contents of *Madiba Magic* are an eclectic cultural spread: African stories from various parts of the continent — Khoi and Nama folktales retold by writers such as Gcina Mhlophe, Pieter Grobbelaar, Hugh Tracey and Phyllis Savory; Van Hunks again; Cape Malay stories; and fiction by Jay Heale, Marguerite Poland and Cicely van Straten. Each story is introduced by a note, but the tone and contents of the notes have thoughtlessly reverted to the old style of ethnographic peritext that betrays confusion as to the age and needs of the reader: "While some attempt has been made to indicate where the story came from, those who are conversant with the ways of folklore will know that it is sometimes — indeed often — totally impossible to pinpoint with any degree of accuracy where the story originated" (*Madiba Magic*, n.p.). By coincidence, most of the stories are reprints from earlier publications by the same publisher, Tafelberg. Nelson Mandela would have had to be a keen reader of Tafelberg children's books over a period of years to make this selection of his "favourite" stories. At any rate, he did write the short foreword, and the proceeds (which must be enormous, as the book is a bestseller in several languages all over the world) go to the Nelson Mandela Children's Fund.

Imaginative, traditional literature for children is invested with hope for South Africa at the opening of the twenty-first century. One of its glories is *Fly, Eagle, Fly!* by Christopher Gregorowski, illustrated by the prominent illustrator Niki Daly. First published in 1982, it was republished in a beautiful new edition in 2000.[65]

A farmer finds an eagle chick and brings it up as a chicken, but his friend cannot bear to see it like that and makes several attempts to get it to fly. Eventually one dawn he succeeds. The story itself appears to be common property; in 2002 another version was published, called *Eagle Learns to Fly*, written and illustrated by Penny Baillie, in which Monty Monkey rescues the eagle chick.[66] Jay Heale's review of this version is not complimentary: "*Eagle Learns to Fly* is this author's light-hearted version of the allegory which inspired Christopher Gregorowski's *Fly, Eagle, Fly!* and it is very much second best. The rhymed verse text makes the story too much like a cute nursery rhyme."[67]

Gregorowski explains in an author's note in the second edition that he reworked what he describes as a "parable" by James Aggrey, the Ghanaian writer, "when our seven-year-old daughter was dying." He set it in the Transkei, "where I worked among the Xhosa people as an Anglican [Episcopal] priest" (*Eagle*, n.p.). Daly adds a note describing the book's history:

> In 1982, when I first illustrated *Fly, Eagle, Fly!*, full-colour illustrations were a luxury seldom seen in South African children's books. That first version of the story was published as a small for-

mat two-colour book. A few years later it was out of print, but it was not forgotten by the readers it had inspired. Now, as our new and precious democracy gives us wings to fly, a new edition with full-colour pictures celebrates the flight of our many eagles — the children of South Africa, to whom I dedicate this book.

(Eagle, n.p.)

Gregorowski's parable of 1982 was powered by his personal grief and his aspirations for the suppressed Xhosa people; in 2000 it took on new urgency and significance:

The golden sun rose majestically and dazzled all of them. The great bird stretched out its wings to greet the sun and feel its life-giving warmth in its feathers. The farmer was quiet. The friend said, "Fly, eagle, fly! You belong not to the earth, but to the sky. Fly, eagle, fly!"...

And then, without really moving, feeling the updraught of a wind more powerful than any man or bird, the great eagle leaned into it and was swept upward, higher and higher, lost to sight in the brightness of the rising sun, never again to live among the chickens.

(Eagle, n.p.)

6

STORIES IN THE FOLKTALE TRADITION

Stories written in the tradition or style of indigenous folktales are an important South African literary form. Though limited in number, they include writing of high quality. Naturally, white writers in this genre can be condemned for their neocolonial appropriation and exploitation of indigenous beliefs and lore, and in the case of some, their shallow approach is obvious. Seen from a modern perspective, the early stories were racist and arrogant. Other writers, more recently, have demonstrably undertaken research and worked hard to do justice to indigenous lore or have been inspired by African beliefs to write about Africa in a way that differs from the Eurocentred approach of the authors of the early fairy and talking-animal stories. As with English and Afrikaans versions of folktales, it can be argued that in the light of the paucity of publications by indigenous people themselves, these stories have for many years provided white children with another mode of understanding their mother country.

It is by no means easy to distinguish stories written in the style of folktales from redactions of folktales themselves. Folktales have no set form, and vary from one performance to another; translations can range from verbatim records such as those of the Bleeks to widely expanded and adapted literary versions. Elizabeth Waterston, historian of Canadian children's literature, has used the term "realizations" to describe literary versions of First Nations tales.[1] This is a musical term (which Benjamin Britten used to describe some of his work) defined in *Collins Encyclopedia of Music* as "The act of completing the harmony of a 17th- or 18th-century work by providing a keyboard accompaniment based on the indications afforded by the figured bass."[2] Scheub probably had this concept in mind in his unfortunately pejorative choice of terminology when he wrote approvingly that A.C. Jordan had "retained many of the core-clichés" in his expanded versions of Xhosa folktales.[3]

A few stories in the early volumes of fairy and talking-animal stories illustrate the emergence of the genre in South Africa. In 1926–1930, some, of the more crass kind, use verbal formulae and a high style associated with folktales, while the contents are clearly invented by the author. Ella MacKenzie introduces her original legend of how a lazy impi (regiment) turned into "ugly, fat black locusts": "A long while ago, before there were any white people in South Africa, away up towards the North there lived a great and powerful Kafir Chief."[4] Among Sadie Merber's fairy stories is "The Ox with the Red Star," which begins, "Far away in Kaffir-land lived an old chief."[5] The plot, about winning the hand of the chief's daughter, is European rather than African, and includes a European gnome who visits a little shepherd boy, Mbutana, and teaches him magic words. Corinne Rey gets off to a bad start when she opens her made-up legend about Africans in *Tales of the Veld*, "In a certain part of our big continent lives a race of natives who have minds just like little children." She writes in high style, ending, "And many other stories do these people tell their children in like manner which is wise. For does not each story set forth a lesson to be learnt?"[6]

Only one story from this period sounds as though it could be authentic. This is the one by G. Daniell mentioned in the previous chapter, which Old Mieta told to Blossom "the day she fell out of the pepper tree." It opens, "Once upon a time there was a wicked old Zulu named Makiaan," and relates how a girl and her lover turn into birds and live happily after her cruel uncle has been killed.[7]

Later Minnie Martin, in *Tales of the African Wilds* (1942), took much more effort to introduce genuine African elements such as African words and names, though with limited success. She derived her trickster stories from Uncle Remus and her fables from Aesop, rather than directly from the African tradition that was their origin, and invented African spirits called Moloi and Gogo. The only direct African folktale element is in "The Gift Bird," which is about a traditional African supernatural creature, the milk bird, that brings "gifts of contentment and unselfishness."[8]

Australia, Canada, New Zealand and South Africa all have children's fiction written by white people that engages with indigenous beliefs, myths and legends, and each country has its favorite genres. Early in the twentieth century, Australia had its share of invented aboriginal tales, which Brenda Niall observes were intended to teach white children about aborigines but simply relegated them to a timeless, primitive past.[9] In Canada, with *The Golden Pine Cone* (1950) Catherine Anthony Clark started a minor tradition of fantasy novels in which white children encounter both invented spirits and the supernatural figures of First Nation lore. Canada also has fantasy stories in which the supernatural, such as an evil spirit, irrupts into a modern teenager's world. Similarly, many novels by the Australian Patricia Wrightson and the New Zealander Margaret Mahy concern modern white children moving in and out of the supernatural world of aboriginal and Maori legend.

South Africa has few fantasy novels like these, *Witch Woman on the Hogsback* by Carolyn Parker (1987) and *The Battle of the Mountain* by Judy Chalmers (1984) being the two most notable examples, though they are not great literature.[10] They vaguely reflect Xhosa beliefs, and MacCann and Maddy have lambasted Parker for her arrogance in attempting to do so.[11]

What South Africa does have is social realist novels about black people that bring in their traditional beliefs, or in which white children make the acquaintance of black people and learn about their traditional beliefs and myths from them. Already mentioned in this book are *Ramini of the Bushveld* by Werner Heyns, *Zulu Boy* by Lola Bower, *Tau, the Chieftain's Son* by G.H. Franz, *The Silent People* by Knobel Bongela, and *The Adventures of Kalipe* by Anne and Peter Cook, who explain in their introduction, "The stories which make up [this book] have been based on legends, histories and stories told by the Nguni tribes themselves."[12] D.R Sherman integrates San lore into *The Pride of the Hunter*, discussed in Chapter 7,[13] and Dorothy Kowen does the same in her rite-of-passage story about a San girl, *Nyama and the Eland* (2003).[14]

Two books by white authors from the period of transition to democracy stand out: *Shadow of the Wild Hare* (1986) by Marguerite Poland[15] and *Mystery at Cove Rock* by Beryl Bowie (1991).[16] Both writers researched the African background carefully. Poland not only grew up in the Eastern Cape, speaking Xhosa fluently, but has done postgraduate work in both Xhosa and Zulu studies. Bowie arrived as an English immigrant to the Eastern Cape in 1980. She lists the books she consulted and thanks a Xhosa teacher and the Xhosa person whose three grandsons' names she uses for characters in the book.

Shadow of the Wild Hare is a dense and subtle novel. Rosie, a white girl on a farm, learns about the complex relationship between humans and animals from a Xhosa who is a professional trapper of jackals, and a slow-witted white woman who has lived among the descendants of the Khoisan. Their ancient myths and beliefs teach about the necessity of death in the cycle of life and death, and how the caging of a creature's or person's spirit is crueller than a quick death. When Rosie takes a hare from the trapper because he used it as bait, the woman, who had been forcibly removed from her kindly caregivers and placed in an institution, tells her, "You should set it free. Even if it dies. It is better than a cage. This thing I know" (*Shadow*, 33). Poland loves African names for people and, above all, animals, which to her are the epitome of African culture. Symbolizing the trapper's determination always to be free, he keeps his name, Tantyi Mayekiso, in spite of the white people's attempts to call him by the nondescript typical laborer's Afrikaans name, Klaas.

Names and language are the gateway to Xhosa culture in *Mystery at Cove Rock*. When a boy from England, Rob, comes to live in a trailer park situated on a wild stretch of coastline, the key to making friends with the Xhosa brothers he meets is to get their names right: Siphiwo, and his younger brothers Thembana and Sithembele. Rob remarks to himself how difficult the names are, and when he approximates with "Spiro," Siphiwo gravely corrects him: "My name is Siphiwo. You say it wrong" (*Cove Rock*, 26). Rob also recognizes, after meeting some Afrikaans boys, that he will have to learn to speak Afrikaans if he wants to make his home in South Africa. At that time, white children had to learn both English and Afrikaans; few of their schools taught other African languages. "Siphiwo was amazed. This boy couldn't speak Afrikaans! Then surely he wouldn't be able to speak Xhosa either. Siphiwo, used to communicating in three languages from an early age, could hardly believe it" (*Cove Rock*, 30). This is only one example of how cultural viewpoints are reversed in this book. Another is how Siphiwo understands the concept of an immigrant by reference to his own nation's history: "Siphiwo's own people, the Abantu abaphesheya kweNciba, had come across the Kei River also, but that had been long, long ago" (*Cove Rock*, 18). The stage is set for Rob to learn from the Xhosa boy.

By alternating between Rob and Siphiwo as centers of consciousness, Bowie delicately explores the place of traditional beliefs in the lives of the Xhosa boys and the white boy's reaction to them. The brothers are typical modern children: the sons of a farm laborer, they go to school and earn pocket money by gardening on Saturdays. In keeping with his firm upbringing, Siphiwo shows great respect for the People who dwell on Cove Rock, correctly called Gompo, who are the Ancestors, just as he respects his parents and his history.

Rob is puzzled as to who the People may be, but as he learns about them, he completely accepts the necessity that Siphiwo is under to appease them with small gifts when entering their territory. Although the disappearance of the gifts of food is explained when a fugitive is discovered living there, Rob accepts Siphiwo's understanding that after Rob saves him from the sea, and later is rescued in turn when he falls into a pothole, the People have rewarded Rob by allowing him to be saved.

Although a newsletter of a children's book group once classified *Mystery at Cove Rock* as "fantasy," there is nothing in it that meets this definition. It simply introduces white readers to another world view.

In the last quarter of the twentieth century, several writers returned to writing fiction in the style of folktales or legends, this time avoiding the racial arrogance of their prewar predecessors. How genuine sympathy can inspire the artist can be seen in the account by an Afrikaans children's writer, Pieter W. Grobbelaar, of how he came to write *The White Arrow* (1974):

> There is something that I can never read without being moved. It is the story of Khabbo, a Bushman of the last century who had to serve out a sentence for sheep-stealing in Cape Town. These were his words: "Thou knowest that I sit waiting for the moon to turn back for me, that I may return to my place. That I may listen to all the people's stories, when I visit them.... That I may sit in the sun, that I may sitting, listen to the stories which yonder come, which are stories which come from a distance.... Like the wind, it comes from a far-off quarter, and we feel it." This authentic narrative with its very distinctive style, recorded by W.H.I. Bleek and L.C. Lloyd in *Specimens of Bushman Folklore*, touched me to the heart and compelled me to start writing at once; and the story of *The White Arrow* took shape almost of its own accord.[17]

The words of Khabbo (now written //Kabbo) that he quotes are the same as those quoted by Elizabeth Helfman in *The Bushmen and their Stories*, referred to in Chapter 5, which she had found so moving;[18] they were also the inspiration behind *The Dancer*, an original story by Nola Turkington and Niki Daly (1996), which Daly illustrated with stylized imitations of San rock paintings.[19] John van Reenen's superb illustrations for *The White Arrow* capture Grobbelaar's empathy for the San. (See Figure 7.)

Modern writers of folktales or stories in the folktale tradition usually still adopt a lyrical — perhaps formal or archaic — style, sometimes echoing African languages or the verbatim translations by the Bleeks from the language of their San teachers. Grobbelaar ends *The White Arrow*, "That is how the south wind came into being, and from that time on Mother Moon grows and pines away, grows and pines away, week after month after year, so that people watching her can know that Death is not the end, but a new beginning" (*White Arrow*, n.p.).

7 Illustration by John van Reenen from *The White Arrow* by Pieter Grobbelaar

A classic collection from 1968 is *Tales from the Kraals* by Madeline Murgatroyd.[20] The cover called it "a collection of African tales and legends," but when she brought out a second volume, *Maduma, Teller of Tales*, in 1987, the cover, calling her "surely the doyenne of children's writers in South Africa," explained that in fact the stories were realizations: "Carefully she has selected motifs from many parts of Africa and fashioned around each a story that is totally new, yet has all the flavour and feel of the true folktale."[21]

Murgatroyd's stories are true art stories, carefully constructed to be dramatic and written in a lyrical style:

> Down to the lovely pool in the glen Tembi and her green birds went. A night snake wriggled out of her way as she tripped down the path. Sleepily, two ha-de-das opened their eyes and shook their bronze wings before they settled down again. An owl hooted eerily, his eyes — like lanterns in the gloom of the glen — shone brightly.
>
> "Be not afraid, my feathered friends," called Tembi, "we come to do no harm but to share the cool water of your pool. And for my green birds, a little honey from the aloe flowers."
>
> *(Kraals,* 75)

Jenny Seed, author of about 100 books of many kinds — and more deserving than Murgatroyd of the title of doyenne — wrote two single-volume stories, *The Lost Prince* (1985) and *The Strange Black Bird* (1986), which have typical folk elements such as a magic bird that helps children.[22] She also wrote a cycle of San stories, *The Bushman's Dream* (1974), which, like Grobbelaar, she says she was inspired by the Bleek material to write.[23] In her author's note she acknowledges that she made up the book using elements of the originals.

Marguerite Poland is the most admired of all the writers in this genre. Once again, the boundary between folk and original material is blurred. Her animal stories, *The Mantis and the Moon* (1979), which won the Percy Fitzpatrick Prize, and *Once at KwaFubesi* (1981), both of which were later combined with a few changes in *Sambane's Dream* (1989), are often referred to as folktales, although they are her own creation.[24] Like her predecessors, Poland anthropomorphizes mostly small creatures such a birds, an aardvark, snakes and bush pigs, giving them African names and authentic settings for their funny, exciting or sad activities. Stories drawing on the Bleeks' San material remain closer to the originals than the African-style stories in subject matter and the cadences of the writing:

> Storms are brought by the rain bulls. The rain-cows come with the misty showers of summer. They are a great herd of eland that live in the sky-pastures. In the winter when the desert is dry and cold, they migrate to distant mountains, where they make the thunderclouds. That is where their herder, the wind, keeps them until winter has gone. Then he drives them with the clouds racing before them and, on a still desert day, the rain-bulls can be heard bellowing in the thunder. Then they gallop across the sky and behind them come the rain-cows with the long-soaking summer

storms that day after day fill the dry pans and waterholes and coax the green out of the earth.

(*Sambane*, 82)

Her second Percy Fitzpatrick Prize winner, *The Wood-ash Stars*, strikingly illustrated by Shane Altshuler, contains two stories that are realizations and two that are simply stories about children, though one includes a magic woman. The title story is an old San myth, which she ends: "And so it is — the old ones say — that the thousands of little stars that form the Milky Way are really a handful of wood-ash glowing in the dark. For once a young San girl named Xama threw the embers of the fire into the sky to light the way for Gau the hunter, lost out in the desert wastes in the darkness of the night" (*Wood-ash Stars*, 15). The other realization is a traditional African tale about doves who bring a barren woman a child, which she has to hide in a pot.

What Poland has done is give the mythical characters names and personalities and explore their emotions, which the original tales do not do: "Xama nursed her burnt and blistered hands. She sang sadly to herself and gazed every now and then at the wood-ash stars she had made. Only in the dawn, when she heard the loud cries of the people, did she leave her brooding and turn and run to where they stood together, pointing excitedly" (*Woodash*, 15).

The San folklore collected by the Bleeks continues to inspire writers and illustrators. A good example is the picture book *The Quagga's Secret* by Hamilton Wende, illustrated by Laurie Gallagher and Adele O'Connell (1995).[25] The story first appeared in the second volume of the ground-breaking anthology *My Drum* (1991), compiled by Barbara Meyerowitz, Jennette Copans and Tessa Welch, which successfully mixed traditional songs in translation with old and new South African stories and poems (often by famous writers) and children's writing and pictures.[26] Ostensibly about the quagga, a zebra-like animal that was shot to extinction, it is also a metaphor for the fate of the San. The mood and pictures illustrating how a San man befriends the last quagga and follows him into the desert, where a white hunter shoots him, are close to the San lore. Without its example it is unlikely the story would have been written.

Cicely van Straten is a well known South African writer who has produced several works that are influenced by folktales. Born in South Africa, she spent much of her childhood in Kenya before returning to her native country, and her writing shows the influence of the landscape and folklore of East Africa. (Her early books were written under the name Cicely Luck.) She has written an entertaining and moving semi-autobiographical youth novel, *The Flowers of the Thorn* (1986), about a white schoolgirl in Kenya at the time of the Mau Mau uprising.[27] Because all her books have been published in South Africa and she is a resident of the country, they are regarded as South African literature in spite of the East African content. In fact, when it comes to folktales and their derivatives, South African literature blurs into pan-African literature, because many similar folktales or core elements can be found throughout the continent. Madeline Murgatroyd, who used folktales from Malawi, is only one out of a number of other writers whose sources know no colonial national boundaries.

In an early collection of stories by van Straten, *The Great Snake of Kalungu and Other East African Stories* (1981), one is a retelling of a folktale, "The Great Snake," in which Serongwane outwits the Great Snake and wins the King's reward.[28] The other stories and those in a companion volume, *Kaninu's Secret and Other East African Stories* (1981), are about black village children, and differ from the grave style and tone of her folk imitations by being lively and funny: "And the dogs smiled and rolled on their backs and so did the goats and donkeys and camels and they kicked and bleated and brayed and hawed because they had caught Akutan, the fish-thief. That's how it is in Akutan's village — you can't do anything without everyone knowing" (*Secret* 43).[29]

Her full-length story *The Fish Eagle and the Dung Beetle* (1982) is an excellent example of an original story inspired by folktales.[30] After the mother fish eagle tells the dung beetle not to roll dung near her nest, he has his revenge by getting all the animals to deposit their dung under the nest, and she has to swallow her pride and ask them to remove it. The lesson of the story is the usefulness of dung beetles. A traditional storytelling technique, which here echoes Kipling's *Just So* stories in the use of big words, is repetition: the duiker warns the dung beetle that hippopotamuses are "bald and blundering and completely clumsy" and crocodiles are "unscrupulous and utterly untrustworthy" (*Fish Eagle* 15), and when the dung beetle meets them these phrases are repeated.

Van Straten is admired for her lyrical style, of which the opening is a good example:

> Once upon a time, beside a beautiful lake where the mist hovered over the water in the morning and the sun danced in a bed of pink fire at evening, there lived two fish eagles. They had built their nest in the white skeleton of a dead tree. They were high and noble birds with fierce gold eyes and white hoods on their proud heads. Their beaks were golden but with a steely black hood to them and their claws were sharp and cruel. They screamed to one another in the early morning as they wheeled above the mist-white waters

hunting fish. And they screamed to one another in the evenings as the sun set and they caught eels for supper. Aaaahaaaa-arra-arra-arra! And they were haughty and proud and cared for no one and nothing.

(*Fish Eagle*, 6)

The fish eagle, with its distinctive haunting call, is the unofficial symbol of the wilderness for modern South Africans, evinced not only by countless advertisements but even in the choice of its Zulu name, *Inkwazi*, for President Mbeki's official airplane. With this unmatched description Cicely van Straten deserves to be the unofficial laureate of South Africa.

Van Straten's major works in traditional style are three quest stories, *Tajewo and the Sacred Mountain* (1983), *Torit of the Strong Right Arm* (1992), and the sequel to *Tajewo*, *Quest for the Sacred Stone* (2000).[31] They are realizations of African legends in which the young heroes have to carry out tasks or face various traditional tests — battling monsters, cannibals and spirits — with the help of talismans and kind people, spirits and animals. She writes throughout in a high, archaic style.

The first one, *Tajewo and the Sacred Mountain*, is loaded with peritext in the form of a lengthy note "About the Maasai" and glossary footnotes giving pronunciation and meaning. The note on the Maasai is very respectful about their beliefs and practices; for example, Engai is referred to as "God" and the Maasai as "His people" in the note and the narrative. This peritext is precisely of the kind to which postcolonial critics object because it places the Maasai in a timeless past, with no hint of their modern lives.

After surviving dangers with the help of creatures to whom he has been kind, Tajewo and his friend Meromo, who are seeking the Charm of the Wind and the Storms to save the land from drought, are put through three tests by the great holy man. Tajewo then has to be ritually purified before he can hold the Charm in his hands, whereafter, as the storms spring from his hands, he falls as if dead for three days.

In *Torit of the Strong Right Arm*, Torit has to recover a sacred white cow stolen by the King of a barren country. If it is not back within three days for its milk to be poured as a libation to the new moon, drought will follow. He is helped by his companion, a talking frog. Years later, as a warrior, he suggests giving the other king a cow and a calf, and that ends the enmity between the kings. This book is not as lyrical or exciting as the previous one.

Quest for the Sacred Stone departs from its predecessors in some ways; for one thing, it has no peritextual notes. It features strong women who play an important role in the story and whom Tajewo trusts and allows autonomy in the face of opposition from other men. An extraordinary element is the use of Judaic myth. A wise old woman tells Tajewo and Meromo the story of Adam and Eve, giving them African names, and bringing the story down to the present by saying that the Morning Star shed a tear at the sight of "Naiterogop" being expelled from the garden, a tear that turned into a stone that becomes the object of their quest. Furthermore, the evil one they have to fight is called Moloch, who in the biblical Book of Kings is the spirit who demands the sacrifice of what we hold most dear.

This book is the least successful of the three. A structural difficulty is that it is made up of two stories tacked together; after completing the quest in the first part, the heroes have to prepare for and fight the ultimate battle against the forces of evil. The book is filled with a huge number of characters whom it is difficult to keep track of, and the two friends are not well developed characters. For modern tastes, she could have done better by trimming the number of incidents and characters and spending more time making the characters of the two heroes more complex and interesting.

Quest stories set so firmly in an ancient past, with their predictable linear plots consisting of a concatenation of tests overcome, are perhaps not the stuff to appeal to modern young readers. Van Straten was not alone in facing this difficulty; another South African writer, Vicki Forrester, tried a similar quest story in 1994. She introduces her story, *The Kingdom Above the Earth*:

> Traditional fairy tales, in any culture, have never existed in a single rigid form. Anonymous storytellers take fragments and string them together in different ways, adding their own personal touch and adapting them to changing times and environments.
>
> I hope this modern interpretation of traditional southern African tales, spiced with adventure and humour, will entertain young and old alike, and revive interest in the delightfully rich heritage of our folk-lore.
>
> My grateful thanks to my husband Daniel, who researched this book, to the library and academics of the University of Fort Hare, Eastern Cape, and to Karen, my editor, for her help and guidance.[32]

This is an unexceptional exposition of how she and her predecessors have created realizations of traditional material. However, the back cover announces, "In this beautifully told story, the author has woven together many of the tales of South African oral traditions into an account of how young people prepare themselves to become the new generation of leaders." The year being 1994, when the first democratic elections were held, the publishers are imposing a new agenda on the traditional material. One wonders whether young readers would absorb its didactic intent.

In this quest story, 18-year-old Demana and his sister Tanga have to fetch the water-pot that will bring water back to their land, which is under a curse. When they reach the land of the Kingdom Above the Earth after adventures with Zim cannibals, Demana has to wait, as he has shown weakness, and Tanga goes on a journey to the Purple Mountain. After undergoing six tests, Kindness, Patience, Wisdom, Courage, Loyalty and Duty, she marries the prince and stays behind with her ancestors. Demana returns home, water flows, and he marries. The author brings in many myths, such as the one of the chameleon and lizard bringing life and death (the chameleon is too slow, and the lizard reaches man first with death).

Forrester is in better command of the structure of the story than van Straten is in *Quest*, so that the narrative is tight, but she does not have the same command of language. Her style fluctuates between high archaisms and the bathetically colloquial and clichéd. Her incongruous use of the word "fairy" for supernatural beings has already been mentioned.

A retelling of an African legend that succeeds on all counts is *Tselane*, by Moira Thatcher (1986), published by Tafelberg.[33] She explains in her preface how she set about writing it:

> The story of Tselane, her mother, and Ledimo, the cannibal, is based on a traditional legend that was handed down originally, complete with Song and Response, purely by word of mouth. I first heard it in the 1930s, and it made such an indelible impression on me that I am still able to recall the details of the story as well as the melody and Sesotho words of the Song and the Reply after all these years. (The English version is my own translation.) As many people believe the story to be true, I decided to do some historical research before setting it down.... The strategy I chose was to interweave the legend and the historical facts by placing the story in the fairly well-documented time of Moshoeshoe, chief of the Bakwena, who later became the first paramount chief or king of Lesotho.... I found it necessary to add some details to the basic legend.... I am deeply indebted to Mr Michael Letsedi and Mrs Johanna Lekgetho, who not only made helpful suggestions, but supplied me with additional information on old Basotho customs.

(*Tselane*, 7)

Unlike the quest stories, which heap one incident on another, the story of the girl who is kidnapped by a cannibal has a simple plot with a dramatic trajectory in which the tension builds until she escapes and is rescued. Tselane is a focalizer with whom the young reader can identify, and the author has kept the style formal but without an archaic ring. By placing the story in the historical nineteenth century, Thatcher has avoided the suggestion of distant primitive times. Any modern child knows the danger of being abducted by a smooth-talking stranger and can identify with the story, which comes to a satisfying closure. The illustrations add to the appeal of the book. They were among the first by Joan Rankin, who went on to become a leading illustrator of children's books, and have been exhibited overseas. As a combination of African legend, history and modern themes, created through the efforts of modern white and black South Africans and an Afrikaans publishing house, this book fulfils the hopes of those who believe that it is possible to make traditional South African literature multicultural.

7

THE SAN AND THE NATIONAL CONSCIENCE

One of the most enduring motifs in South African culture is the San. They made their appearance in the earliest records of whites who reached the shores, and, centuries later, the new democratic state that followed the elections in 1994 honored them by incorporating reproductions of their art, as well as wording the motto in one of their languages in the new national coat of arms.

The first inhabitants of the country, the San's hunter-gatherer way of life inevitably brought them into conflict with successive immigrants: pastoralist Khoi, black African pastoralists and agriculturalists, and whites. Also known as the Bushmen, they did not have a name for themselves as a race, but only names for smaller regional groups. The term "Khoisan" is used when the two peoples, who predated the arrival of Bantu-speaking peoples from the north, are grouped together for reference purposes, or for when their separate identities had blurred. Both "Bushman" and "San" (a Khoi term meaning "vagrant") were derogatory appellations, but are used today in the absence of an alternative.

Gradually, the San disappeared as a distinct racial group. They intermarried with other races, they were killed in attacks and counterattacks, when the Boers killed adults they took the children as slaves, imprisoned adults willed themselves to die. San have survived into the twenty-first century to the north of South Africa in Namibia and Botswana, and in a few small communities that were brought to South Africa in recent years. Certain other South Africans acknowledge their San ancestry.

In South Africa, traces of their languages remain in the languages of black African people, especially Xhosa, and in place names; certain rainmaking practices, for which the San were highly regarded by other people, linger to the present. Their most dramatic and visible heritage is the tens of thousands of rock paintings and engravings that cover the entire country—a treasury of exquisite works of art of deep spiritual significance. To scholars, writers and poets, the records of their lore that were preserved by the Bleek family and imparted to more recent anthropologists are both an inspiration and an inexhaustible source of information about their beliefs, religious practices and way of life, which more and more popular books are bringing to the attention of the public.

One thing is certain: the San have long played a role in the development of the identity of different races in South Africa, and their significance intensified after the inauguration of democratic South Africa in 1994. Thabo Mbeki invoked them in his famous speech as Deputy President on the making of the nation at the adoption of the new Constitution of the Republic of South Africa on May 8 1996:

> I am an African....
>
> I owe my being to the Khoi and the San whose desolate souls haunt the great expanses of the beautiful Cape—they who fell victim to the most merciless genocide our native land has ever seen, they who were the first to lose their lives in the struggle to defend our freedom and independence and they who, as a people, perished in the result.
>
> Today, as a country, we keep an audible silence about these ancestors of the generations that live, fearful to admit the horror of a former deed, seeking to obliterate from our memories a cruel occurrence which, in its remembering, should teach us not and never to be inhuman again....[1]

Images of the San and the ideological uses to which other people have put them have changed over the years, though they follow no simple chronology. There is an extensive literature about the way the San have been portrayed in government documents and the writings of travelers, and, more recently, by anthropologists, archaeologists, museologists and popular historians. Chapter 5 referred to the controversy over the appropriation of the San through the retelling of their folktales, which has been likened to the exhibition of their bodies in museums. The anthropologist Edwin Wilmsen has criticized the choice of San figures as symbols in the coat of arms as an attempt to go back to a neutral "pan-human" period, before successive waves of Khoi, black and white people arrived. It simply dehumanizes them, he argues: "They can be pan-human only by being pre-human."[2]

Cultural historians have investigated how the San have been portrayed in film, television, art, popular culture and commerce.[3] *The Gods Must Be Crazy*, Jamie Uys's 1980 comedy featuring the San, is the most successful film ever made in South Africa.[4] Literary historians have analyzed their place in Afrikaans and English literature, arguing that the reasons behind the obsession of whites with the San are, as David Maughan Brown puts it, "revealed, perhaps better than anywhere else, by the fiction."[5] A.E. Voss writes of "the primacy of the Bushmen" in literature;[6] Duncan Brown says, "The apparently atavistic understandings of aboriginal peoples [as revealed in literature] are often fundamental to modern and postmodern belief and practice (including the 'unit' of modernity — the nation state)";[7] and Helize van Vuuren asserts that Afrikaans novels of the 1990s about the San "are of central importance for a better understanding of the country, its people and the way in which they deal with each other."[8]

Children's books have much to contribute to an understanding of the portrayal of the San, though most literary critics have ignored them.[9] In general, children's books are an invaluable source of information on popular culture because they catch people with their guard down. Not only do they reveal what society wants its children to think about a topic, but because of their simplicity they are rather more frank than they would be if written for an adult audience.

The first children's novel set in Southern Africa was *The English Boy at the Cape* (1835) by an Englishman, Edward Kendall.[10] It provides the only example in the literature of the application of the notion of the "noble savage" to the San; by about 1850 this concept had died out. Other children's books describing the San in early colonial days are historical novels written in the following century, which look back on that period from points of view other than that of Kendall's contemporary account.

In three volumes, it tells the story of Charles, who is orphaned when the ship bearing him to the Cape at the age of seven is wrecked. Setting the picture of the San as innocent victims, a passenger remarks as their ship is foundering, "If they [the Boers] do not fire upon us, as they do upon the Bushmen, they would at least leave us to sink or swim as we pleased" (*English Boy*, I, 232).

Traveling to the interior with a party of Boers, Charles witnesses them hunting San. A captured, dying San man, asked why they shoot the Boers with arrows, replies, "To kill the great, the strong-limbed Land-drost [magistrate], whose father killed the chief of our people, and killed his wife, and stole away their little ones" (*English Boy* II, 34). Commenting on this episode, the author is even-handed in blame, seeking to understand human motives in this chain of attack and revenge.

Charles runs away from a gross Boer woman who maltreats him, and is taken in by a band of San who give him shelter for a while. The author makes a little "Bush girl" the focalizer as she takes him home, wondering how her parents will react to her saving a white boy. This is a strong assertion of her humanity, in a century when adventure stories barely investigated the consciousness of any characters. Continuing this point of view, the narrator says, "They argued, that ferocious and little to be trusted as were Europeans, and untaught in the virtues and points of conscience which regulate the steps of Bushmen, they would surely show as much mercy toward a young one of their brood" (*Boy* II, 244).

The author portrays the San as rather dirty, but he is not derogatory about them — they sing and dance and tell stories, but they also labor and discourse on matters of philosophy — as do all the other peoples of Africa, he reminds his readers. He constantly applies the adjectives "good" and "hospitable" to them.

By the time Olive Schreiner wrote the first great South African novel, *The Story of an African Farm* (1883), the San had disappeared from the Karoo, where the first part of her novel is set.[11] The three children of the farm retreat from the cruelties inflicted on them by adults to a rock shelter that had been home to San, who left their paintings on the walls. The paintings are a reminder of both the ancient history of the land and the impermanence of human existence. Literary scholars have been drawn to consider the significance of this key passage in a key novel. Stephen Gray observes that by placing the San and the animals they painted in the past, Schreiner marks her departure from the typical adventure novel, which featured immediate encounters with savages and wild animals: this would rather be a novel of ideas and psychological complication.[12] Malvern van Wyk Smith considers that "the Bushman…becomes the node of doubt and displacement that invades all the lives on the farm."[13] Voss, commenting on how the paintings are particularly intriguing to the sensitive Waldo, who tries to picture the artist that created them, concludes, "In a post-Romantic aesthetic approach to cave-painting, 'the individual' is the necessary, if doomed, artist whom Waldo imagines…. The disappearance of the threat of the Bushmen as a group makes possible this encounter with the individual Bushman" (*Voss*, 31).

The children's books that followed early in the twentieth century converted noble savagery into the sentimentality popular at the time. In "Love-of-my-Heart" by G. Daniell (1926), a prince and his little daughter rescue a group of San who have been kidnapped and taken to Abyssinia as slaves to the Queen of Sheba, but the child's nurse from Java is jealous and turns them into doves, which now sit outside the classroom window of a modern girl.[14] Even before their metamorphosis, the San sound more like Hobbits than real people: "Little men less than four feet high, light yellow in colour, their flat faces wrinkled and puckered, their oddly big feet making no sound on the bare polished floor" ("Love," 30). In Corinne Rey's *Tales of the Veld* (1926), the illustrator of a story in which a white boy falls asleep and sees San maidens has drawn them as European fairies.[15] Reference has already been made (in Chapter 4) to how Victor Pohl, harking back to this period, introduced *Farewell the Little People* (1968) by suggesting that the San conjured up thoughts of "Lilliputians, fairies, gnomes and elflike creatures."[16]

B. Schwartz published a poem for children, "Bushman Paintings," in *South African Bilingual Verse* (1947):

> I love to see the Bushman caves,
> Study the paintings on the wall.
> The hunters seem such tiny men,
> The animals quite strong and tall.
>
> 'Tis strange how after all this time
> These stones recall their life so free.
> I wonder! In a hundred years,
> Will anybody think of me?[17]

The San have been so completely obliterated that they are simply a prompt for self-indulgent thoughts.

Modern children's books about the San start with the classic *Skankwan van die Duine* (Skankwan of the Dunes) by the Hobson brothers, first published in 1930 and translated into English in 1977 as *The Lion of the Kalahari*.[18] The literature is of various kinds: fiction for ages ranging from young children to teenagers; fiction written "to order" for prescription as a school reader; non-fiction, both of a popular kind and in a form apparently intended as school textbooks or as juvenile reference works for libraries; a few poems and collections of folktales.

The peritexts and style of illustration sometimes indicate confusion on the part of publishers and authors over the status of their subject matter and the intended readership, to which the titles give a clue: *The Search for the Little Yellow Men, These Small People, Children of the Kalahari, Farewell the Little People, God's Little Bushmen*.[19] The small physical size of the San and their neotenic features suggest to the authors in some vague fashion that the San are childlike, and therefore an appropriate subject for children to read about. Mary Phillips typically introduces *The Cave of Uncle Kwa* (1965) by saying, "They are a tiny people — a childlike people."[20] At times, authors such as Pohl and McAdorey (*The Old Man of the Mountain*, 1992)[21] present the San implicitly as children, emphasizing their changeable emotions, delight in simple pleasures, and lack of care for the future. "Child-man" is the term used by McAdorey. Abdul JanMohamed, writing of van der Post's adult novel *A Story Like the Wind* (1972),[22] which features San people, says that his "decision to depict his own experience of African oral cultures takes the form of a novel about a young boy's adventures" because of "his belief that only a child would be interested in such cultures."[23] These books are good examples of how the "ideology of littleness" in literature serves to place certain categories of people in a particular light.[24]

Even the very series in which a particular volume is included may say something about how the San are to be seen. Dennis Winchester-Gould's novel *God's Little Bushmen* is one of a series from a Pretoria publisher, Rhino Publishers, given on the cover as "ECOSPACE — Reality of space for wild things — for all life," in which all the other volumes are about animals. This is an anachronistic reversion to placing the San in the same category as flora and fauna — the image of the San that led to their lifecasts and their art being displayed in natural history museums.

The imperialist children's fiction of the nineteenth century took its inspiration from utilitarianism, science and moral instruction. Writing in the mode of the immensely popular travel writers of the period, boys' adventure writers gave detailed accounts of the way of life of African tribes. This tradition has continued in the twentieth century books, which are packed with "facts" about their way of life and beliefs. The San are also a gateway to the ways of wild creatures, which the authors enjoy digressing to describe. As Chapter 5 pointed out, folktales were often deliberately selected for children's books because they are about animals.

Often the authors seem bursting to share their knowledge of the facts. The first-hand experience and knowledgeability of Victor Pohl; P.J. Schoeman, author of a well-known Afrikaans book translated into English as *Hunters of the Desert Land* (1957);[25] and the Hobsons and their modern translator, Esther Linfield, are given prominence in the peritexts. Agnes Jackson's *The Bushmen of South Africa* (1956) still perpetuated some of the most notorious stereotypes of aboriginal peoples to be found in western writing: "When the Bushmen want to prepare themselves for a festivity they throw dust all over themselves, instead of water, just as animals do"; "Although they have hard lives, the Bushmen are naturally a gay and happy people who are fond of dancing and music."[26] Some of the illustrations in her book reflect the denigratory tone. In contrast, *Children of the Kalahari* by Alice Mertens, *These Small People* by Candy Malherbe, and the notes in *The Bushmen and their Stories* by Elizabeth Helfman (1971) are more accurate and sympathetic.[27]

The information about the way of life of the San that many fiction authors present — in the case of John Coetzee in *Flint and the Red Desert* (1986)[28] one can say *hasten* to present, as soon as the San appear on the scene — is so similar that it is predictable. Not only are these "facts" selective, but in a number of cases they are simply wrong. To present the information, the authors often use the device of children being taught by their elders. Mostly it is man-talk, or women's activities seen by a male (such as little boys who fret at having to go gathering plants with the women when they would rather be hunting), but there are also some detailed accounts seen through female eyes.

This information is easy to summarize: their appearance and the color of their skin; how they make poisoned arrows and hunt; animal lore; how the women gather, especially what the reader is improbably told they themselves call "Bushman rice" (ants' larvae); what they eat, especially insects, reptiles ("lizard biltong" [dried meat]) and putrid meat; how they overeat when meat is available; how they suck up water from under the sand; that they are nomadic; how they dress and ornament themselves; how they abandon old people to die, and abort babies or bury them alive in times of stress; that women are treated as inferiors and even worse, and that they are silly; courtship and marriage customs and rites of passage; children's games; how and why they paint; how they dance; that they practise divining and have witchdoctors, and, in some books, that they possess supernatural powers; their folktales and religious beliefs; and what their language sounds like, with special emphasis on how, to a white person, it sounds like clicks. Under the guise of objective information, the San are dehumanized. The more unpleasant details, reiterated so often, mark their primitiveness.

Sometimes writers suggest more indirectly that the San are not quite human. Pohl sets the scene for *Farewell the Little People* by saying that in the old days they mixed freely with baboons, their allies "since time immemorial" (*Farewell*, 4), and that "like all his people Tsipele was not given to much speech, particularly about something not connected with his everyday activities" (*Farewell*, 47). In John Coetzee's *Flint and the Red Desert* the San are heard "laughing and clicking" (90) rather than speaking.

The effect of almost all the books is that white readers would come away with the impression that the San are extremely different from themselves. Some authors seem to have chosen them as the subject of a story, or introduced them into a story, simply because they are curiosities that can provide an unusual topic.

The peritexts to translations of San folktales and nonfiction on the San are particularly prone to the danger, described in Chapter 5, of portraying the people as stuck in an ahistorical stasis, a primal past without any contact with other people and certainly no modern history. Increasingly, modern archaeological and anthropological research is showing that the notion of a "pure" primal race is a fallacy; even the identity of the San can be considered as the construction of a class of people through trade and other interaction.[29] An enlightened account of this view is given in the introduction to the Hobsons' *The Lion of the Kalahari* by the anthropologist Esther Linfield, who translated and adapted the novel. She tackles the fact that the San have no generic name for themselves, and how this ties up with the question of their identity.

While the modern reader has to make allowance that some books were written when knowledge about the San — such as the import of their rock art—was not as advanced as it is today, the same precept of Wayne Booth that applies to the treatment of ecology in fiction, cited in Chapter 3, must be applied in these instances as well; the authors can, and should, be criticized for their attitudes and their treatment of their material.

A straightforward explanation as to why white children's writers have presented stories about the San to white readers is that they believe that children should learn their history, but the authors themselves have often had difficulty coping with this history. This dialogue from "Peter's Bushman" by Enid Ablett (1939) indicates the ducking and diving:

> "Where are the Bushmen? Can I see them too, Uncle Koos?"
> "I'm afraid you can't, Peter, they went away a long time ago."
> "How long ago?"
> "A hundred years, maybe longer."
> "Where did they go?'
> "Further and further away from their enemies."
> "Who were their enemies?"
> "Strong natives with spears and shields and, above all, the white men, who carried fire sticks...."
> "Didn't the white men like the Bushmen?"
> "No, for the little, yellow men were great thieves, they loved to steal cattle. They lived mainly by hunting, never staying long in one place, but moving on after the game."[30]

The uncle does not explain why the Bushmen should have stolen cattle.

One of the earliest substantial novels for children about the San written in English was *Farewell the Little People* by Victor Pohl, which follows a San family's journey as a microcosm of the history of the people as they are driven out by waves of invaders. Dr A.C. Hoffman stresses in his foreword that it is based on "the experiences of his early youth" and "intensive research work," apparently consisting of "many interviews with anthropologists and archaeologists" (n.p.), and Pohl announces in his preface, "I consider myself fortunate that in my childhood and youth I was in daily contact with the members of a typical bushman family" (n.p.). Nevertheless, the history, geography and anthropology are wildly inaccurate. The author implies that the San physically left the mountains and traveled all the way to the Kalahari desert, which is why the San are found there today, whereas some San have always lived there, and the few San who ever left the Drakensberg moved northeast to Lake Chrissie.[31]

This historical and geographical impossibility recurs in several books. Even Esther Linfield writes authoritatively in her introduction to *The Lion of the Kalahari*, "Gradually, however, they were pushed out by invading peoples, black and white alike, and were forced to take refuge in the caves and rock shelters of the high mountains. Then, driven from their strongholds, they retreated to the harsh, almost uninhabitable plains of the Kalahari" (*Lion*, viii). In fact, San had lived in the mountains since time immemorial, as archaeological evidence proves.

Pohl is one of several writers who suggest that the San were "wiped out" (*Farewell*, 76) mainly by black Africans, Griquas (a mixed-race people) and Khoi, not by whites. Their stories served white authors and readers as a way of "othering" both the San and blacks and, and in this way, displaced white guilt. What is more, in Pohl's story the refugees find their last haven on the farm of an Afrikaner, "a man of reasonable education and compassion, [who] deplored the fact that the Bushmen were being ruthlessly destroyed by newcomers of every colour" (*Farewell*, 124). There, in a lyrical passage, they are described living out their lives comfortably as servants, though longing for the mountains. And so the San are an instrument for portraying the blacks as cruel savages and the whites as caring, civilized people who are exculpated from blame.

Pohl implies that the black tribes migrating into the country killed the San simply because they were different. An earlier story, "The Enchanted Impi" (1923) by Ella MacKenzie, made the same suggestion. In the smoke of a fire made by a witchdoctor, a black king "saw, as if far away in the distance, a strange and mountainous land, and in the rocky caves he could make out queer little yellow men and women going about their daily occupations."[32] He thereupon decides to send an impi to attack them, apparently simply on a whim.

Pohl's accounts of the fighting between San and black Africans are absurd. The inaccurate details are too numerous mention; suffice to say, the San send smoke signals as though in a western movie, while the climax is a great set-piece battle that sounds like Agincourt: "Bushmen archers and dagger men," with "reserves in the mountains," "let fly an even denser hail of arrows," and "at the blast of a horn, a thick cloud of arrows descended" (*Farewell*, 87).

Novelists distorted history in their effort to portray the San as innocent victims, whether of whites or other people (including other San) who were the whites' allies. Actually, once the raiding and counter-raiding had started, the San attacked with extreme cruelty to humans and animals,[33] but this is acknowledged in only two stories. In *The Adventures of Kalipe* by Anne and Peter Cook, four young black men, who flee to the Drakensberg mountains after the Zulus destroy their village, are attacked there by San;[34] and *The Last Horizon* by Reginald Maddock (1961) describes the San's brutal revenge attacks on Boers.[35]

Increasing evidence is being uncovered by anthropologists, archaeologists and linguists of how black Africans and San mixed and intermarried from the time when they first encountered each other, and how to this day San descendants live among the Xhosa, respected for their gifts. This record of interracial harmony should provide writers with an opportunity to celebrate multiculturalism in the country's history rather than the grim record of genocide, but only one book, written in the 1980s when the final struggle against apartheid was at its ugliest, has taken this line. Set in the Drakensberg "about the end of the eighteenth century," *Kabo of the Mountain* by Joan Nockels and Alex Wilcox (1988) tells how San and black Africans become friends, and hints that intermarriage may follow, which is, in fact, what often happened.[36]

In writing about the treatment of the San from the eighteenth century to the present, writers are faced with the incontrovertible historical facts. What lesson can they draw for their child readers? Two American critics of South African children's and youth literature, Donnarae MacCann and Yulisa Amadu Maddy, condemn various writers for depicting events and attitudes that are typical of the racist climate in the country at the time when the stories are set, but they ignore the moral stand that the writers take toward racism. In one case, though, their condemnation is justified.[37] *Tinde in the Mountains* by Ken Smith (1987) tells of the friendship among a San, a Xhosa and a white boy on the Great Fish River border in 1800.[38] Although the boys are depicted as equal, the author passes no judgment over the political settlement that in the end gave the whites all the territory they wanted, leaving the San and Xhosa as client peoples.

Good writers are frank about the horror and brutality, and the melancholy of their writing speaks for itself. *The Sound of the Gora* by Anne Harries (1980), one of the best books to emerge in the wave of emancipated writing that came out in the 1970s and 1980s, opens with a cutting depiction of the psychology and religious hypocrisy of the Boers in their treatment of captured children.[39] Marguerite Poland wrote a short story, "The Broken String" (1986), in which the poignancy of the pointless shooting of a San man at the hands of the Boers serves as a protest at what happened.[40] In *The New Fire* (1983) Jenny Seed tries to make the best of her story of how Boers, in retaliation for the theft of sheep by the San, attack them and abduct a little girl. Her band retreat to the interior, where they will light a new fire, but of course the pattern of attack and counterattack will continue until the San are all gone.[41] The reader is left with the aching sadness of her story.

Moving away from history to the present, D.R. Sherman, whose *Pride of the Hunter* (1979) is set in modern Botswana or Namibia, lifts the San out of the romantic timelessness in which white culture had placed them.[42] His novel offers no solution to their intractable plight, seen through the eyes of a San man who still lives a nomadic life:

> The red men [whites] had made laws, and even now his people were caught and carried away for killing certain animals, and he had heard they were put in small stone houses which the red men built, and more often than not they died there, deprived of their music and their stories and the magic sight of the sun rising in the desert.
>
> And if they did not die, they were broken men when they came out, their spirit gone no one knew where, living on the settled fringes of the desert and working as herdsmen, despised by both the red man and the black man, unable to break away, suspended between an old way of life and a new one, their hearts breaking with a longing to return that they could not satisfy.
>
> (*Pride*, 46)

The best authentic account of modern San is given by Lesley Beake in *Song of Be* (1991), a young adult novel that is a remarkable imaginative feat.[43] The narrator is an educated young San woman named Be who works with her mother on the farm of a white man in Namibia and falls in love with a San election worker at the time of Namibia's first democratic elections. Whereas other stories have often emphasized that in earlier times San women were subordinate to men and were treated badly, although the historical basis for this is doubtful, Beake has created in Be a remarkably strong and independent young woman. It is refreshing to encounter in this book, as well as in *The Sound of the Gora* by Ann Harries and *God's Little Bushmen* by Dennis Winchester-Gould, a shift from the voices of white males to narratives told from the point of view of young San women. Be's inner strength is emphasized by the contrast between her and the farmer's wife, who is driven mad by life on the farm and commits suicide. As the story of Be's life and that of her parents emerges, many aspects of the lives of modern San are covered, culminating in their taking their place as literate citizens of the newly independent country.

Beake's novel has struck an international chord. The American Library Association selected it as a "Notable Children's Book" in 1993 and a "Best Book for Young Adults" in 1994, and Judith Rovenger, Youth Services Consultant of the Westchester Library System in New York, has admired its universal relevance:

> Be's story and Be's struggle with a world in transition sheds light on the current global struggle of societies in transition and the struggle to keep what is important from the past and merge it with what is good in the present and necessary for the future.... I believe that young readers will have their world expanded by this meeting and their notions about the world enriched. I hope it will spark their outrage at injustice, evoke their compassion for each other, and help them to understand with Be that "when I was still very young, I thought like that. It was then that I thought what you *had* was important. Now I know it is what you *are*."[44]

Margaret Lenta, citing the notice "To the Reader" in Elsa Joubert's South African novel *The Long Journey of Poppy Nongena* (1980), observes that by the early 1980s white authors of fictional biographies of black women in South Africa began to feel obliged to explain why they should "speak for" their subjects.[45] Lesley Beake acknowledges with thanks the assistance of the Ju/'hoan people and the Nyai Nyai Farmers' Cooperative, with whom she worked for several years, in this way anticipating objections to the absence of the voice of the indigene in postcolonial literature. She emphasizes her own interest in the present-day San by including a note at the end entitled "The Future," in which she says that the Ju/'hoan people are going back to the land with new skills, and she gives the address of their co-op. This is the most optimistic work on the San that has yet been published for children and young adults.

The publishing fate of *Song of Be* shows how the concern of the author for authenticity can be counteracted by publishers with a different agenda. It has been published overseas in many different editions, including translations into seven languages. The cover of the original South African edition published by Maskew Miller Longman bears a photograph of a young San woman, chosen by the author (see Figure 8), but the covers of some of the other editions reflect misguided attempts to package the story with a glamorous romantic image, showing Be either as some kind of North African pastoralist or spear carrier, or as improbably Western, dressed in shorts. Beake has herself described the

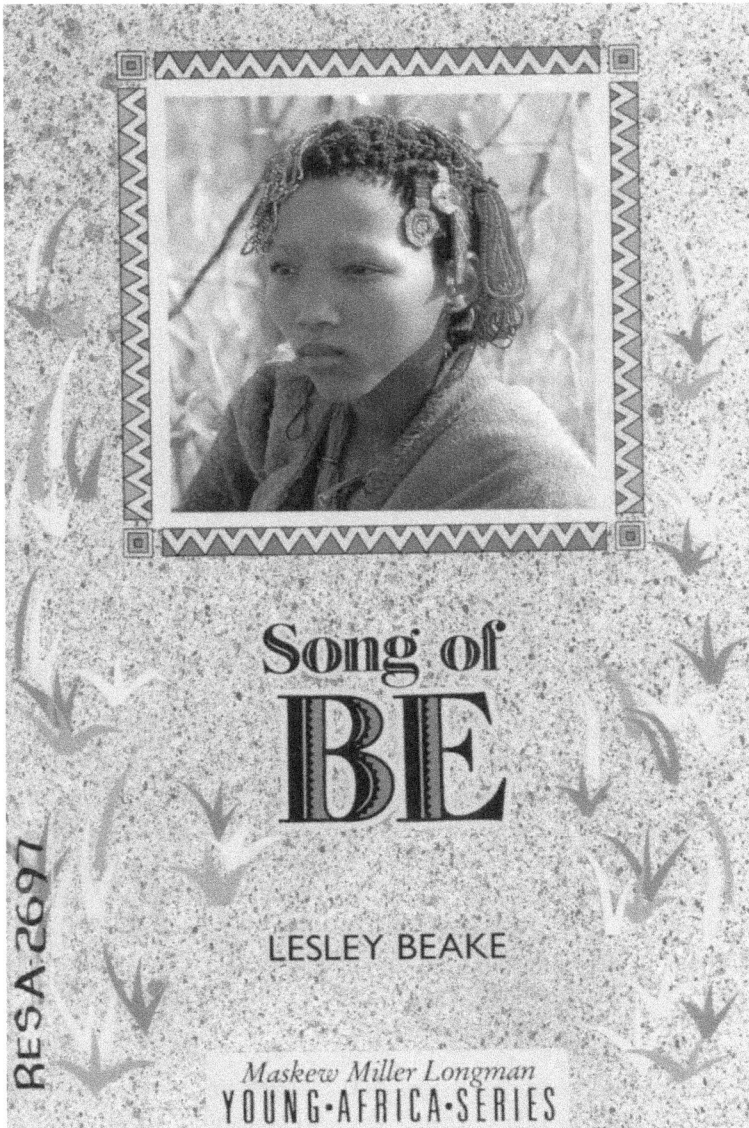

8 Cover design by Lesley Sharman for the Maskew Miller Longman edition of *Song of Be* by Lesley Beake

Puffin edition cover as "utterly wrong." Commenting on this, the South African book critic Jay Heale observes, "We seem to be back portraying Africa as the popular reader wants to imagine it, and not the way the author has written it or the reality of Africa itself" (*Heale*, 218).

Almost all the writers bring in San religion, ostensibly treating it with respect. Two versions are given: a monotheistic belief, or a simplistic animism that degenerates in some stories into a phantasmagoria of witchdoctors and other stereotyped features of "superstition" drawn from nineteenth-century colonial fiction that have no documented basis.[46] This is a demeaning pseudo-ethnology that serves to trivialize San beliefs as something barbarous, even though they are disguised as something quaint, attesting to the spirituality of the San.

In this concentration on San religious beliefs one can detect the urge, epitomized by Laurens van der Post but going back to Rider Haggard, to search for spiritual truths that only Africa may be able to provide. Van der Post's books *The Lost World of the Kalahari* and *The Heart of the Hunter* (1961) were influential in changing whites' attitudes toward the San from despising them as near-animals to holding them up as people whose mystic beliefs could save the modern world. D.R. Sherman, author of *Pride of the Hunter,* who was not a South African although his book was published in Cape Town, is one author who clearly followed van der Post closely. Today it is generally accepted that van der Post's writings on the San were mainly a product of his own imagination.[47]

Sherman is yet another writer who occasionally succumbed to the temptation to turn the search for African mysticism into mumbo-jumbo. He has a San man who inherited a sixth sense from his mother; the Hobsons have one who practices ventriloquism, terrifying the other San while the sophisticated reader can smile at their gullibility. Sherman's story is about a San man who develops a relationship with a wild lion similar to that of Androcles; Mary Phillips, in *The Cave of Uncle Kwa,* gives her small hero a tame lion cub that he takes for walks; and the San in Pohl's *Farewell the Little People* keep two cheetahs and a baboon as pets. Instead of describing typical rock overhangs and their small paintings, Maddock's *The Last Horizon* deteriorates into nonsense about tunnels and subterranean caves decorated, according to the illustration, with lifesize paintings.

Most disappointing is a modern book, *The Old Man of the Mountain* by Ursula Karsen McAdorey. The cover announces that it was specially written as a reader for use in secondary schools in the various countries of southern Africa, with a controlled language level, which implies that it is intended for readers for whom English is not their mother tongue. It should have been a welcome extension of the curriculum, introducing all southern African children to the San. On the cover is a colored photograph of an old San man, which adds verisimilitude.

The story is a fantasy about a multiracial group of modern children who, after stumbling upon a band of San living according to their old ways, join them for three months on their travels through an unidentifiable part of Africa. The author repeatedly makes it clear, once one accepts the fantasy, that they are undergoing a didactic experience, to learn from the ways of the San. Implicitly, one may assume that the school students who read it are also expected to learn these lessons. Yet McAdorey ignores modern scholarship and perpetuates totally discredited stereotypes of the San as well as making factual errors. Filled with clichés and hocus-pocus, it features an old man who possesses mindreading and prophetic powers. Prospero-like, he summons up a vision of prehistoric creatures fighting to the death, which, he tells the children, carries the same message about the need for conservation as the extinction of the quagga. More supernatural elements include a "witchdoctor" who wears an "enormous ostrich-feather head-dress" (*Old Man*, 160, 54), and a legend of a black hyena that casts a real shadow. When McAdorey's absurdly overheated narrative announces, "The San had lived through the volcanic eruptions of the continent's birth.... They had survived the sabre-toothed cats, the three-toed horses, the giant baboons" (*Old Man*, 63), the value of the book as a source of factual accuracy is irredeemably destroyed.

Presumably because of the mystical connotations of the San, an unusually high proportion of fiction about them has taken the form of fantasy: some of it, such as *The Old Man of the Mountain*, crass, some very good, as this chapter will show. A couple of mediocre stories use fantasy to fulfill the longing to be able to talk to one of the vanished San by bringing him into the present.

In "Peter's Bushman" by Enid Ablett, the boy meets one in a cave, who tells him in improbable pidgin, "Hunting very bad, no buck come to my waterhole for one whole month" (*Bushman*, 12). Another is *A Drakensberg Tale* by M. Edward, written in a particular facetious style that cropped up in some books and illustrations in the 1940s and 1950s.[48] It must have been well regarded at the time, because it was illustrated — inaccurately — by the eminent artist Ernest Ullmann, and broadcast as a radio serial. Mr. Philos. O. Pher spends a holiday in a painted rock shelter: "The walls were artistically decorated with paintings of men and animals by some Bushman-tenant of long ago. He must have had an undisturbed lease to do all the creative work" (*Drakensberg*, 13). He gets chatting to a baboon, who introduces him to a San man, Sian, "the Inspector of Caves." Sian tells him he participated in a parade of San at the Union Pageant many years ago, and Pher recollects that he had heard of the "Wandering Bushman," who Sian must be. Sian repeats a San prophecy that "the White man's great cities may crumble back to earth":

> A golden dream has vanished from the land,
>   And what remains? A scar upon the sand;
> A sorry place, where once had been proud Whites
>   Too mindful of their heritage and rights.
> And now the jackals howl amidst the ruins.

(Drakensberg, 38)

At their best, the books convey quality of life rather than dry ethnographic facts or inventions. Edna Quail's *Kattau the Hunter* (1983) exemplifies this.[49] The little boy Kattau senses the warmth of the sun, the shade of the trees and clouds, the heady taste of honey, even "the springbok sensation" (*Kattau*, 39) that San hunters speak of when he hunts. He learns, "This was the place where his people and the birds and the beasts had lived since Mantis first threw a feather into the sky and made the moon" (*Kattau*, 9). His people's beliefs form a meaningful part of his experience of the world rather than being conveyed as quaint stories, as they are in Mary Phillips' stories about a little boy.

A recurring theme is that because of the oneness of the San with nature, "they never took from the land more than they needed," as Linfield puts it in her introduction to *The Lion of the Kalahari*. Citing the Bleek material, she writes, "Indeed, the sun, the stars and the wind, all animals, birds, insects, trees and plants were once 'people of the early race'. Everyone spoke the same language and there was kinship between them" (*Lion*, viii). In *When Whales Go Free* (1988), Dianne Hofmeyr specifically introduces a description of the harmonious way of life of hunter-gatherers in order to contrast it with the rapacious whalers of modern times.[50]

A common didactic purpose of the children's books, then, is to hold the San up as models of good ecological practice. Modern societies are apt to affect nostalgia for the pre-colonial past that they have contributed to destroying. Voss suggests that one of the functions of nostalgia for the extinct San is "assuagement of the ecological guilt that nourishes 'Nature' in reserves and on wilderness trails" (Voss, 21). In Thesen's *A Deadly Presence,* guilt over enmity between humans and nature is equated with guilt over enmity between black and white people because the leopard is symbolically black. This is the guilt that the conservator takes upon himself by making himself a living bait for the leopard.[51]

When writers introduce San in modern times who, quite impossibly, still lead a primal existence, this serves another purpose. In Coetzee's *Flint and the Red Desert*, for example, happy clicking San turn up out of the desert every now and then, do the whites a favor and accept gifts of beads and tobacco, although, as a white girl says, "They don't really expect anything in return" (*Flint*, 55), before disappearing again. Keyan Tomaselli observes, "Confirmation that some First Peoples have survived intact is somehow seen to hold a key to the West's own redemption."[52]

The San can be awarded this special status because they are unthreatening to modern society. Pohl describes their rock art as "the work of a rare artist, natural and untaught" (*Farewell*, 5); in his novel *Savage Hinterland* (1956), a San boy is able to escort a white boy in safety on a walk of 700 miles to the nearest white settlement because of his "instinctive" knowledge.[53] Such innate knowledge and skills are not to be measured by modern western standards and are no competition for modern technology. The implication of Smith's *Tinde in the Mountains*, as MacCann and Maddy have pointed out, is that nomadic peoples were incapable of political organization, so that in fact there was a need for white people to move in and establish a government.

Another aspect of the San way of life to be found in the stories is their ethic that harmony must prevail in the clan and even between clans, even if the clans are depicted in destructive conflict. One of the best is *Narni of the Desert* by Gwen Westwood, ahead of its time when first published in 1967.[54] It is a simple story for young children, carefully crafted and beautifully told, about how a San boy grows up to the point when he can join the men on his first hunt. Although the setting is alien to modern readers, she makes the story very human, full of the comfort and reassurance given by family and friends. When Narni is lost, he hears his mother pounding roots: "It was echoing over the desert calling Narni home" (*Narni*, 72).

It was easy for writers to extend this domestic harmony to relations between races. Within the San band, Kabo, in *Kabo of the Mountain* by Nockels and Wilcox, is scolded by an adult, "Have you eaten the hare and not shared it with your family? That is not right! Have you not learnt that what one has one shares?" (*Kabo*, 31). But the story goes further; it alternates between Kabo and two black African girls as focalizers, and they sustain into young adulthood their friendship begun as little children. Kabo's grandmother announces, "It is time now, if we are to share this mountain, that we befriend these people so that they do not become our enemies" (*Kabo*, 29). The tender story is brought to a heartwarming close when Kabo persuades his grandfather that the others are not all "wild, angry people" (*Kabo*, 103).

The political lesson is clear. But an even more pressing concern of children's writers has been how to cope with the guilt of genocide. Some of South Africa's best children's authors have turned to fantasy in order to come to terms with it. Two short stories on this theme that are similar in setting are "Xhabbo and the Honey-guide" by Cicely van Straten and "The Broken String" by Marguerite Poland.[55]

Van Straten's story takes place, like *Kabo of the Mountain*, at the time when the San in the foothills of the Drakensberg are threatened by the influx of black African pastoralists: "And now Xhabbo and his people were like hunted buck, and the terrible dark strangers were the huntsmen" ("Xhabbo," 63). Young Xhabbo is left with the women and children of his band when their men do not return from a hunt. While he is desperately searching for food, he is approached by a honey-guide, which is a bird famed in African folklore for guiding animals or humans to a bees' nest so that it can feed on the honey and grubs when they rob the hive. For this reason, in African oral and written literature, it is an archetypal symbol of coexistence between humans and animals.[56] Although Xhabbo ignores the bird, it persists until he follows it. High in the mountains he comes upon an idyllic hidden valley, holding the promise of honey, the paths of buck and a rock shelter where swallows nest. He fetches his people to live there, and "They were still there when Xhabbo's great-great-grandchildren were men." They left their paintings on the walls of the shelter, "And if today you climb in the Drakensberg near the Umhlwasine river valley and find that cave, you will see them there still on the golden rock — Xhabbo's people leaping with swift feet" ("Xhabbo," 70). All that modern people can do is enjoy the beauty they have left behind.

Marguerite Poland's story is equally elegiac. The title, "The Broken String," is taken from one of the laments in the Bleek collection of San lore:

... Everything feels as if it stood open before me
empty, and I hear no sound
for they have broken the bow's string for me
and the old places are not sweet anymore
for what they did.

("*String*", 17)

A young San man is killed by the Boers when they arrive in the Drakensberg, and his close friend Mashake finds his broken bow.

An eland (the beloved antelope of their god, Kaggen) leads Mashake and his people to a hidden valley: "There the eland and their people live in freedom and the footprints of the white-backed wagon never mark the earth. There the children of Mashake and Soai still play their hunting-bows to call the clouds so they may hear the voice of Kaggen in the rain" ("String," 32).

Poland's writings as a whole do not suggest that the solution to horror is to escape into fantasy; rather she conveys in many of her stories the strength that the San drew from their spiritual beliefs, particularly belief in the renewal of life through the cycle of death and birth. Her use of another San poem, a prayer to the star Xkoagu, as the epigraph to her collection of animal stories, *Sambane's Dream* (1989), suggests that the animals are to be seen as metaphors for humans.[57] Xkoagu, "grandmother of all, red with fatness" protects the dreams of small creatures like Sambane, the aardvark, and Nzwili, the ant-eating chat, and gives them courage.

> Take my heart, my heart
> small and famished without hope
> so that like you I too may be full
> for I hunger.

> (*Sambane's Dream*, 1)

Nzwili gives his life, but his descendants live. Perhaps a poor consolation for modern children, but Poland believes that Africa offers the hope of regeneration.

Anne Harries also used the Bleek material to convey hope through renewal. *The Sound of the Gora* is set in two times, the clash of Boer and San in the past, and Cape Town in the 1980s. The little abducted San girl in her story prays the same prayer to Xkoagu that Poland quotes. She escapes and lives a free life, and later, when she is dying, she offers a prayer to the moon (also taken from the Bleek material):

> Once when your child the hare
> cried to you, his mother, not to let him die
> you told us too that when we died
> > we should return again.

> (*Gora*, 84)

This belief in regeneration, arising from the image of a hare to be seen in the dark shapes on the moon, also forms the theme of Poland's *Shadow of the Wild Hare*.[58] The prayer of the girl in *The Sound of the*

Gora is answered, because her descendant is involved in reconciling races and in fighting for freedom.

Mention was made in Chapter 5 of how, as the twentieth century drew to an end, children became the focus of hope for the new nation. The end of a millennium, for all its factitious nature, is a time of great psychic upheaval, more so than the ordinary turn of a century. At such a time, people not only look to the future with apprehension or expectation, as the people of South Africa did, but they also look back to the past. Both of these responses — concern for the future and engaging with the past — can be seen in South African children's literature. At the beginning of the twentieth century, on the day of the Union of South Africa, May 31 1910, H.B. Hook dedicated his historical children's novel to the wish for "race-union" between Afrikaner and English.[59] Two novels about the San marked the beginning of the twenty-first century. *Song of Be* by Lesley Beake looked to the future, while the past was the focus of a remarkable novel, *The Joining* (1996), by Peter Slingsby.[60] Tony Voss presciently wrote in 1989, "The turning points in the history of the Bushman image occur at crucial moments in the history of South Africa" (*Voss*, 20).

The Joining is such an important book that it deserves a detailed analysis. It is a "time-slip" story about four modern children who, after the election in 1994, slip through time to live with a band of San several centuries in the past, before the coming of the Europeans. What makes it astonishing is that it is a rare example of a time-shift novel in which the protagonists do not return to the present. Slingsby's children ultimately renounce the opportunity to return, and remain in the past with a race they know is doomed.

Slingsby's novel is a good example of the new style of children's time-slip stories identified by Maria Nikolajeva in her study of world youth literature of the 1990s, *Children's Literature Comes of Age*.[61] The modern trend is a shift from the passivity of the child actors to agency; instead of being pawns who are carried back to the past, they are protagonists in the quest for identity (Nikolajeva, 73).

The differences that set *The Joining* apart from earlier children's fiction about the San are signalled by the title, which refers to the art of the San and its place in their religious and social beliefs and practices. A San man explains: "A painting is a joining. It joins the shaman to his trance-dream, it joins the animal-people to us. It is a way in which we can speak to them and share their power. Even if we paint after something has happened, that painting is a joining" (*Joining*, 84).

Slingsby is the first novelist to have posited his portrayal of the San upon the new understanding of the interrelationship of their spiritual beliefs and practices with their art and their way of life that has become available in the last three decades. Hitherto, writers of fiction had concentrated on a sociological portrayal of the San in attempting to convey their significance to modern children. The simple didactic message of *The Old Man of the Mountain* by Ursula McAdorey, for example, is that children can learn good manners and ecological responsibility from the ancients. Leon de Kock has argued that Michael Chapman, in his history of southern African literature, has attempted to understand fiction featuring the San by looking for similar lessons, but in doing so has missed the real difference between San life and modernist white literature: "What is extracted [by Chapman] from diverse sources and people are diluted themes of a common citizenry, a singularity of ethical humanism ultimately signified as 'South Africanism'. What is utterly lost in this process is the untranslatable sacred experience now generally described as 'shamanism', which is not amenable to sociological or rational analysis, and which constitutes *difference* proper in the Bushman case."[62]

Shamanism is central to *The Joining*. Whereas rock paintings in earlier children's books were simply another feature of material culture that added to the record of the way of life of the San, in *The Joining* they open up possibilities and meanings that are otherwise ineffable. Paintings on the walls of shelters not only join the natural with the supernatural but blur the distinction between fact and fiction.

Some of Slingsby's descriptions of people and events are obviously drawn from paintings he has seen, while he has taken details of shamanism, such as bleeding from the nose while in trance, from the anthropological literature, and has based other aspects of the San way of life in his novel on the findings of archaeology and anthropology. Moreover, the paintings that characters make to record incidents in the story are actual paintings, reproduced in the book, which are situated in the region whose topography is described so precisely by the author. Any reader, with the aid of Slingsby's descriptions, books on the rock art of the Western Cape and a good map, could visit the sites today, and Slingsby has, in fact, published such guides. He is inducting not only the modern characters of the story but the modern reader into the world of the San.

This is in keeping with the latest trends in time-slip fiction described by Tess Cosslett in her essay, "'History from Below': Time-slip Narratives and National Identity."[63] Traditionally, English time-slip stories presented the grand imperial pageant (for example, in the *Puck of Pook's Hill* stories of Rudyard Kipling) — the equivalent of which are the events of white conquest in southern Africa, canonized in old school history books and endorsed in fiction such as *Tinde in the Mountains* by Ken Smith; now they uncover the history of ordinary people — in this case, the San.

"Joining" is not only a word used in the book for paintings; in the title it has a double meaning, referring also to the joining of the modern children with the San. By using the same word, the author reinforces the idea that by joining the hunter-gatherers, the children are becoming part of their way of life and cosmology. To the San, people are joined with one another and with nature, and everyone and everything is joined with the spiritual world. In the opening, the boy who is the focalizer of the story, Jeremy, remonstrates with their white youth leader for calling the San "primitive," and it does not take him long when living with them to appreciate their quality:

> They are people and they behave just like ordinary people, except that they seem to be a lot gentler [....] Surely that makes them more...he struggled to remember the word...more *civilised* than other people? They're organised. They live simply but they've got everything anyone really needs. He suddenly thought of the word he was looking for. What they've got is *harmony*. That's it! They don't kill more than they need, they don't eat too much, they don't own things. They just belong. They use what they need, then they move on. Like the eland and the birds and...everything in the wide world stretched out beneath him. *Harmony*.
>
> (*Joining*, 36)

Even when, later, he sees one of them roused to anger to the point of threatening to kill one of the children, he does not change his mind, but modifies his understanding of them; people are not simple, like animals, but "because they have brains they are likely to be...*unpredictable*. That's why they made rules, but the rules were never good enough, never complete, because you never knew what a human being might do next" (*Joining*, 108). With this insight, Slingsby advances beyond the simplistic views of San harmony portrayed by some earlier authors.

The events of both the present and the past are clearly set in a historical context. Though the exact date to which the children go back is uncertain, it must be in the seventeenth century, when whites had settled at the Cape, Africans had already reached the Eastern Cape, and migrating Khoi pastoralists were already clashing with the San. Jeremy is perfectly aware of this and the fact that it marked the start of a painful period of two centuries that would see the persecution and disappearance of the San. As for the present, the story is set after the first democratic elections of 1994. Why, then, should Slingsby's characters voluntarily leave it behind to enter a doomed past?

In American stories of the late nineteenth and early twentieth centuries, boys such as Tom Sawyer were allowed to escape for a while to the wilderness; it would be good for them, but they would return.[64] Similarly, in an Afrikaans children's book of 1963, *Agarob, Kind van die Duine* (Agarob, child of the dunes), Jan J. van der Post fictionalized an episode in his own life when he ran away with a San boy and lived for a while with his people before returning to go to school.[65] But Slingsby, and South Africa, had moved far beyond this 40 years later.

When, on two occasions, Jeremy has the opportunity to return irrevocably to the present, it is the contrast with modern life, and his awareness of his forefathers' complicity in wiping out the San, that sends him back to the past. The meaninglessness of obsessions with race in the face of the reality of South Africa is brought home by the hint that even Jeremy, in spite of his red hair and fair skin, has colored ancestry.

Part of the persuasive impact of the story comes from the gradual revelation of the dysfunctional family backgrounds of all four children, resulting from typical social circumstances in the late twentieth century. Jeremy's mother is divorced and has gone overseas with a man, leaving her son with an aunt whose main impact on him is made by her cigarette stubs in the ashtray, while his life runs its routine of suburban trains, takeaway foods, television and homework. Like him, the Xhosa twins, Sitheli and Phumzile, do not know what has happened to their mother. They live in fear of crime, behind high walls in a black township, with a father who buys them what they want but has no time for them. Christine, who is clearly descended from the San, lives with an uncle who sexually molests her. She never has any doubt that she wants to stay where she need never fear, and the story ends with her betrothal to a San man.

The twins, with Jeremy, waver at the last, but then decide to remain in the past. Each has found a place and a role in the little band, and Jeremy has already become aware of mutual attraction between himself and a pretty girl called Grassbird. (One could, of course, argue that Slingsby gives both Jeremy and Christine "colored" blood to avoid the suggestion that their marriages with San partners would be interracial.)

The Joining is one of only a few time-slip stories in which children do not return to the present; another is *A Chance Child* (1978) by Jill Paton Walsh, in which an abused twentieth-century boy returns to the age of the Industrial Revolution, and, after experiencing the hardships of working children, makes a reasonable life for himself.[66] Classic, earlier children's time-slip stories of the twentieth century, such as those of L.M. Boston, E. Nesbit and Philippa Pearce, differ from *The Joining* and

A Chance Child, both in their portrayal of the past and in that their protagonists return to the present. In them, as Linda Hall has commented,
"change and loss…evoke a genuine sense of elegy"; but the past must be
left behind, albeit with regret.[67]

Slingsby could easily have taken the same path, for the present
circumstances in South Africa are conducive to feelings of nostalgia.
Momentous times such as the coming of the millennium or the changes
taking place in South Africa arouse feelings of dislocation, discontinuity
and uncertainty that give rise naturally to a sense of nostalgia, as Fred
Davis has argued in *Yearning for Yesterday: A Sociology of Nostalgia.*[68]
Whether one does feel nostalgic depends on one's perception of these
changes. The conditions for nostalgia postulated by Christopher Shaw
and Malcolm Chase in *The Imagined Past: History and Nostalgia* are
that the present is considered deficient, that one has lost faith in the
ability of the world to change for the better, that material objects are
available on which to project one's nostalgia and one's sense of time
must be linear and secular.[69]

Slingsby matches most of these criteria. He is not sure that the present
political situation is all that hopeful. When an old shaman, speaking in
fables, asks Jeremy whether, in his future time, the white and the brown
and the black mice have made peace yet, Jeremy answers uncertainly,
"I think so" (*Joining*, 58). It can also be argued that Slingsby abhors the
quality of modern life, because the children are motivated by a wish to
escape their miserable home circumstances, just as in an earlier novel,
Leopard Boy (1989), he wrote of a boy who escapes the social ills of
the modern world by donning a leopard skin and, refusing help from
adults, disappears into the mountains to lead a feral existence.[70] Nor is
an environmental renaissance the answer. Although Slingsby is by pro-
fession an environmental educator, the children's leader who is also one
in *The Joining* is by no means an admirable role model with a meaningful message for them.

And so the lesson for today's children appears to be depressing: modern life is hateful, but there is no solution other than the acknowledged
fantasy of running away to the past. Even the precondition of having
material objects as a focus for nostalgia is met by the paintings. Judith
Inggs' verdict on the end of *The Joining* is that it is "a profoundly pes-
simistic conclusion, which represents the death of the children in the
present time."[71]

Yet Slingsby dedicates the book to the "children of free South Africa"
and dates it Freedom Day, 1996. Is he being hypocritical in writing a
novel that endorses opting for the past, but telling modern youngsters
they are lucky to be living in the exciting present? After all, in Lesley

Beake's *Song of Be,* the young San man who is working as an electoral official tells Be, "It's no use trying to go back, back in time, back to an old life that doesn't — that cannot — exist any more" (*Be,* 73).

Although there is an element of nostalgia in Slingsby's view that the past had order, simplicity and harmony that are missing today, unlike the time slip stories of L.M. Boston and Philippa Pearce but like *A Chance Child,* he acknowledges that the past was no idyll. To go back is not taking the easy way out. In any case, nostalgia is largely an adult emotion that the authors of classic time-slip stories engaged in; children want to move on.

Some insight into the children's decision is provided by comparing *The Joining* with another postmodern novel, *The English Patient* by Michael Ondaatje (1992).[72] Both have a scene in which a modern white person is taken into a cave lined with ancient paintings, where his or her body is painted. Rufus Cook comments, "When he [Almásy] paints Katharine's body in the Cave of Swimmers, he is certainly conferring an immortality of sorts on her, but the method he is using to do so is that of 'translating' her into the body of a literary text, by inducting her into that non-sequential, non-linear mode of duration that is the hallmark of poems and paintings and works of fiction like *The English Patient.*"[73]

In *The Joining* time present and time past are confused and have different duration, as the children mature in the past but occasionally return to the present in what appears to be a matter of hours. Apparent realities of different times, of dream and trance and everyday life, coexist for Jeremy, as they do for his shaman mentor, Gau: they are "non-sequential, non-linear."

The novel neatly fulfills the hopes for South African literature of the new era that Elleke Boehmer expresses in her essay, "Endings and New Beginnings: South African Fiction in Transition." She dismisses "magic realist conjuring tricks" in post-apartheid writing, which suggests what is so bad about McAdorey's *The Old Man of the Mountain,* and declares, "Now that fiction has made new kinds of formal cultural daring more possible, it will be liberating to see the lens of vigilant social observation crack across to give life skewed, fragmented, upended, not by apartheid as before, but as part of the manipulation of aesthetic form, of the testing of visionary, hallucinatory, dislocating, non-camera-ready ways of representing the world."[74]

Slingsby writes in this mode because he is exercised by the notion of guilt. Although he probably did not know it, his novel had been preceded in Canada by a complex fantasy-cum-time-slip novel for young adults about the extirpation of the indigenous people of Newfoundland in the early nineteenth century. *Blood Red Ochre* by Kevin Major (1989) tells how a white boy enters the past, where he is reconciled with the Beothuk people against whom his white ancestors had committed atrocities, whereupon the last of them leaves in a canoe and he returns to the present. Now Slingsby was to perform the same literary act of contrition for white South Africans.

To Slingsby, South Africans of the present must come to terms with the past, learn from the genocide and expiate their guilt by sharing in the redemptive spirituality of those gentle people who preceded everyone else. In his daring novel, by going back to join the San, the children — Jeremy in particular — are partaking in a mystic sacrificial union with the seductive outsider, and in that way with a missing part of themselves. Slingsby's epigraph is an old /Xam song:

The day we die a soft breeze
will blow away our footprints in the sand.
When the wind has gone, who will tell
the timelessness that once we walked
    this way in the dawn of time?

(*Joining*, n.p.)

Consequently, in his dedication he adjures "all the children of free South Africa": "You are the timelessness; look upon the joinings of those who walked this way in the dawn of time; see their long shadows from afar and remember them" (*Joining*, n.p.). For his readers it is not necessary to leave the present; they must make the future such that children will not wish to leave it.

Whereas in Slingsby's earlier novel *The Leopard Boy* characters run away from society, and in *The Joining* they choose to return to the past, he committed his child characters to the present and the future in his next novel, *Jedro's Bane* (2002).[75] The child narrator, a boy called Jedro, frames a serial story that his grandfather (Oupa) tells about an ancestor of Jedro's, Koot Dawid, who lived early in the nineteenth century. He was a Khoisan freedom fighter who defended his people against unjust white farmers, freeing them so that they could take refuge at mission stations. An old seer told Koot that this was his duty: "Ta-rau/ka is the turn-around, the time when the world changes so that it will never be the same again. Some are chosen to lead others through the changes" (*Jedro*, 86). Jedro has to apply lessons from the past to his own life by listening to his grandfather's tale and drawing his own conclusions. All that is needed is for the stories of ordinary people such as Koot to be made known, in addition to the grand narratives of white history.

Unfortunately, in the execution of the novel, the momentous story of his ancestor and the lesson it carries is disproportionate to the resolution of Jedro's own story, because he learns that he has to understand what drives the village bully to behave as he does and take the first steps at reconciliation.

Oupa takes up where *The Joining* left off. He refers to the coming of democracy in 1994, already history, and tells Jedro of the obligation he has to that moment and his ancestors: "You're young, you can't remember that day, just a few years ago, when the world turned around yet again — *ta-rau/ka* — and we became free at last. Koot fought for that, it's the memory of people like Koot that brings hope when people are not free" (*Jedro*, 134).

8

CROSS-CULTURAL DRESSING, NUDITY
AND CULTURAL IDENTITY

South African children's stories written by white writers often draw attention to the customary nudity or near-nudity of certain children. They also depict children assuming the dress of another culture, which usually entails black children covering their nakedness or white children undressing. Often boys of different cultures undress and swim together. In these stories, clothing and the state of dress or undress are signifiers of culture. The authors use them to portray what they think the views of the characters are about differences in culture, while at the same time revealing their own attitudes.

The stories raise questions about the nature of culture. Is it something that can be exchanged, put on or taken off? How easy is it for a person to change cultures? Can culture be changed while one's essential character remains the same? What notions of pleasure, transgression, power and knowledge do the stories embody?

The stories were written by white writers for white audiences. Some of them are historical fiction that explores the nature of racism in earlier South African society. While the examples discussed in this chapter are, with one exception, from books in English, parallels are to be found in Afrikaans books, for example *Agarob: Kind van die Duine* by Jan J. van der Post (1963) and *Karel Kousop* by Dolf van Niekerk (1985).[1]

Nudity and near-nudity are often foregrounded in stories that include indigenous children. Many of the stories are about the San. They either concern the few San who were still living their traditional lives as hunter-gatherers at the time of writing, or are historical or fantasy fiction about earlier times. In the past, African and San children went naked when they were young, and then wore small aprons. It is what white children first notice about them, in a dispassionate way: "The little boy was brown and skinny.... The most curious thing about him, though, was that he was naked. Well, not quite. He seemed to be wearing a sort of string about his waist, from which hung a small flap."[2] A white boy of the early nineteenth century meets a young Zulu: "The boy was wearing nothing but an *umutsha* of twisted calf skins."[3]

The children's nudity is also remarked on by authors. From the 1930s to the 1960s, their tone borders on the patronizing: "The Brown Babies lived in the land of the Golden South where the sun always shines and the days are always hot — that is why the Brown Babies wore no clothes";[4] "Bobo, the young picaninny, was wearing only a string of beads today, because her mother said it was far too hot for her to wear her little yellow print frock;"[5] "It is easy to get dressed if you are a small African herdboy in the Transkei. Bengu crawled from under his red blanket and flung it around his shoulders";[6] when children go swimming, the author remarks that they wear so little that it does not take long before they have undressed and are in the water.[7]

Historical fiction shows white adults until the early twentieth century to be more critical than children, seeing the nudity of the indigenes as immoral and regarding the San as savage and pagan because they are "dirty," as they smear their bodies with substances that include animal fat to protect their skins, and consequently have a strong body odor. The authors are historically accurate about this; it was typical of travel writers in the eighteenth and nineteenth centuries to react in this way, because they took customs that were dictated by the San way of life out of context and then condemned them as uncivilized.

While distancing themselves from the historically racist attitudes of adults in the stories, authors in the latter half of the twentieth century have nevertheless often continued to remark on the physical differences between the San and Europeans. Two writers stress the beautiful color of San children's skin: in *The Sound of the Gora* by Ann Harries, a girl is a "tiny golden creature";[8] in *The Old Man of the Mountain* by Ursula McAdorey, children have "complexions like thick yellow cream."[9] In both cases, the San children are juxtaposed with whites — an "evil-smelling Boer" and a red-haired, freckle-faced boy. The difference in this case is intended to show up the indigene to advantage. Their naked comeliness, their golden and cream colors, suggest that they are in harmony with nature.

Although twentieth-century authors do not show any moral disapproval of nudity, publishers and illustrators have apparently felt that it is immoral to depict it. Just as in Victorian books, the illustrations sometimes contradict the texts by depicting the children as clothed.[10]

In most historical fiction about the colonial period written by modern authors, black characters are forced to don European clothing, and the stories show sympathetically what this means to them. A reversal of perspective that would bring a white reader up short is the remark by a black character in *The Great Thirst* by Jenny Seed (1971) that clothing worn by whites is "like the scum on stagnant water."[11] The San see it as uncomfortable and impractical because it impedes movement and makes a noise in the grass, betraying one's presence. To be forced to put it on is to be forced to accept white culture; the act of dressing is symbolic of enslavement. In *The Last Horizon* by Reginald Maddock, when a young San called Strong Arm is captured, he despises an enslaved San for wearing trousers, but on joining him as a servant he too is made to dress: "She [his mistress] taught him also that Christians covered their bodies.... He could not see that his body was evil, and he felt no shame in showing it.... Bushmen were born naked, lived naked and died naked, and the trousers rubbed his skin and kept the sun's warmth off his legs" (*Horizon*, 32).

The stories show how, for white people, washing was a necessary preliminary to dressing. Nama, the tiny golden girl, is captured by what she regards as an "evil-smelling Boer," but his wife's reaction when he brings her home is, "Let's take her inside and clean off her Bushman filth" (*Gora*, 30). In effect, by washing the San and removing their smeared body covering, the whites are undressing them before dressing them in European clothing. The narrator of *The Sound of the Gora* remarks, "After her first bath...the Bushman girl looked considerably more naked than when covered with her Bushman filth" (*Gora*, 31).

Dirt is associated by the white historical characters with immorality; when Strong Arm, now called Jonny after the family's former pet baboon, is made to wash by his new mistress, "She made him understand that washing was something Christians did, but she never made him understand what a Christian was" (*Horizon*, 32).

Well might the washing be confused with christening, as it is in the minds of the San in some stories, because it was usually accompanied by the bestowal of a "Christian" name to replace the indigenous one. Nama, which means "Daughter of the people" — "a name for wild savages!" exclaims her mistress — is renamed Marguerite (*Gora*, 49). Nevertheless, the Christianizing of black children in no way granted them equality of status with their white masters. The stories by Maddock and Harries bring out the hypocrisy of settlers who tried to convert children while treating them as slaves. Strong Arm is tied to the leg of the table on which the Boer paterfamilias rests "the Good Book" during devotions (*Horizon*, 34); Nama receives the news that her brother has been sold to a farmer just as "evening prayers were about to commence" (*Gora*, 36).

A story of 1935 that is resolutely pro-Zulu rejects the association of nudity with sin, although the defense is not very articulate. In *David Goes to Zululand* by K. Marshall, a boy's old nurse in England tells him that she has heard that "all the African natives were wicked heathens and ran about without any clothes on," to which his father replies, "Where we shall live the natives are not wicked. They don't wear much in the way of clothes and most of them are heathen; but both these things suit them."[12]

In *the Sound of the Gora*, Ann Harries acknowledges that the Boers' treatment of their servants and slaves could be paradoxical, mingling cruelty with paternalism. Seeking a surrogate child of her own, the Boer woman dresses the tiny golden girl in precious old velvet that her ancestors brought from France. Nevertheless, because the child runs away, Harries makes the point that the clothing is an unsuccessful, superficial attempt to change her, as it is in the story of Strong Arm.

As the twentieth century drew on, indigenous peoples became increasingly Westernized, abandoning their traditional dress. Authors writing about their own times responded in different ways. "The Magic Shoes" by Sadie Merber (1930) features a little herd boy: "His skin was as black as pitch, his hair was as curly and wiggly as you can imagine, his eyes shone like two bright stars. He wore but scanty clothes [in this case the illustration shows him naked], and the whole day long he played and ran about."[13] He covets a pair of shoes that a white "fairy man" offers to sell him in exchange for the goats he is minding. After the deal, he finds the shoes pinch. "He took the lesson very much to heart and was never in the future heard to ask that he should wear shoes like the great people of the towns" ("Shoes," 50). To Merber, for a black child to *want* to wear the clothing of whites was unacceptable hubris that was socially destabilizing.

Similar anxiety is evinced in "Macepa and the Voice" by Ella Mackenzie (1923).[14] A little black boy runs away to town and finds work as a houseboy: "His mistress…made him a nice unbleached calico suit trimmed with red braid" (*Macepa*, 34). But Macepa is given a fright by a gramophone and runs home again, having learnt his lesson.

A white suit trimmed with red braid was the standard uniform for male domestic servants in the first half of the twentieth century, and became emblematic of their servitude. In *Working Life 1886-1940: Factories, Townships, and Popular Culture on the Rand,* Luli Callinicos quotes a letter written to *The Star* in 1911: "No native should be allowed to wear ordinary European dress during working hours, and employers should combine to this end. European dress gives him an inflated sense of importance and equality."[15]

In a book of verse about farm life by D.A. Nesbitt (1926?), a poem sarcastically entitled "Gentleman Sixpence" holds a young farm laborer up to ridicule for dressing up in European clothes when he goes visiting (*vagash*):

> His kit was very meagre,
> Consisting of two things—
> A pair of dirty sandals
> And two small bits of skins.
>
> But when he went vagash
> He'd be real swell
> With shirt and shorts complete,
> A sporting coat as well—
> A walking stick and socks,
> Shoes far too tight.
>
> The boys down in the compound
> Would laugh at him and jeer—
> He'd only look more foolish
> And grin from ear to ear.[16]

By contrast, Sally Starke wrote a poem in which she sympathizes with white farm boys who have to dress up to go visiting:

> We put on shoes and socks, and shirts
> That button to the chin,
> We wear a hat and all that
> And a *visiting* grin....
>
> Before we go to town we talk
> For days and weeks about it,
> But when we're there we wouldn't care
> If we had done without it.[17]

Another story of this period, *Two Little Strangers Meet* by Helena Hersman and H. Lily Guinsberg (193-), suggests what the attitude of black children to the clothing of whites should be. It tells of the friendship on a farm between a black girl — "All she wore was a string of red beads" (converted to an apron in the illustration) — and a white girl. Eventually, as the accounts of such friendships so often have it, the white girl has to go away to school: "[Margaret] had so much to say. She told M'sonda about her blue dressing gown with its tassels and slippers to match; about her many new frocks, the white hat, and her lovely new shoes …. M'sonda listened eagerly" (*Strangers*, 29). Good black children simply accepted the status quo.

That writers were secretly uneasy that all was not just in the social order of the 1920s is suggested by the extraordinary lengths to which Sir Henry Juta went in *Tales I Told the Children* (1921) to explain why a Zulu man was serving as a nurse to white children, dressed in the standard servant's uniform and called by a facetious English name.[18] Juta, scion of the Juta publishing house, was the speaker of the old Cape Legislative Assembly and later Judge President of the Cape and an Appeal Court Judge. He could consider himself an accomplished author: he wrote a detective novel and a volume of reminiscences, as well as the children's stories that first appeared in the Juta's Juvenile Library series and were collected in the volume, *Tales I Told the Children*, which was reprinted several times.

His book is addressed unequivocally to very young readers, yet in "The Water Baby," which is a fairy story typical of the period, he devotes four long paragraphs to justifying the position of the children's nurse, of which the following is part:

> Sixpence was the children's nurse. Yes, their nurse. Not a young woman with a blue cotton dress, white apron, and little bonnet with long streamers; but a tall Kafir, dressed in white linen trousers that came just below his knees, with bright red braid sewn down the sides and round the ends, and in a white linen tunic that nearly touched his knees, also finished with red braid round the neck and round the wrists. But no nanny nurse was more faithful or more careful than this Zulu boy.
>
> In his own country he had been a little king and a soldier, and when Jimmy's father had gone into his country, Sixpence had watched over him and taken care of him. He grew so fond of Jimmy's daddy that he walked all the way to Jimmy's home….
>
> You want to know how he got the name of Sixpence? Once upon a time he worked in the Diamond Fields…. His Zulu name was a long word with funny little sounds in it like a hen cackling. So the English miners, who could not speak Zulu, gave him the name of Sixpence. But Sixpence did not mind being called Sixpence. In his own country he was a chief and was saluted by the name of "Inkoos," which means king; and now that he had served

Jimmy's daddy, he called Jimmy "Pikanini 'nkoos" or "little chief," and Sheila was called "inkosikaan."

(*Tales*, 4)

This book was published in the Juta series that had the iconic frame for the title page that included among its images of South Africa a slave of a previous century who has had a makeover to appear as a romantic pirate wearing a spotted bandanna, but no contemporary servant in white and red suit.

A certain discomfort at the obvious distance between affluent white children and naked, uneducated black children was creeping in. This could be represented by a specious envy, presented facetiously in a poem by Pattie Price in *The Afrikaner Little Boy: Ten Songs with Music about Small Children* (1935).[19] The instruction for performance calls for it to be delivered "peevishly":

When I'm all dressed up
For going to Town
With my socks pulled up
And my collar turned down
And I *know* I'm wearing
An ugly frown,
'Cos I feel as if Town wasn't worth it!
For my coat's all thick
An' hot, you see,
My shoes too tight
An' my neck isn't free,
An' "Christmas" stands and grins at me,
With nearly nothing on!
....
And think of how lovely to run a race,
With nearly nothing on!

(*Little Boy*, 12)

This was not the first children's poem to express envy of black people; back in the days when the ordained roles of black and white in South Africa were unproblematic to white people and the term "kaffir" was normal usage by whites, Edith King, headmistress of a famous school for white girls in Bloemfontein, wrote "To a Kaffir Baby" in *Veld Rhymes for Children* (1911) in the persona of a "little English baby":

And, when you're a grown-up Kaffir,
    You'll be strong and tall.

You will drive a team of oxen,
> You will sow and dig—
Just the things that I should like to
> Do, when I am big.[20]

Contrived envy of black children's nudity continued in *Stories from Sunny Zululand* by Dulcie Carter (1947).[21] It was very much a home-grown Natal book, published in Durban by Knox. A boy called Campbell (the author gives him the name of one of Natal's wealthiest sugar-growing families) and his sister June, who live in Zululand, go through the little family incidents typical of stories of the time. When they go fishing in the Umfolosi River, they find some Zulu boys swimming there:

> They were little black boys, and looked so happy and cool as, in Zululand, very few little native boys wear clothes. Campbell thought to himself how wonderful it would be to be like that and not have to wear a shirt which was always coming out.... They dived into the water and swam back to the shore, their little bodies glistening in the sun. They lay flat on their tummies to dry. "They can't get sunburnt because they are so brown already," said June. The children thought it must be lovely to live like the little Zulu boys. No school, no homework.... Of course, when the umfaans [boys] grow up they go to work in gardens or in a house, and some Zulu boys make very good cooks or house-boys.

> (*Sunny Zululand*, 10)

But, at the same time, Durban could also produce stories by white writers that made Zulu children the focalizers and portrayed them more realistically, as is shown by two books by Esmé Karlson that were also published by Knox, *The Coat of Many Patches* (1944) and *Peanut Goes to School* (1945).[22] In these stories, told from within Zulu society with no comparison with white children, it is accepted automatically that Zulu children do go to school and that they and their parents take pride in clothing them. In the first story, when a boy is due to start school, his father "bought him a slate, and a slate pencil, a pair of blue trousers, a white shirt, and last of all, a new blue coat" (*Coat*, 27). In the second story, when the children set off for school, "Peanut had on an old torn shirt and a little 'umutsha' [loin apron], and Geepie wore her spotted dress" (*Peanut*, 9). Peanut takes stiff porridge for his school lunch, and shares it with his classmates. "'Why don't you bring lunch to eat?' Peanut asked the other children. 'Because our mothers are too poor to give us clothes for school, and food as well,' they answered"

(*Peanut*, 9). These two stories, told without sentimentality or condescension (apart from the facetious nicknames), are the reverse of the standard trope in South African literature, seen in Hersman and Guinsberg's *Two Little Strangers Meet*, of white children going off to school dressed in new clothes, leaving their black playmates behind with no future but to become unskilled workers — gardeners, "cooks or house-boys."

During this period of cultural transition for black people, some writers considered that a black child dressed in European clothes marked an inevitable and satisfying step forward in the civilizing process. Earlier imperatives to turn pagans into Christians by bathing and dressing them became economic imperatives of incorporating Africans into society as useful workers.

A story of 1907 by H.A. Bryden, *The Gold Kloof*, already took this view.[23] The white heroes come across a feral child living with a troop of baboons. He is an African boy of seven or eight who had been abandoned by his father. On the first day they tame him sufficiently to be able to put him into trousers: "His face expanded into a broad smile — by far the most human-like expression that had yet appeared there — and he looked down at his new garments with real contentment. Thus was his first step towards civilization accomplished.... In another day's time Tom had induced the child to wear an old flannel shirt" (*Kloof*, 178). Tom remarks approvingly, "I'm sure he'll make a smart lad and a good herd boy" (*Kloof*, 188).

Jessie Hertslet, who wrote the text of the picture book *Kana and His Dog* discussed in Chapter 1, wrote a pair of novels in the 1940s that presented black children with models of what an educated Christian black person should be, much in the style of nineteenth-century missionary stories. *Mpala: The Story of an African Boy* (1942) was published by Oxford University Press in London in a series called "Oxford Story Readers for Africa," and *Nono: The Story of an African Girl* (1948) was announced as its sequel.[24] Mpala's first job is as a garden boy, for which "he had to wear a blue and red suit" (*Mpala*, 24). He becomes dissolute, but later is found to be the lost son of Chief Zulu. He gives himself to God, accepts his role as a chief and determines to use his education to better his people.

Nono warns readers against the evils of paganism. Nono is a country girl, the daughter of an herbalist and a Christian mother who despises her husband's tricks. The girl becomes a Christian, trains as a nurse specializing in preventive health care, and declares that she will "fight the dark ignorance which results in unhappiness and disease" (*Nono*, 103). She finds this "dark ignorance" even in the city, where she obtains her first appointment, in the shape of a "dirty bone-thrower" (*Nono*, 83). As a young woman living in her village, she meets Mathilda, a young woman visiting from town, and they are invited to a traditional dance: "There they took off all their clothes and put on narrow cloths round their hips and beads on their wrists, necks, and ankles. Nono felt rather uncomfortable and ashamed, but Mathilda cried, 'I like this! I like being bare, without clothes! Oh, how I wish I were a country girl!'" (*Nono*, 30). Nono leaves the dance in disgust.

In the mid-twentieth century, Fay Goldie wrote *Zulu Boy* (1968), the story of Umfaan, who goes to seek his fortune in town.[25] He is inspired by "Sezulu, ... a man of dignity and held in high esteem by his neighbours. ... He wore the military jacket with the brass buttons which he had bought many years before from a Big Baas in the dorp" (*Zulu Boy*, 12). His adoption of the secondhand jacket has fitted him into the lower orders of modern society. When Umfaan reaches town, he admires and longs to wear the "kitchen-boy uniform" that a friend wears. After a while he decides to learn to read and write, for, as his old black mentor says, "things are changing quickly in our land" (*Zulu Boy*, 82), and his illiterate brother concurs: "Who can tell what work you will want when you are a man?" (*Zulu Boy*, 97). But, none of them questions the political status quo. In taking the view that clothing indeed effects cultural change, Goldie was part of the political thinking of her time that whites had a paternalistic duty to "uplift" black people — within limits.

Daphne Rooke, another mid-century author, considered nowadays to have been an enlightened author for her time on matters of race, also engaged with notions of dress and schooling in *The South African Twins* (1953).[26] She was depicting no more than a typical situation when she introduced Kondulu, an orphan and turkey-herd on a remote farm, "a thin, eager youth, dressed in skins" (*Twins*, 29), and Karel and Tiensie, the white children of the farmer, who attend boarding school. Employing the standard trope of farm stories discussed in Chapter 2, she makes Kondulu and Karel companions during the holidays. In a change from the normal story of acculturation, Kondulu renames Karel, but the power relations are not reversed: he calls him Muscles, in admiration for his build. At the end of the story, Kondulu finds a hoard of gold sovereigns and tenders one at the local store "to buy a jersey for himself and some handkerchiefs and sweets for his female relatives" (*Twins*, 166). Karel tells him that after the government has taken its share, he will be rich, and asks him what he will do with the money. He replies, "First, I will have fifty jackets, all different colours, and a sack full of sweets" (*Twins*, 174).

A thief makes off with the sovereigns, but leaves behind the far more valuable diamond that he had stolen from the twins' father when he found it many years before. So the white family becomes rich, but Kondulu's luck has failed. In a section at the end of the book, which was left out of the American edition, the author tells what happened to everyone afterward: "Kondulu is at Lovedale College [a famous private church school for black children] where he is receiving a fine education. Karel sees to it that he has a new jacket every six months, and one day he is sure to have fifty jackets, and so realise one of his ambitions" (*Twins*, 188).

Rooke's version of the friendship of white and black boys shows that they are never equals. Kondulu is naive and silly, and the reader is invited to share with the author a smile at his simple, acquisitive ways and obsession with Western clothes, just as Jack Bennett invites the reader of *Jamie* to share in amusement at Kiewiet's superstition. Rooke does not kill Kondulu off as a resolution to his and Karel's friendship, as André Pieterse's film *e'Lollipop*, discussed in Chapter 2, does to the black boy; she only robs him of the treasure, and Kondulu remains dependent on Karel until his education will bring him independence.

Occasionally in the fiction a white child cross-dresses in the clothes of another culture. If it were possible to subvert an entire genre of literature on the subject before it was written, Edward Kendall did so in *The English Boy at the Cape* (1835), which was discussed in Chapter 7.[27] He took a view of cross-cultural dressing that was not to be repeated until Peter Slingsby's *The Joining* appeared in 1996. Nine-year-old Charles is abandoned in Cape Town and placed at an inn by the authorities pending the departure of a ship. Neglected, he becomes a filthy street child. A Cape Malay goldsmith finds him, bathes and clothes him in fresh white robes, and sets him to study and work with the Malay boys. And so he is restored by the cleanliness, spiritual tranquility and industry of the Muslim community.

Until Slingsby's novel, white children's cross-dressing was always an interlude, not the permanent closure that cross-dressing usually meant for black children. Most writers have associated themselves with the traditional view of white South Africans that a bit of cultural cross-dressing by white children is charming and harmless — it won't last.

A landmark episode occurs in the classic Afrikaans children's book by Alba Bouwer, *Stories van Rivierplaas* (1955), about Alie, a little white girl who lives on a farm.[28] When her friend Lulu comes to play, they ask the daughters of her nanny to dance for them:

> The Basuto children on a Free State farm don't wear clothes, and Sanna and Little-Melitie each had only a little band of beads

around the lower part of their bodies and a couple of copper rings around their arms.

Lulu declares she can dance as well as they, provided she is dressed like them.

> "That's a good idea," says Alie straight away, and right there and then Little-Melitie and Sanna are given their dresses and panties to put on, and Lulu and Alie put the bead bands low around their bodies and the copper rings around their arms, just as Sanna and Little-Melitie wear them. Now they all clap hands and white head and black head nod-nod next to each other, ... and the bead bands go flap-flap and the bangles go ting-a-ling and the little white feet stamp-stamp in a circle until the grass is flattened. Oh, but this is really fun!
>
> (*Rivierplaas*, 5, trans.)

The scene is illustrated without elaboration by the leading book illustrator, Katrine Harries.

Throughout the *Rivierplaas* series Bouwer makes an effort to show that, within the extremely structured traditional social hierarchy of farm life, Alie has respect for the Basotho people and their traditions, and she and her nanny relate warmly to each other as human beings. Alie, for example, treasures the Sesotho name that the people gave her. This scene of cross-dressing occurs in the very first story, which must have been a shock to some white readers in the 1950s; but it is only an escapade. Alie's nanny is, as usual, sworn to secrecy so that her parents don't hear what she has been up to. She can only sample Basotho life before returning to her own culture.

Gail Ching-Liang Low has observed that when a colonizer dons the clothing of the colonized, "the change effected by the clothes is (unsurprisingly) characterized by a release of libidinal energy."[29] The ecstatic dancing of the girls of Rivierplaas is a good example. Behind the cross-dressing can lie enjoyment of the transgression — the author's and the reader's orientalist fantasy of illicit pleasure in sampling the Other. Low, citing Edward Said, maintains that "the visual and imaginative pleasure of stepping into another's clothes forms one of the central legacies of orientalism" (Low, 83). This colonial heritage lingers in the South African literature still. The normal racial boundaries in society are not threatened because these are only brief episodes.

A story by Lesley Beake, *A Cageful of Butterflies* (1989), presents an account of the friendship between white and black boys that, she says in a note, is based on real events.[30] The white boy, called Fan, deliberately becomes black to look the same as his Zulu playmate, Mponyane, by taking off his T-shirt and rubbing himself with coal dust: "Mponyane looked at Fan and Fan looked at Mponyane. Fan grinned. 'Same colour, Mponyane!' he said happily, holding his own black arm against Mponyane's. 'We're both black!'" (*Cageful*,33). Their friendship is actively encouraged by adults, but does not continue into adulthood, as Mponyane dies.

A radical reversal of the trope of cross-dressing as an interlude of illicit pleasure or, at any rate, of short duration, occurs in *The Joining* by Peter Slingsby. When the children travel to the past and join the San, for both parties the shedding of their Western clothing is a clearly defined act of irreversibly shedding their culture; they will never return to the present.

Slingsby gives readers a strong sense of the values of the San and their way of life, which outweigh for these children the attractions of modernity that are symbolized by the stinking artificial fabrics of their clothing. Nudity is no longer innocent in the 1990s; the oldest girl will not strip to swim with the others because she lives with an uncle who sexually molests her. The illustrations shrewdly reinforce the San point of view by reproducing authentic San rock paintings that unselfconsciously depict the San in their nude state.

In a reversal of the washing and dressing forced on San children by Boers in the historical novels, the children are purified by fire and water in order to join the San. The symbolic moment arrives, and an old shaman announces, "The children will wear their coverings tonight. Tomorrow the boys will go with Wali, and he will dress them as the /Xam dress boys who are not yet men. Uub will dress the girls as the /Xam dress girls who are not yet women" (*Joining*, 44). To the white boy, Jeremy, it was time, for his clothes by now "felt scratchy and tight." "Acrid black smoke rose into the clean blue sky as the nylon and cotton fabrics melted and bubbled and burned. Wali raised his arms, the only thing he did that resembled any form of ceremony, and shouted.… He raked the stinking coals, piled on more wood, and turned to the boys. 'Come,' he beckoned" (*Joining*, 50). But Jeremy keeps his boots, until finally, of his own accord, he burns them. "The others looked back to the column of dirty smoke. 'He is letting the devil out, the wind that howls,' Uub said simply" (*Joining*, 75). When Jeremy bathes in their sacred river, he perceives that he has taken the final step: "*With /Xixo and Phumzile I have washed in the waters of the tra-tra, at the centre of this n!ore*" (*Joining*, 151; original italics). The San accept each of them, after a period of testing, on the strength of their innate personal qualities, which one of the San enumerates in a formal speech. This novel is the clearest rejection of cultural essentialism in the literature.

Just how revolutionary the story is can be judged by comparing it with *The Old Man of the Mountain* by Ursula McAdorey, which also sends modern children into the past to live with the San. She laboriously spells out the trite lessons they learn about respect for elders, unselfishness and so on, but she brings them back to the present without their ever taking their dirty, ragged, lice-ridden tracksuits and trainers off, even to swim.

Stories about close friendships between black and white boys often feature them naked and swimming together. In one way, this is an extension of scenes in which boys of the same race strip and swim together, which emphasize their existing or growing intimacy. In *Forever in the Land* by Robert Hill (1991), for example, an English-speaking city boy comes to stay with his Afrikaans relatives on the farm, and as part of his induction to country life, his cousin persuades him to undress and swim: "Don't worry, no one ever comes here."[31]

e'Lollipop, which is filled with clichés, has an incident of exchange of clothing and brief nudity intended to emphasize the intimate friendship of the black and white boys. When they are given a mild caning on the buttocks for being naughty, the white boy takes off his trousers and hands them to his friend, who is naked under his ragged long coat, so that he can enjoy similar protection. The next scene, selected to publicize the film, shows them cooling their bottoms in the river, one with his pants down, the other lifting his coat.

The liberal writer Jenny Seed took the symbolism of nude swimming a stage further in her historical novel *The Broken Spear* (1972), in which Boer pioneers from the Cape arrive at the lagoon of Port Natal:

> Dirk looked around. He saw that a number of black children had followed him from behind the mangroves. Dirk hesitated, but the attraction of the water was too strong and, after all, had he not swum naked many times with the Hottentot farm boys in Oom Sarel's dam? In a moment he had stripped off his coarse linen shirt and leather trousers and was in the water. Dirk grinned and waved and from behind the mangroves came friendly squeals and in a moment the black children were in the lagoon, splashing and kicking and shouting. For the first time in many months Dirk laughed.... Oh, he had indeed been stupid to be afraid of this new land.

> (*Spear*, 25)

This episode not only affirms Dirk's common humanity with Hottentot and Zulu, but is a kind of baptism symbolizing his identification with the continent of Africa.

When considering the colonial baggage that South African children's literature carries, it is often enlightening to look at Australian children's books as well, where the distance between white and black is more extreme. Sure enough, Patricia Wrightson set a similar archetypal nude swimming scene in one of her early novels, *The Rocks of Honey* (1961): "The boys stood side by side between the river oaks: a sturdy, fair body and a whip-thin, shining dark one."[32]

This too has undertones. In her writing at that time, Wrightson, one of Australia's best-known children's authors, was taking Aboriginal people seriously a decade before adult Australian fiction did. It is the white boy who suggests that they should undress, while the Aborigine boy demurs. The author does not say why, but she could be suggesting that, having achieved some degree of equality with the white, he is reluctant to be made to dress down to the usually despised state of traditional nudity of his people. Unlike the South African boys, he is aware that stripping naked is not going to make them equal. Afterwards, they'll put on their clothes and return to their different homes. As Gail Low has observed, "Needless to say, the fantasy of native costume is reserved for the dominant White Man;... it is the white man who dresses up and the native who reveals his body for consumption by dressing down... The act of donning another's clothing... is seldom indicative of the disruption of power hierarchies. Instead it works — however problematically — towards reinforcing them" (Low, 83).

By the 1970s, South African writers began to evince unease with the trope and question why the common humanity revealed in childhood could not be acknowledged in adulthood. It was now politically possible for authors to place this equality ironically within the prevailing social order of apartheid. In their stories, nudity and natural functions were now simply a shared fact of life, not a matter for sentimentality — and thus more to be feared by adults. In *Borderline,* by Ann Dymond (1986), a story about white children who have no sense of racial difference and, in defiance of adult norms, shelter a young African freedom fighter who is on the run, he asks them to supply him with toilet paper, which they do without comment.[33] This intimacy would have been received with outrage by their adult guardians had they known of it.

Catherine Annandale made a politically liberal point in *Tongelo* (1976).[34] To begin with, a white boy and a black boy enjoy an idyllic childhood: "They swam, dived and frolicked in the water. When they

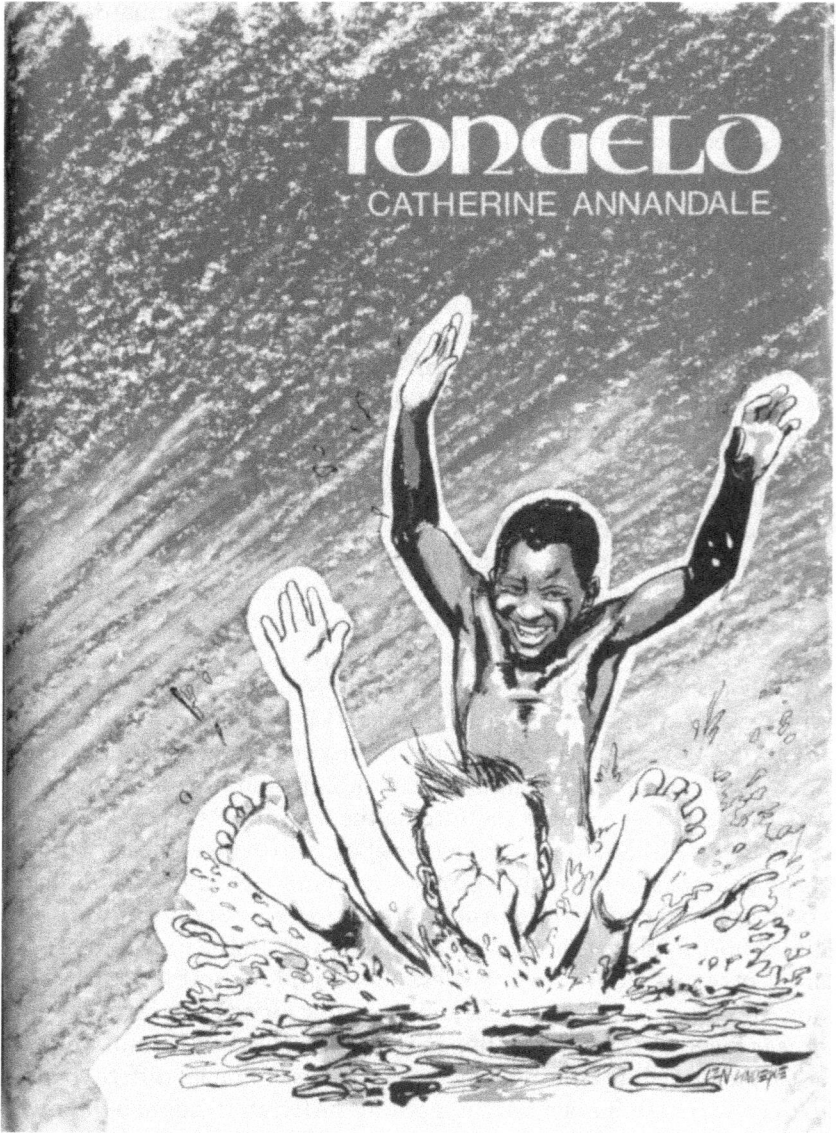

9 Illustration by Len Lindique, cover design by Dirk Joubert for *Tongelo* by Catherine Annandale

were exhausted, they clambered onto a smooth rock…. There they lay, naked in the sun, brown body beside white, two happy boys in the warm summer sun" (*Tongelo*, 3). This classic scene is depicted on the cover of the book. (See Figure 9) However, as in real life, the white boy has to go away to school: "'Never mind, Tongelo, we'll always be friends. No school is going to make any difference to us! It will always be the same.' But of course, it never was quite the same again" (*Tongelo*, 44).

This ominous note was taken up more directly in *Waiting for the Rain* by Sheila Gordon (1986), which follows two swimming companions from their childhood on a farm to a tragic encounter as young men, one a conscripted soldier, the other a freedom fighter.[35] There could be no rapprochement in that bitter decade. The ostensibly egalitarian situation of the swim has undertones that subvert the traditional suggestion of equality. It is the white boy who teaches the other to swim: "'Last one in's a monkey!' Frikkie shouted, as they pulled off their shirts and waded into the water in their shorts" (*Waiting*, 26). Perhaps, by keeping them dressed, Gordon is dissociating herself from earlier sentimentality about their being the same, and it is the white boy who is the leader.

What had begun as a sentimental affirmation of common humanity now became symbolic of difference: enemies would not expose their true selves to each other. In *Into the Valley* by Michael Williams (1990), when a white teenager who would like to intervene in the violence in KwaZulu-Natal comes upon young black activists bathing in the nude, he longs to join them and heal the enmity between himself and them, but they rush to get dressed before confronting him.[36]

An almost identical scene occurs in *Outside the Walls* by Lawrence Bransby (1995).[37] The novel is set in KwaZulu-Natal in the run-up to the election of 1994, when the province was wracked by violence between the two major black political groupings. A 17-year-old white boy spurns the telescopic philanthropy of his mother, a liberal who works for an anti-apartheid political party but ignores him. He adopts antisocial behavior and breaks white taboos by befriending some black squatters who have been made homeless by the violence, but he is rebuffed by them when he offers bread to a man who replies that he doesn't want handouts but a job. He comes across two of the black boys swimming naked in a dam: "They reached for their clothes — a bundle of khaki on the grass — and then ran as if they were afraid I would hurt them. Perhaps it was the colour of my skin. It made me sad" (*Walls*, 72).

He perseveres and wins the squatters' confidence by helping fight the fire set by his white schoolmates in order to burn their shacks down. "Now you too are black," observes Phillip, the Zulu (*Walls*, 80). Later he resists the police who break down their shacks and helps the occupants rebuild elsewhere, telling his father that he gave his tools away to a guy who was "REAL, man" (*Walls*, 124). Through his growing friendship with the Zulus, he becomes whole again. In less than ten years between the publication of *Waiting for the Rain* and *Outside the Walls*, young-adult literature had progressed in pace with the political climate in the country, from apparently hopeless hostility to reconciliation and the sense of wholeness that comes with it.

Interracial male friendship was a recurring myth in nineteenth-century American novels such as *Huckleberry Finn* by Mark Twain; Kenneth Kidd, in *Making American Boys*, draws attention to how two American culture critics, Robert K. Martin and Leslie Fiedler, have interpreted it. According to Kidd, Martin claims that "Herman Melville presents the interracial male couple as 'an inherently democratic union of equals' capable of transcending and transforming social hierarchies," whereas Fiedler is suspicious of this innocence, his point being that "boyhood is a powerful discourse that authorizes a homoerotic and racist myth of interracial fraternity" and that "the homoeroticism between whites and nonwhites absolves the white man's racial guilt."[38] The adoption of these themes in South African youth literature is just another example of the debt it owes to the literature and myths of nineteenth-century America. While South African writers may have thought they were presenting Martin's viewpoint, in practice they were much closer to what Fiedler saw this literary trope as doing.

A late twentieth-century South African youth novel about an interracial male couple tackles head-on issues of cultural difference, combining them with questions of sexual identity as well. Robin Malan's *The Sound of New Wings* (1998), set in an international school in Swaziland, relates how love develops between a Swedish boy, Bo, and a Swazi boy, Nathi, while the students and teachers at the school explore cultural attitudes toward nudity, body language and homosexuality.[39]

When a Pakistani boy refuses to shower with the other boys, a teacher explains, "It's a cultural thing. Quite often happens" (*Sound*, 10), and Nathi assures him, "Ja, it's difficult, hey? Some of the Swazis — especially those from a rural background — also don't like to do it at first" (*Sound*, 18). This is a prelude to an incident when Bo goes to spend a weekend at his new friend Nathi's home. At bedtime, he says, "'I, um, didn't bring any pyjamas or shorts.' There was no more than a beat before Nathi said, 'We don't need pyjamas.' He pulled off his pyjama trousers, folded them up neatly and dropped them back in the drawer" (*Sound*, 34).

Bo is intrigued at the Swazi custom that males can hold hands in public without arousing suspicion that they are homosexual. Nevertheless, the lovers are faced with homophobia in the school and community, and they have to work with their friends on projects to promote acceptance of diversity in the school. There are promising signs that they are succeeding, and the book ends with their looking forward to returning in the new year to take their efforts further. The story is no fatuous or overoptimistic statement that nudity disproves cultural difference; the boys' differences in customs and color are acknowledged at the same time that their autonomy as individuals is established: "They both looked at the dark brown hand against the fair bronzed skin" (*Sound*, 35).

Symbolic nude swimming has continued in the twenty-first century. The bane of Jedro, in *Jedro's Bane* by Peter Slingsby, is the bully Randall, and the bitter enmity between them sours relations throughout their small community.[40] At a hint from his grandfather, Jedro invites Randall to take a walk down to the river to talk things over. They see what they think is a body in the water, and jump in to pull it out. It turns out to be an old chair, but they have got wet, so they strip and have a "proper swim" (*Jedro*, 149). This story shows how the concerns of children's writers have changed since the 1980s, while drawing on earlier tropes. Jedro and Randall are the same race; their nude swim shows that they are learning lessons about human relations at the personal, not the cultural, level.

9

CITY CHILDREN

A trickle of white immigrants from abroad made their way to South Africa's cities in early children's books. In 1926, Dorothea Fairbridge's immigrant squirrel taught his children of their right to be South Africans.[1] The greatest immigration to the cities was the internal movement of millions of black people and Afrikaners to the cities after the Second World War. In the case of Afrikaners, this led to a marked shift in the setting of their children's literature. The black migration has featured often in English literature and films, but only rarely in juvenile literature. By the 1970s, the spiritual homeland of white English speakers, already urban dwellers, had shifted forever from the Karoo and the bushveld to the cities, and its youth literature followed it there, though slowly: of the English juvenile books published in South Africa in 1990, 30% had an urban setting.[2]

A film made in South Africa in 1949 by Donald Swanson and Eric Rutherford entitled *Jim Comes to Joburg* gave its name to an entire genre of stories about unsophisticated black people coming to the city — a theme that had first appeared in literature in 1908.[3] Literary historian Michael Chapman observes, "The Jim-comes-to-Joburg story would become the South African story."[4] The most famous novel of the genre is *Cry, the Beloved Country* by Alan Paton (1948). Today the term is used in cultural studies to identify this genre although, even at the time the film was made, it was racially insulting, because "Jim" was a generic name that whites gave to black men.

A writer who is almost completely forgotten today, Iris Clinton, wrote a novel on the theme, *Ridge of Destiny* (1956),[5] which, according to M. Sewitz's bibliography, *Children's Books in an African Setting: 1914–1964*, was intended for young adult readers.[6] It appears to have been influenced by Paton's novel and similar novels by the black author Peter Abrahams, *Mine Boy* (1946) and *The Path of Thunder* (1948), and is even more explicitly Christian than Paton in its principles, but it is poorly written by comparison with *Cry, the Beloved Country*. Nevertheless, it packs in everything that could be expected of such a work at the time: descriptions of the city with its affluent white suburbs and illegal township shebeens, accounts of the racist, brutal treatment of people of color, hypocritical Christian whites, the corruption of black professionals, the work of the trade unions, the dangers of working in the mines, and the young woman who will "try for white" (another standard theme, about the pale-skinned person of mixed race who masquerades as a white person). It concludes, "[The mixed-race protagonist] knew now what he had to do. He would go on in the strength of Christ to serve his people and to battle for their rights" (*Ridge*, 89).

From *Ridge of Destiny* it is a jump to 1977, when Juliet Marais Louw, already introduced in Chapter 1 under her earlier name, Juliet Konig, wrote the first children's story about a young African coming to Johannesburg, *Sipho and the Yellow Plastic Purse*, in which Sipho goes to Johannesburg to find his relatives after his foster mother dies.[7] A remarkable feature of the book is that not a single white person appears in it; all the characters are black, but this is unmarked, as they are referred to simply as Mr. Ngcobo, Mrs. Sithole, and so on, which is how the boy Sipho would have known them. Louw may not have been able to portray African society with much depth, but she writes with realism and tact. The novel does not deal with the economic and legislative constraints under which black people moved to the cities; it is a personal story that celebrates the ties between urban and rural people and the strength of bonds of friendship, blood and common humanity — the qualities that helped black people survive in a world governed by apartheid. Being a novel for younger children, it ends happily: even the missing purse, which Sipho thought had been stolen from him on his way to the city (a typical incident in a Jim-comes-to-Joburg story) is restored to him with its contents. Louw's empathy and sensitivity would have made this a humane and inspiring book for white and black readers of the time. But it was only eight years before a book with a similar plot of a journey by black children to seek their mother in Johannesburg took a completely different turn. In *Journey to Jo'burg*, a simply told little story by Beverley Naidoo (1985), black country children land in the violent uprising against the government that was sweeping city townships at the time, before the story ends with happy closure.[8]

In *Serena's Story*, published in 1990 and reprinted in 1995, Lesley Beake produced a feminist Jim-comes-to-Joburg story.[9] Young Serena comes to the city to seek her mother, and obtains help from various women and the Domestic Worker's Society. The novel has echoes of Es'kia Mphahlele's *Down Second Avenue*,[10] his memoir of growing up in a Pretoria township, in the anger with which it portrays the lot of female domestic workers at the mercy of mainly heartless white employers. Women such as Serena's mother, who is serving six months in jail for trading in dagga (marijuana), and Beauty Mangele, who deals in illicit liquor, drugs and stolen property, break the law to lift themselves out of the plight of domestic employment.

Half a dozen British writers who chose to set one of their stories in South Africa sent their characters there from England, usually as visitors but also as immigrants: Marjorie Bevan and L.D. Stranger in the 1920s and 1930s, and Maud D. Reed, Lady Kitty Ritson, Jane Shaw, and James Cahill in the middle decades. They were following the pattern of most children's fiction set in this country in the nineteenth century, which was written by British authors who used the country as an exotic setting for their adventure yarns. In typical colonial style, the young heroes of those earlier stories took what they could in ostrich feathers, hides, trophies, captured wild animals, gold and diamonds before hightailing for home, in the process having proved their manhood in battling dangerous animals, strange tribes and the Boers.

James Cahill's *M'Bonga's Trek* is an anachronistic work of this kind, published in 1947 and into its third impression by 1952.[11] Although set in contemporary mid-twentieth-century South Africa, it is an error-ridden piece of sensationalism, featuring a grotesque "witchdoctor" and Zulus, dressed like Sudanese, who hunt with spears. It was one of a series that, the publishers announced, "is the answer to the demand for good, up-to-date Sunday School Reward Books. Lutterworth Press has enlisted a team of first-class writers who give the uncompromising Christian message in really gripping modern stories" (*M'Bonga's Trek*, cover). It can be seen rather as a betrayal of enlightened Christians who were combating racism in South Africa at the time.

The other British writers were women who produced stories typical of the period, involving a group of children who have mild domestic adventures or sometimes catch a crook. Lady Kitty Ritson, author of countless pony stories, has the heroine of *Tessa in South Africa* (1955) spend a summer with a pony in South Africa and catch a band of smugglers,[12] and Maud D. Reed's little Candy of *Candy Finds the Clue* has a holiday adventure in the Kruger National Park and Rhodesia involving counterfeit banknotes, after the previous book in the series saw her in Norway.[13]

Many novelists have made use of a visitor to ask questions about this strange country. Children's writers use this device to give curious information — in 1946, Dorothy Wager's American twins in *Umhlanga* are still intrigued by the trap-door spider, a common object of amazement in the previous century — but also to point mildly at racist practices,[14] as do the children in *Venture to South Africa* by Jane Shaw:

> "No matter what age they are," observed Mike, "I see they're always called *boys* and *girls*."
> "But of course *boy* doesn't mean "boy," said Uncle Alec helpfully.
> "Well, what does it mean?" said Mike.[15]

Uncle Alec does not reply, and the story moves on.

This is one of a few mid-century juvenile novels featuring families emigrating from England to Johannesburg that took delight in detailing the oddness of the city and its life through their eyes. It makes interesting reading from a social-historical point of view. Among the many details of Johannesburg that are described, the children like the voortrekker wagon-wheel gates of Afrikaners' houses, but hate "those awful shanties, those tumbledown shacks with tin roofs" (*Venture*, 55); and the reader learns that all suburban white women sleep in the afternoons.

Iris Clinton, author of *Ridge of Destiny*, wrote *The Clarkes Go South* (1951), which is an earnest, plodding account with practically no characterization, using the parents rather than the children as focalizers.[16] Similar to Paton's *Cry, the Beloved Country* in atmosphere and its belief in the efficacy of Christian *caritas* (charity), it describes how the immigrant family members become involved in liberal organizations such as the Left Club, the Boys' Brigade and the church. While including scenes of the cruelties of apartheid, the author on the whole is guarded in her political comments, and does not explore political issues in depth. The book never lives up to the bright moment early on when the family see ragged children begging next to the train and young Tom, remembering his father's talking of "Ian, so sturdy in his khaki shirt and shorts," whom he had met on a previous visit, pipes up, "I thought you said the children you saw in Africa were hefty chaps, Dad. Those kids are skinny enough" (*Clarkes*, 13).

Emigration from South Africa in the second half of the twentieth century, whether temporary or permanent, has also been a significant part of the country's social history, but has received little attention in juvenile literature. A comic story for young children by Lesley Beake, *Harry Went to Paris*, deals only with the common wish of young citizens of the Commonwealth to travel to Europe, although it was published in 1989, when much more serious considerations were driving young black and white South Africans abroad, blacks to join the anti-apartheid struggle, whites to avoid military conscription.[17]

Harry the Hare stows away to Paris after a stork recommends foreign travel, quoting the advertising slogan of the national carrier: "The stork smiled secretly to itself. 'Round off the...ah...rough edges so to speak.... Fly SAA!'" (*Harry*, 10). Harry is thrilled to speak to a French mouse: "'Ja,' Harry nodded. Hang, he was having a conversation! In Foreign!'" (*Harry*, 28). But he doesn't like garlic sauce, gets homesick, and returns to be welcomed by another hare: "'This is the Highveld. This is Parys, Free State, and this,' he thumped the ground beneath his feet, 'is Home. And my name is Frikkie the haas'" (*Harry*, 61). In this story, at any rate, "home" was still the veld with an Afrikaans flavor.

Norman Silver, a white South African living in England, wrote a teenage novel, *No Tigers in Africa* (1990) about a white family who move to England when the country appears to be collapsing.[18] The father, after his son had summoned him, had shot dead a young black burglar instead of letting the boy escape. The family disintegrates in alcohol and infidelity (the mother with a black man), and the son, after attempting suicide, confesses in a therapy group his part in the boy's death and all the petty acts of discrimination for which he was responsible. Whether whites would actually be destroyed in this way by their memories of their minor role in apartheid is debatable, but obviously something Norman Silver believed; in many respects (such as the use of broad South African English for the narrative), the book lacks verisimilitude.

Black political exiles and their return to South Africa after 1990 have been major components of the country's modern history, but their experiences overseas and on their return have not caught the interest of writers for young adults. Exile, during which the parents split up, is simply the prologue to *Dear Ludwig* by Robin Saunders (1998).[19] The only notable juvenile novel to go into more detail is *Joe Cassidy and the Red Hot Cha-Cha* by Janet Smith (1994), which is about a mixed-race family on their return to Johannesburg.[20]

The intensification of the struggle against apartheid that led to the unbanning of resistance organizations in 1990 and the democratic elections in 1994 took place at the same time as the shift to cities in the setting of South African literature, both Afrikaans and English, adult and juvenile. This required a new kind of fiction. Writing of literature for adults, Malvern van Wyk Smith said, "A literature of veld and farm, productive largely of romance and the pastoral, gave way to a literature of city and, eventually, private, inner and agonized space, generating modes of realism, surrealism and a dislocated existential inwardness.[21] Chapman remarks, "Looking back from the perspective of subsequent urbanisation after the Second World War, one is left wondering whether, demographically, the story of city life in South Africa could have been 'knowable' in the 1920s and 1930s" (Chapman, 187). In children's and young adult books of the 1970s and 1980s, white characters had to get to know the city at the same time as they encountered the crude reality of apartheid that the city exposed.[22]

That era is over now, and Jakes Gerwel, in his foreword to a collection of writing for "young people entering adulthood amidst the wide-ranging changes in South Africa today," published in 1995, hailed the change: "The inspiring coming together of a divided nation during and immediately after the April elections signalled the crossing of a divide which had liberating effects far beyond the obviously political: the awakening of an awareness of others, a loosening of the paralysing bonds of fear and suspicion, the dawning of a sense of self, the possibility of remembering and speaking about pain without unleashing destruction, the emancipation of the personal from the overbearing domination of the political."[23]

Judith Inggs says that new South African youth literature explores "the role of the physical environment in the reconstruction of the child in a new space…how children are reclaiming that space as their own, empowering themselves with a secure identity in the world" .[24] This change in South African books was paralleled in their Australian counterparts at the turn of the millennium, in which, writes Wendy Michaels, "fiction, literature, art, all offer the individual resources for the ongoing project of the construction of self-identity."[25] She might as well be writing about South Africa's emerging from the ultra-realism of the violence of the 1980s: "Whereas the reader of hard-core realism is invited to cast the gaze on the unified selves of adolescent characters as they deal with the traumatic events of the 'real world', the new realism invites the reader to become complicit in the aesthetic construction of self-identity through the narrativisation of the self." Quoting Mike Featherstone,[26] she calls this the "aestheticization of life" (*Michaels*, 57).

Featherstone, in his book *Consumer Culture and Postmodernism*, writes of the "aestheticized commodity world" that young people experience through "new cultural intermediaries" such as "marketing, advertising, public relations, radio and television producers, presenters, magazine journalists, fashion writers, and the helping professions," to which he later adds music and film people (*Featherstone*, 75, 44).

All these intermediaries and their products can be found in one or the other modern South African book, embraced or rejected by the protagonists, but in some way shaping their modern world. Even the "helping professions," which at first glance may seem out of place in this list of purveyors of consumer culture, are ubiquitous; their practitioners are the phonies that teenagers, in true Holden Caulfield style, reject. The influence of J.D. Salinger's *The Catcher in the Rye* (1951) was heavy for 30 years and more down the line. In earlier books, the helping professions' representatives were the earnest liberals working in nongovernmental organizations, churches and political parties, such as the mother of John in *Outside the Walls* by Lawrence Bransby, who has no time for him because she is working for a left-wing political party.[27] They spout pious clichés and psychological jargon, like this mother in *Pedal Me Faster* by Beryl Bowie (1995): "Marcus, what's going on in there? You being hyperactive again?" ... "Leave those knives alone, Marcus, you're being obsessional again."[28]

Predictably, authors turned to first-person narration, especially the fictional diary, as the genre of choice for portraying teenagers drawing on multiple resources to find a meaning in life. It provides the ideal medium for witty, sardonic, colloquial teenage monologue. The diary is an obvious way to make the reader "complicit in the aesthetic construction of self-identity through the narrativising of the self," as Wendy Michaels puts it.

Dianne Hofmeyr used postmodern techniques to draw the reader into the creative process in the diaries that constitute her two Johannesburg novels, *Blue Train to the Moon* (1993) and *Boikie You Better Believe It* (1994) (which created a sensation in cultural circles by winning the valuable M-Net Prize for adult literature).[29] In the former, at one stage the diarist finds a letter stuck in her diary by her mother, who had read the diary and written the response, and in the latter, the diarist makes metanarrative remarks such as "I've just read over that last paragraph and I must say, not bad, boikie, not bad!" (*Boikie*, 32).

Sarah Britten wrote two books in diary form, *The Worst Year of My Life — So Far* (2000) and *Welcome to the Martin Tudhope Show!* (2002), which are so obviously derivative in concept that she even has the diarist of the former self-reflexively make several references to Adrian Mole.[30]

Characters invoke other media in an effort to detect a pattern in life or define their feelings. In *Way to Go!* by Gail Smith (1995), when Lance groans, "My brain won't take any more. It desperately needs some light relief," his friend sarcastically suggests, "Like a Leon Schuster movie," referring to a series of mindless but extremely popular farces.[31] The diarist of *The Worst Year of My Life — So Far* often makes remarks such as "If my life were a movie, the director would cut to a close-up of my face now" (*Worst Year*, 2), and *Not Another Love Story* by Dawn Garisch (1994) is held together by the leitmotiv of the narrator's turning everything into plots for television soaps. She also creates newspaper headlines about herself: "CITY GYNAECOLOGIST'S DAUGHTER DROWNS WHILE FORNICATING IN BATH."[32] Readers would be caught up in these games and would be stretching their imaginations to picture the resulting creations.

The reader of *The Sound of New Wings* by Robin Malan has to create some coherent meaning from not only the third-person narration but also the variety of kinds of writing that are produced every day in a lively school, such as notices, questionnaires, journals, letters, post-cards, e-mails, school essays, reports, case files and minutes.[33]

Language, writing, books, poetry, names, the titles and lyrics of songs — teenagers in these books are acutely conscious of how the world can cheat them or be opened to them through words. When the white narrator of *Not Another Love Story* loses a writing competition because her entry was deemed political, she looks up the definition of "politics" in a dictionary and concludes, "I couldn't help feeling it left something unsaid" (*Not Another*, 126). She and a "coloured" man who had earlier quarreled over what he called her racist attitudes end up flinging traditional South African racist insults at each other in a hilarious game that symbolizes the catharsis that their country was experiencing:

> I took a deep breath. "I thought you were a gangster." …. I was relieved Aaron was laughing.
>   "Well, you are just a colonial oppressor!" he roared.
>   "And you are a lazy Hottentot!" That shocked us both….
>   "Wow," he said grinning. "You are a real Mohammed Ali! Well. You whiteys are self-centred, insensitive, racist, capitalist pigs, we will drive you into the sea!"
>   I snorted, pig-like, drenched with relief. "Whereas you, you belong in the trees!" We rolled around in the back garden, roaring with laughter and hurling abuse at each other.
>
> (*Love Story*, 133)

The diarist of *The Worst Year of My Life — So Far* collects new words that enable her to formulate her feelings and often interrupts the text to point out that she is using a new or favorite word, or even gives the etymology: "… in a less ebullient frame of mind. (Ebullient: exuberant, high-spirited. Also, in chemistry, boiling. From the Latin *ebullire*, to bubble out.)" (*Worst*, 36)

These young people gain insights from discussions in English class on death, suicide or homosexuality that enable them to reflect on what is happening in their lives. They often refer to books they have read or studied at school, and use history lessons to give themselves an understanding of the new world in which they find themselves. But first the old, official white version has to go. In *Freefalling* by Shelley Davidow (1991), after the white narrator's black foster sister is told to get off the beach by white boys, they go home and let off steam by tearing up her accumulated apartheid-era school history books and notes. "History lay shattered, torn to shreds by the present. All the monsters from Van this to Van that lay in pathetic two-dimensional scraps under our bums. What a victory!"[34] This is the girl referred to in Chapter 4, who dismissed the European fairy tales that had been of no help to her in growing up in Africa.

History, young protagonists in modern books learn, is not something found only in books, remote and unrelated to their lives. Some fine books engage the readers with the protagonists in encountering modern history through other media.

Joe Cassidy and the Red Hot Cha-cha by Janet Smith is a cleverly structured story that engages the reader in the mystery of the backgrounds of the fathers of two teenagers who are falling in love, which is sustained until it is revealed to the reader that the father of Diane, a girl of mixed ancestry, was killed by a letter bomb while in exile. When her white boyfriend, Joe Cassidy, confesses that his father, who has committed suicide, was an explosives expert in the Special Branch, she tells him to go away. Catharsis comes with a history lesson in school in which the students reenact the birth of the Freedom Charter, and she tells her classmates a little about her father and breaks down. Joe takes her home, and when she tells him how her father died he too weeps: in all probability, his father sent the bomb. The couple share their grief, and the past is put to rest.

Of the popular books on the life of Nelson Mandela that have been published for children, one employs oral tradition and another uses visual imagery. In *Madiba, The Story of Nelson Mandela* by Chris du Toit (1999), a Xhosa mineworker tells the story to his children.[35] The blurb explicitly links modern history with traditional tales: "The story is told in this way because Nelson Mandela himself grew up hearing the history of the Xhosa people from his own mother and father, who had heard it in turn from their parents. The legends, fables and stories of historic battles had a great effect on the boy" (*Madiba*, n.p.). In another picture book, *The Picture that came Alive* by Hugh Lewin, illustrated by Barry Wilkinson (1992), the narrator is a little girl whose father brings home a large picture of Mandela (shown in the illustrations to be a famous photograph of him as a handsome young man), frames it and hangs it on the wall.[36] The girl realizes the man in the picture is special, because people admire it, while a policeman advises her father to take it down. She follows events when he is released, and six months later he visits their village. Asking the grown-ups to step aside, he hugs the child.

> He was laughing and smiling. He picked me up and held me up to his face. He kissed me and then he put me down.... Then he was gone. I was very sad. I stood with tears running down my face. My father asked me what was wrong.
>
> "He looks more like the father of the man in the picture on the wall," I said. "But I'll always remember today. The day the picture on the wall came alive."

(Picture, 26)

In this way, Lewin uses the portrait of Mandela to teach about both the immediacy of history and the nature of the passage of time.

Usually, especially in Britten's two novels, teenagers slickly but uncritically invoke popular culture and the mass media as reference points. In *Welcome to the Martin Tudhope Show!* the sardonic teenager, as Judith Inggs has pointed out (Inggs, unpublished), mocks U.S. consumer culture, but is determined to get it for himself by making a success of his life: "I am going to make it happen. I will become rich and famous. I will drive a Ferrari" (*Tudhope*, 159). Among the welcome exceptions, Lawrence Bransby, who normally does not pay attention to such things, has his teenage rebel in *Outside the Walls* make a caustic comment about the kitsch ceramic plaques of Mexicans sleeping under palm trees that white suburbanites stick on the outside walls of their houses. Michael Williams's *The Eighth Man* (2002), a complex novel that won the Percy FitzPatrick Prize, challenges the reader to consider critically the difference between how a radio talk-show host and a newspaper journalist with a deep sense of ethics handle a crime story.[37] Both are lightly done: the presenter with his slick patter is funny, and the journalist's ethical worries tie up with her strained relationship with the detective, providing the love interest.

Music and dance fill the lives of many of the teenage characters, providing a springboard for the action in novels such as *Crocodile Burning* by Michael Williams (1992), an author who works in the performing arts and has composed youth operas.[38] This book, which is about a performing group of township children who go on tour to the U.S., has been particularly popular in America. When Robin Malan's *Siyagruva* series of easy-reading stories for young adults was being planned, a dance studio in Cape Town was deliberately chosen as the focal point

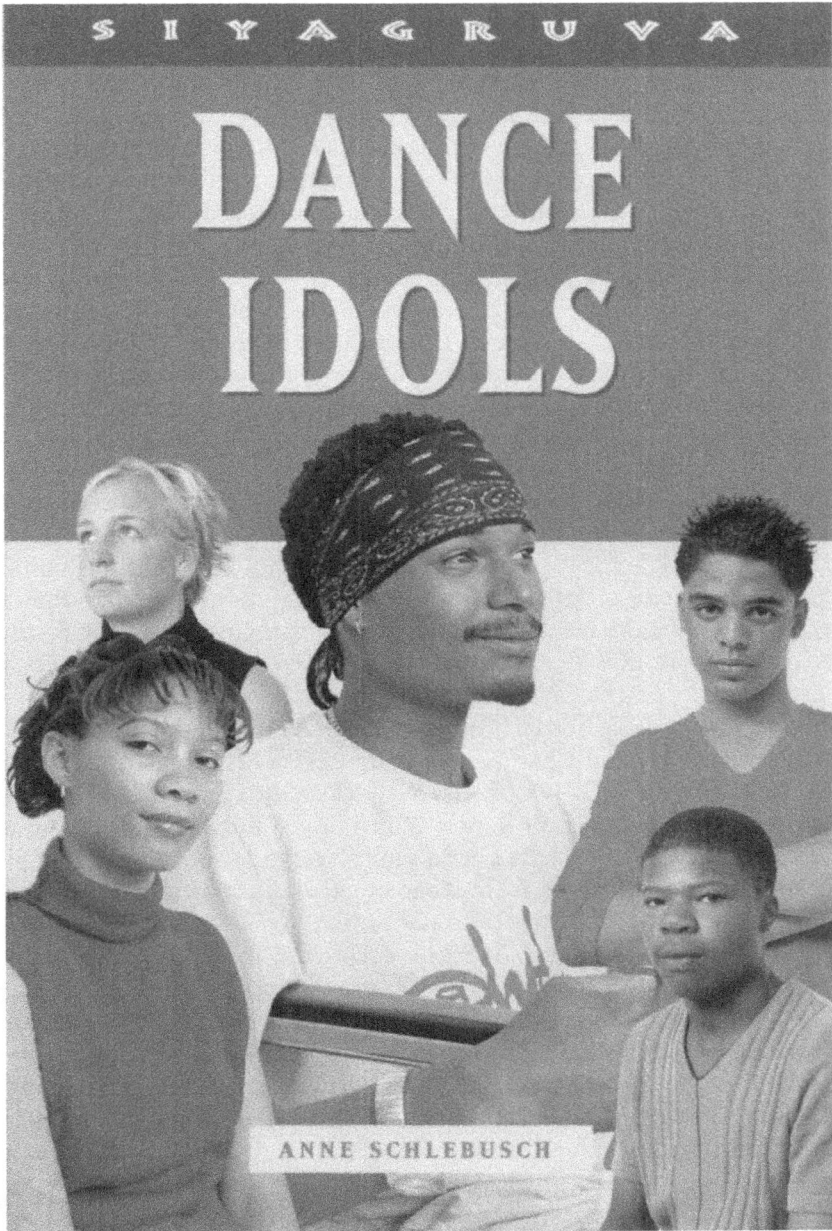

10 Cover design by Orchard Publishing for *Dance Idols* by Anne Schlebusch

because it provided a springboard for portraying a racially mixed group of young adults living modern city lives, as they do in *Dance Idols* by Anne Schlebusch (2003).[39] (See Figure 10) The successful series has also been popular in Namibia, possibly because young people in that country like to dream of the sophistication of the Siyagruva crowd.[40]

In other novels, characters draw on the titles and words of songs to interpret their lives. Even book titles can be direct quotes from songs: *Mellow Yellow* (1994) and *Dark Waters* (1995) by Jenny Robson, and *Wake Up Singing* by Jane Rosenthal (1990).[41] "Mellow Yellow" is fittingly polysemic, reflecting the restless, ever-changing urban scene; it is not only the title of a song by Donovan but the brand name of a soft drink, a slang name for a kind of police vehicle and the nickname of a street child who wears a big yellow sweater — "Who needs a blerry sleeping-bag?" (*Mellow Yellow*, 3).

Most city stories are set in Cape Town or Johannesburg, while Pietermaritzburg, Durban, Bloemfontein and Kimberley occasionally feature. A plethora of landmarks and names of streets and shops create credible settings that map out their city for its inhabitants, just as the use of proprietary brand names for clothes, food and beverages captures the feel and meaning of the daily lives of young South Africans. Townships — residential areas formerly reserved for people of color — and informal shack settlements have featured in stories, from *Ten Tickeys* by C. de Bosdari (1954), through *Sidwell's Seeds* by Maretha Maartens (1985) and *Charlie's House* by Reviva Schermbrucker, illustrated by Niki Daly (1989), which are all set on the Cape Flats, to *Stanza on the Edge* by Zachariah Rapola (2001), a fast-moving story about a youngster who gets involved with gangsters in Alexandra, in Johannesburg.[42] The townships are home to practices unknown in traditional African society, such as the Rastafarianism of a Ugandan man living in Pretoria, which South Africans encounter in *A Twin World* by Mosibudi Mangena (1996).[43]

In modern picture books, black children are part of the urban scene. Those of Niki Daly's picture books set in cities celebrate city life without marking it as exceptional, for example, when Jamela of *What's Cooking, Jamela?* (2001) chases her chicken through the Miss Style hairdressing salon.[44] Daly's most famous city child is the boy in his multiple-award-winning *Not So Fast, Songololo* (1985), who goes shopping with his grandmother.[45] (See Figure 11) It is the city setting that white South African admirers of the book fix upon: Jay Heale says it "has been hailed as a milestone in South African children's publishing" because it was "the first full-colour book to feature a black urban South African child";[46] and Andreé-Jeanne Tötemeyer says, "Little

11 Illustration by Niki Daly from *Not so Fast, Songololo* by Niki Daly

Shepherd with his new red and white tackies [trainers or sneakers] and his OK [supermarket chain] shopping bag is the prototype of the urbanised black. Not only is he unquestionably a black child, but he is also unmistakably city-bred."[47] With *Songololo,* children's books had come a long way from the boy in "The Magic Shoes" by Sadie Merber in 1930, who, after giving up his goats for shoes that were too tight to wear, "took the lesson very much to heart and was never in the future heard to ask that he should wear shoes like the great people of the towns."[48]

Two outstanding books that belong together, bracketing the remarkable last decade of the twentieth century, extended the range of aesthetic experience in children's and young adult literature and took the celebration of the South African city to new dimensions.

Ashraf of Africa (1990) is a colored picture book, for which Ingrid Mennen and Niki Daly wrote the story, published in Niki Daly's Songololo Books series.[49] Nicolaas Maritz painted the illustrations in rough, bold strokes, very different from Daly's own realist style of illustration. *Skyline* (2000), which won the Percy FitzPatrick Prize, is a young-adult novel by Patricia Pinnock, author of *The King Who Loved Birds* and other children's books as well as poetry and fiction for adults.[50] Both are about Cape Town and were published by Cape Town publisher David Philip.

Ashraf is a boy in shorts and sandals, one of the children of the Bo-Kaap, the picturesque suburb on the slopes of Signal Hill above Cape Town where the descendants of the previously enslaved people from the East live. The book is dedicated to these children. "Ashraf loves his city. Deep black shadows cut across pavements and streets. Traffic lights blink as noisy cars and city people come and go" (*Ashraf*, n.p.). He makes his way through familiar streets and alleys to the library to take out his favorite book, which is a picture book on the wild animals of Africa.

But a child reading the text or studying the pictures carefully will see that, while Ashraf dreams of Africa, he is in Africa already. Knowledge comes from books, but not only from them — Ashraf's senses of feeling, sight and hearing are engaged. "In summer, the city lies soaked in African sun, dry under endless blue sky" (*Ashraf*, n.p.). Everything he passes embodies the continent, such as "the place where drummers drum almost forgotten stories and dancers dance to the music that explodes from marimba and horn. That is the music of Africa" (*Ashraf*, n.p.). This world is a fusion of old and new, symbolized by the model cars made of Coca-Cola cans in the shop window, of the kind first made by country children and later sold alongside highways; a world where arts, crafts and traditional products are commodified for tourists in shops selling "tusks and tortoises and a stool with elephant toes" and beads. In African style, the length of his shadow tells him it is time to go home. The book concludes, "Somewhere in Africa, Ashraf knows, lions are lazing in tall golden grass and overhead this same hot sun is shining down on them" (*Ashraf*, n.p.).

Mike Featherstone has described how "the aestheticized commodity world" of the twentieth century "meant that the city landscape conferred on childhood memories the quality of alluring half-forgotten dreams. In the mythical and magical world of the modern city the child discovered the new anew" (*Featherstone*, 74).

What Ashraf discovers in the space of one short picture book is discovered in more complexity in *Skyline*. The narrator is an unnamed white girl who lives with her young autistic sister, Mossie (Little Sparrow) and remote, absent mother in a rundown block of flats called Skyline, in Long Street, Cape Town. Like Ashraf, the girls make the colorful streets of the city, its shops and its people their own. The narrator also hears the traffic, and in her imagination its sounds rising from the street echo her moods. Other sounds also convey complex messages to her. Living in the flats are immigrants and refugees, mainly from other parts of Africa, and, like Ashraf, the girl listens to their music and songs, hearing in them stories of their journeys to this country, though she does not understand the words.

Like Ashraf, she sees in shops and on market stalls African crafts, some of them imitations of traditional objects, some of them, sadly, the ancestral beadwork that country women have been forced to sell. Beads communicate; Mossie buys them in the market and in a bead shop (a famous landmark of Long Street, which is probably the one Ashraf also walks past) and learns their history and the meaning of their patterns, imagining how they were brought to Africa by Arab dhows from the East and carried along trade routes. Mossie, who cannot speak, is "frantic to buy up this silent speech" (*Skyline*, 137). The beads can be known through feel as well; she pours them over herself and even over her sister when she needs soothing. The girls also learn that even handmade grass mats have meanings woven into them.

Colors also communicate. Among the neighbors are a blind couple who wear plain clothes until a pair of flamboyant transvestite hostesses persuade them to make a change: "So now Gracie and Cliff have cupboards full of silks, satins, brocades, velvets and fake fur. In this way their Braille-sensitive fingers can read the cloth of their gorgeous clothes" (*Skyline*, 145).

The most spectacular use of color is in the paintings of their Mozambican friend, Bernard, which are described at the end of each chapter in extracts from a catalog of his work written by an old woman, a refugee from Hitler's Germany. In his paintings, Bernard gives expression to the horrific story of the massacre of his family and his employers, the harrowing stories of other refugees and the events of each preceding chapter set in their cityscapes. The reader has to make do with words to imagine the pictures, but the language of the descriptions, the allusions to famous Western works of art that inspired Bernard, the broken

English of the titles that he gives to the paintings and the descriptions of the homemade frames combine to convey a rich aesthetic experience.

Pinnock's prose is filled to repletion with African similes:

> Colours carry an orchestration of African city-sound to the centre of the painting. Azures, plumbago blues and fire-yellows weave through traffic choruses with the beating of goat-hide drums and rhythms of kwaito. A cacophony of cars and rushing people swirls around in a tempest of colour: granadilla-orange, placenta-red, leguaan-blue and the browns of Kalahari sand. We even hear, caught within the mixing of golden-yellow and purple, the soft tinkling of someone's brass bracelets.
>
> (*Skyline*, 3)

A typical description remarks, "In this painting we see again a modelling on Marc Chagall's work, this time his monumental *War*" (*Skyline*, 71), while Bernard's title for a painting of a girl wearing a yellow Star of David, seated on a bench between two Nazi soldiers, is *The Sorrow is Sitting on the Bench* (*Skyline*, 85). The frames can be made from "orange Rizla packets stuck side by side onto card" (*Skyline*, 82) or "slightly rusted, flattened-out Coca-Cola cans" (*Skyline*, 11), recalling the model cars that Ashraf sees in the shop window — the detritus of Western consumer culture that refugees from other parts of Africa encounter and recycle in their search for a better life.

This city is not only a haven for foreign refugees and a support for the girls that they do not find in their own home, but a place of darkness and fear, where a white ex-serviceman who fought in Angola, now alcoholic and mad, begs on the pavement, an Italian immigrant abuses his wife, the transvestites are brutally assaulted, drugs are traded and Bernard is murdered in the street. The social import of Pinnock's novel is to counter the xenophobia that the latest generation of immigrants encounters in the city, but *Skyline* goes further: in celebrating the contribution that African immigrants make, Pinnock joins with the creators of *Ashraf of Africa* in proclaiming that now, at last, South Africa can claim its heritage as being part of Africa:

> Their words cry through the stairwell like egrets flying home.... Their hair is plaited or braided like rivulets running over granite koppies. They play music on drums and little whistles or xylophones which speak of sands and golden dates or reed boats paddled across rivers pulling in fish.

Their music makes each flat become a village with bellowing oxen coming home at night. Their drumming speaks in the ochre and mud of clay pots and baskets woven tightly to hold beer and sour milk.

A tin guitar twangs forlornly about a crowded shack in a Lusaka township; a small drum, plaited round its edge with twine and carried across borders, down footpaths and along highways, pounds out songs of migrations and moving nomads, about orange sands and shifting sheets of dunes peppered with the bones of lost travellers.

(*Skyline*, 7, 8)

NOTES

Introduction

1. Fikile-Ntsikelelo Moya, "Of Sacred Cows.... Interview with Wole Soyinka," *Mail & Guardian*, 22–28 July 2005.
2. National Arts Council, "Voices in Action: Towards Developing a National South African Literature" (unpublished proceedings of the conference of the National Arts Council, Pretoria, 21–23 June 2002).
3. Mary Carey-Hobson, *The Farm in the Karoo* (London: Juta, Heelis, 1883).
4. Elwyn Jenkins, *Children of the Sun* (Johannesburg: Ravan, 1993), 5.
5. Gretel Wybenga and Maritha Snyman, Eds., *Van Patrys-hulle tot Hanna Hoekom* (Pretoria: LAPA, 2005).
6. Jane Rosenthal, *Wake Up Singing* (Cape Town: Maskew Miller Longman, 1990), n.p.
7. Bevis Hillier, *The Style of the Century, 1900–1980* (London: Herbert, 1983).

Chapter 1

1. Annette Joelson, *How the Ostrich Got His Name and Other South African Stories for Children* (Cape Town: Juta, 1926), 5.
2. Thomas Mayne Reid, *The Bush Boys* (London: David Bogue, 1856).
3. Jane Shaw, *Venture to South Africa* (London: Thomas Nelson, 1960), 54.
4. Mary Carey-Hobson, *The Farm in the Karoo* (London: Juta, Heelis, 1883).
5. Mabel Waugh, *Verses for Tiny South Africans* (Cape Town: Maskew Miller), 12.
6. Sally Starke and Doreen Rowbottom, *The Young Karoo* (Pietermaritzburg: Shuter & Shooter, 1950), n.p.
7. See, for example, Guy Butler, "Sweet Water," in *Collected Poems* (Cape Town: David Philip, 1999), 167.
8. Maude Bidwell, *Breath of the Veld* (Cape Town: Juta, 1923), n.p.
9. E. Owen Wright, *Backveld Born* (Bloemfontein: A.C. White, n.d.), n.p.
10. Juliet Konig (Marais Louw), *South Wind* (Cape Town: CNA, 1943), n.p.

11. G. Daniell, *Jantjie's Aunt and Other Stories* (Cape Town: Juta, 1930), 51.
12. Sally Starke, *Little Huts That Grow in the Veld* (Cape Town: CNA, 1943).
13. Norah Perkins, *The Candle on the Windowsill*, 2nd ed. (Boksburg: Geo. Constable, 1926), 1.
14. C.M. Stimie, *Children of the Camdeboo* (Johannesburg: Afrikaanse Pers-Boekhandel, 1964).
15. Edith King, *Veld Rhymes for Children* (London: Longmans, 1911), 56.
16. See "The Bushveld Syndrome," in Elwyn Jenkins, *Children of the Sun* (Johannesburg: Ravan, 1993), Chap. 3.
17. Percy FitzPatrick, *Jock of the Bushveld* (London: Longmans, Green, 1907).
18. Werner Heyns, *Ramini of the Bushveld* (Pretoria: Voortrekkerpers, 1963), 7.
19. Yvonne Jooste, *Mummy, I'm Listening* (Pretoria: J.H. de Bussy and Cape Town: HAUM, 1943), 6.
20. F.A. Donnolly, *Papa Baboon* (Pretoria: van Schaik,1933).
21. Maud Reed, *Candy Finds a Clue* (London: Epworth, 1958).
22. South African Institute of Race Relations, *Fast Facts* 2 (February 2005): 1; H.L. Watts, "A Social and Demographic Portrait of English-speaking White South Africans," in *English-speaking South Africa Today*, Ed. André Villiers (Cape Town: Oxford University Press, 1976), 41–90, 54.
23. Andreé-Jeanne Tötemeyer, "Trends in Children's Literature at Home and Abroad," in *Towards More Understanding*, Ed. Isabel Cilliers (Cape Town: Juta, 1993), 159–169, 167.
24. Eleanor Stredder, *Jack and His Ostrich* (London: Nelson, 1890).
25. Jane Spettigue, *A Trek and a Laager* (London: Blackie, 1900?).
26. Jane Spettigue, *An Africander Trio* (London: Blackie, 1898).
27. Dorothy Gard'ner, *Verses for South African Children, Grown Up or Otherwise* (Pretoria: van Schaik, 1939), 32.
28. Felicity Keats, *Rudolph's Valley* (Cape Town: Tafelberg, 1991).
29. A.J. Coetzee, Tim Couzens and Stephen Gray, "South African Literatures to World War II," in *European-language Writing in Sub-Saharan Africa*, Ed. Albert S. Gérard (Budapest: Akadémiai Kadó, 1986), 173–213, 206.
30. Sheila Egoff and Judith Saltman, *The New Republic of Childhood* (Toronto: Oxford University Press, 1990), 13.
31. Brenda Niall, *Australia Through the Looking Glass* (Melbourne: Melbourne University Press, 1984), 149.
32. W.M Levick, *Dry River Farm* (London: Dent, 1955); *River Camp* (London: Dent, 1960).
33. Fay King (Goldie), *Friends of the Bushveld* (London: Cape, 1954).
34. Dorothy Wager, *Umhlanga* (Durban: Knox, 1946), 124.
35. Marie Philip, *Caravan Caravel* (Cape Town: David Philip, 1973), 6.
36. Daphne Rooke, *The South African Twins* (London: Cape, 1953).
37. Charles Hoppé, *Sons of the African Veld* (New York: McBride, 1947).
38. Francois du Preez, *Mystery at Rushing Waters* (Johannesburg: Afrikaanse Pers-Boekhandel, 1964).
39. Brenda Munitich, *Ben's Buddy* (Pretoria: de Jager-HAUM, 1987).
40. Sheila Dederick, *Tickey* (Cape Town: Oxford University Press, 1965).
41. Maritha Snyman, "Die Afrikaanse Jeugreeksboek," in *Van Patrys-hulle tot Hanna Hoekom*, Eds. Gretel Wybenga and Maritha Snyman (Pretoria: LAPA, 2005), 89–112.
42. Kenneth B. Kidd, *Making American Boys* (Minneapolis: University of Minnesota Press, 2004).
43. May Baldwin, *Corah's School Chums* (London: Chambers, 1912).

44. P.H. Nortje, *The Green Ally* (London: Oxford University Press, 1963); *Wild Goose Summer* (London: Oxford University Press, 1964).

45. For example, George and Lorrie Raath, *Chums of Meredrift School* (Johannesburg: Afrikaanse Pers-Boekhandel, n.d.).

46. Bessie Marchant, *Molly of One Tree Bend* (London: Butcher, 1910); *A Girl of Distinction* (London: Blackie, 1912); *Laurel the Leader* (London: Blackie, n.d.).

47. Lola Bower, *Zulu Boy* (London: Hutchinson, 1960); Anne and Peter Cook, *The Adventures of Kalipe* (Cape Town: Via Afrika, 1957); G.H. Franz, *Tau, the Chieftain's Son* (Dundee, Natal: Ebenezer, 1929).

48. Jessie Hertslet, *Kana and His Dog* (Cape Town: African Bookman, 1946).

49. National Library, *Amandla eBali* (Cape Town: National Library, 2004), 26.

50. J.A. Kruger, *Kinderkeur* (Pretoria: Unisa, 1991), 240 (trans.).

51. Maria Mabetoa, *Our Village Bus* (Johannesburg: Ravan, 1985).

52. Phyllis Savory, *Xhosa Fireside* Tales, reprinted in *African Fireside Tales* (Cape Town: Timmins, 1982), 15–102.

Chapter 2

1. David Adey, Ridley Beeton, Michael Chapman and Ernest Pereira, *Companion to South African English Literature* (Johannesburg: Ad. Donker, 1986), 97.

2. Thomas Pringle, *African Poems of Thomas Pringle*, Eds. Ernest Pereira and Michael Chapman (Pietermaritzburg: University of Natal Press, 1989), 89.

3. Olive Schreiner, *The Story of an African Farm* (London: Chapman & Hall, 1883).

4. A.J. Coetzee, Tim Couzens and Stephen Gray, "South African Literatures to World War II," in *European-language Writing in Sub-Saharan Africa*, Ed. Albert S. Gérard (Budapest: Akadémiai Kadó, 1986), 173–213, 185.

5. Percy FitzPatrick, *Jock of the Bushveld* (London: Longmans, Green, 1907).

6. For a discussion of the book, see Elwyn Jenkins, *Children of the Sun* (Johannesburg: Ravan, 1993), 49, 50.

7. Pauline Smith, *Platkops Children* (1935; Cape Town: Balkema, 1981).

8. Iris Vaughan, *The Diary of Iris Vaughan* (Johannesburg: CNA, 1958).

9. Michael Chapman, *Southern African Literatures* (London: Longman, 1996), 188.

10. Margaret Lenta, "Postcolonial Children and Parents: Pauline Smith's *Platkops Children*," *English in Africa* 27(2) (2000): 29–43, 29.

11. P.J. Stanton, "Bibliography of Books in English Especially Suited to South African Children" (Research Project, University of Cape Town, 1946), 17.

12. M. Sewitz, "Children's Books in English in an African Setting: 1914–1964" (Research Project, University of the Witwatersrand, 1965), 63.

13. Shirley Davies, *Reading Roundabout: A Review of South African Children's Literature* (Pietermaritzburg: Shuter & Shooter, 1992), 193.

14. Jay Heale, *From the Bushveld to Biko: The Growth of South African Children's Literature in English from 1907 to 1992 Traced through 110 Notable Books* (Grabouw: Bookchat, 1996), 11.

15. Joan Bevan, "Children's Literature in English," in *Catalogue for the Exhibition of South African Children's and Youth Books*, Ed. M.A.G. Swart (Potchefstroom: South African Library Association, 1978), 32–34; Anna Smith, "Children's Books," in *English and South Africa*, Ed. Alan Lennox-Short (Cape Town: Nasou, 197–), 125–129.

16. Eve Jammy, "The English Children's Book in South Africa," in *Kinder- en Jeugboeke: Referate Gelewe tydens die Haum-Daan Retiefsimposium oor Kinder- en Jeugboeke*, Eds. H.S. Coetzee and H.J.M. Retief (Pretoria: University of Pretoria, 1990), 88–96.

17. Anna Louw, "The English Children's Book of South African Origin," in *Papers Presented at the First Symposium on Children's Literature* (Potchefstroom: Institute for

Research in Children's Literature, Potchefstroom University for CHE, 1979), 16–26, 20; Hilda Halliday, "South African Writing for Children," *Crux* 8(3) (1974): 57–60, 57.

18. Sheila Scholten, "*Platkops Children* — The Childhood Sketches of Pauline Smith: A Commentary," in *Pauline Smith*, Ed. Dorothy Driver (Johannesburg: McGraw-Hill, 1983), 138–43.

19. Henry Juta, *Tales I Told the Children* (Cape Town: Juta, 1921), 10.

20. Jane Spettigue, *An Africander Trio* (London: Blackie, 1898).

21. Edith Green, *The Cape Cousins* (London: Wells Gardner, Darton, 1902).

22. Nellie Fincher *The Chronicles of Peach Grove Farm: A Story for S. African Children* (Pietermaritzburg: Times Printing and Publishing, 1910).

23. Humphrey Carpenter and Mari Prichard, *The Oxford Companion to Children's Literature* (Oxford: Oxford University Press, 1984), 218.

24. Sima Eliovson, *Little Umfaan: The Story of a Road* (Johannesburg: The Author, 1952?).

25. Jack Bennett, *Jamie* (London: Michael Joseph, 1963); republished (Boston: Little, Brown, 1963); 2nd, revised ed. (Cape Town: Tafelberg, 1990).

26. Jack Bennett, *The Voyage of the Lucky Dragon* (London: Angus & Robertson, 1981).

27. Jack Bennett, *Mister Fisherman* (London: Michael Joseph, 1964), cover.

28. Laurens van der Post, *The Hunter and the Whale* (London: Hogarth, 1967).

29. Roy Campbell, *The Mamba's Precipice* (London: Frederick Muller, 1953).

30. Quoted in Mary Webster, "Daphne Rooke," in *English and South Africa*, Ed. Alan Lennox-Short (Cape Town, Nasou, 197-), 67–69, 69.

31. Daphne Rooke, *The South African Twins* (London: Cape, 1953); 2nd ed., *Twins in South Africa* (Boston: Houghton Mifflin, 1955).

32. Victor Pohl, *Savage Hinterland* (Cape Town, Oxford University Press, 1956); *Farewell the Little People* (Cape Town: Oxford University Press, 1968). See Elwyn Jenkins, *Children of the Sun*, Chapter 3.

33. Hjalmar Thesen, *A Deadly Presence* (Cape Town: David Philip, 1982).

34. Jay Heale, *Young Africa Booklist* (Glasgow: Blackie, and Cape Town: Book Promotions, 1985), 60.

35. Stuart Cloete, "The Claws of the Cat," in *The Soldiers' Peaches and Other South African Stories* (London: Collins, 1959), 154–173.

36. "The Claws of the Cat," reprinted in *Close to the Sun*, Ed. G.E. de Villiers (Johannesburg: Macmillan, 1979), 118–132; and in *Africana Short Stories*, Ed. J.W. Loubser (Alberton: Varia Books, 1969), 113–126.

37. Jack Dewes, "Journalism gave PE-born Author Work Discipline," *Weekend Post*, 31 May 1990.

38. Geoffrey Allen, "Touching Eastern Cape Tale," *Eastern Province Herald*, 6 June 1990.

39. Roderick Haig-Brown, *Starbuck Valley Winter* (1943: London: Collins, 1965).

40. Mboma Dladla, *The Story of Mboma* (Johannesburg: Ravan, 1979), 38.

41. G.M. Rogers, "*Snow*," *The Brave Little Kaffir Boy* (Cape Town: Juta, 1927?).

42. *Pretoria News*, "*e'Lollipop* Makes a Return," 6 May 2004.

43. Peter Davis, *In Darkest Hollywood* (Randburg: Ravan, 1996), 116.

44. Sheila Gordon, *Waiting for the Rain* (1987. Toronto: Bantam, 1989), 42.

45. Dennis Bailey, *Khetho* (Johannesburg: Heinemann, 1994), 3.

46. Anton Ferreira, *Sharp, Sharp, Zulu Dog* (Johannesburg: Jacana, 2003; first published as *Zulu Dog* in the USA, 2002).

47. Donnarae MacCann, "The Sturdy Fabric of Cultural Imperialism," *Children's Literature* 33 (2005): 185–208.

48. Es'kia Mphahlele, *Father Come Home* (Johannesburg: Ravan, 1984).

49. Es'kia Mphahlele, "The Dream of Our Time," in *Storyland*, Ed. Jay Heale (Cape Town, Tafelberg, 1991), 85–90.

50. Es'kia Mphahlele, *Down Second Avenue* (London: Faber, 1959).
51. K.S. Bongela, *The Silent People* (Cape Town: Maskew Miller Longman, 1983).
52. National Library, *Amandla eBali* (Cape Town: National Library, 2004), 16.
53. Njabulo Ndebele, *Bonolo and the Peach Tree* (Johannesburg: Ravan, 1992).

Chapter 3

1. Isaac Taylor, *Scenes in Africa* (London: Harris, 1820), 78.
2. Dan Wylie, "Elephants and Compassion: Ecological Criticism and Southern African Hunting Literature," *English in Africa* 28(2) (2001): 79–100, 83.
3. John MacKenzie, *The Empire of Nature* (Manchester: Manchester University Press, 1988); "Empire and the Ecological Apocalypse," in *Ecology and Empire*, Eds. Tom Griffiths and Libby Robin (Edinburgh: Keele University Press, 1997), 215–228.
4. Stephen Gray, *Southern African Literature* (Cape Town: David Philip, 1979).
5. Margaret Scanlon and David Buckingham, "Deconstructing Dinosaurs," *Bookbird* 41(1) (2003): 14–20.
6. Laurens van der Post, *The Hunter and the Whale* (London: Hogarth, 1967).
7. Dianne Hofmeyr, *When Whales Go Free* (Cape Town: Tafelberg, 1988).
8. Dale Kenmuir, *Song of the Surf* (Cape Town: Maskew Miller Longman, 1988).
9. Roy Campbell, *The Mamba's Precipice* (London: Frederick Muller, 1953).
10. H.A. Bryden, *Animals of Africa* (London: Sands, 1900); *The Gold Kloof* (London: Nelson, 1907).
11. Harriet Bolus, *Elementary Lessons in Systematic Botany* (Cape Town: Maskew Miller, 1919).
12. Dorothy Norman, comp., *A Bird-book for South African Children* (Cape Town: Juta, 191–).
13. Frederick Fitzsimons, *The Monkeyfolk of South Africa*, 2nd ed. (London: Longmans, 1924).
14. Sydney Skaife, *The Strange Adventures of John Harmer* (Cape Town: Maskew Miller, 1928).
15. James MacKay, *Some South African Insects, Described in Rhyme with Nature Notes from a Southern Clime* (Durban: Davis, 1915).
16. Cecil Shirley, *Little Veld Folk* (Cape Town: CNA, 1943).
17. Dorothy Wager, *Umhlanga* (Durban: Knox, 1946).
18. Nellie Fincher, *The Chronicles of Peach Grove Farm: A Story for S. African Children* (Pietermaritzburg: Times Printing and Publishing), 62.
19. Jack Bennett, *Jamie* (London: Michael Joseph, 1963).
20. Stuart Cloete, "The Claws of the Cat," in *The Soldiers' Peaches and Other South African Stories* (London: Collins, 1959), 154–173.
21. Hjalmar Thesen, *A Deadly Presence* (Cape Town: David Philip, 1982).
22. Patrick Brantlinger, *Rule of Darkness* (Ithaca: Cornell University Press, 1988).
23. Sarah Gertrude Millin, *The South Africans* (London: Constable, 1926), 115 (original ellipsis).
24. Jan Juta, *Look Out for the Ostriches* (Cape Town: Dassie, 1949), 63, 142.
25. Malvern van Wyk Smith, *Grounds of Contest* (Cape Town: Juta, 1990), 65.
26. Leonard Flemming, *A Fool on the Veld* (Cape Town: Argus, 1916).
27. Baffie Coetzee, *Children of Mount Imperani* (Pretoria: Daan Retief, 1987).
28. Norman Herd, "Save our Soil!," in *South African Boys Twenty-story Annual* (Durban: Knox, 1945), 91–95, 94.
29. Edward Roux, *The Veld and the Future* (Cape Town: African Bookman,1946), n.p.
30. B. Schwartz, *South African Bilingual Verse* (Johannesburg: CNA, 1947), 41.
31. William Herbst, *From Beacon to Beacon* (Johannesburg: Voortrekkerpers, 1959?).

32. George Klerck, *At the Foot of the Koppie* (Cape Town: Maskew Miller, 1929).
33. Fay King (Goldie), *Friends of the Bushveld* (London: Cape, 1954).
34. Jane Carruthers, *Diverging Environments* (Boston, Mass.: African Studies Association, 1993); *The Kruger National Park* (Pietermaritzburg: University of Natal Press, 1995).
35. Julia Kristeva, *Powers of Horror* (New York: Columbia University Press, 1982), 4.
36. K. Argyle, *Stories from the Game Reserve* (Cape Town, Oxford University Press, 1985).
37. David Bunn, "Comparative Barbarism," in *Texts, Theory, Space*, Eds. Kate Dorian-Smith, Liz Gunner and Sarah Nuttall (London: Routledge, 1996), 37–52.
38. K. Marshall, *David Goes to Zululand* (London: Nelson, 1935).
39. Dale Kenmuir, *The Catch* (Cape Town: Maskew Miller Longman, 1993), 17.
40. Julia Martin, "Long Live the Fresh Air! Long Live!" *scrutiny2* 2(2) (1997): 10–29.
41. David Phiri, *Tikki's Wildlife Adventure* (Cape Town: Houston, 1995).
42. Brenda Munitich, *Thoko* (Cape Town: Tafelberg,1995).
43. Mboma Dladla, *The Story of Mboma* (Johannesburg: Ravan, 1979), 38.
44. Julia Martin undertook a survey of all the material she could find on the subject that was published or performed between 1986 and 1996; unfortunately, she missed some important children's books, and, in claiming to have been the first to investigate the subject, also missed all earlier criticism, for example, Dianne Hofmeyr, "A Greening for our Children," *Weekly Mail*, 3–9 November 1989; Elwyn Jenkins, *Children of the Sun* (Johannesburg: Ravan, 1993), Chap. 4; Yulisa Maddy and Donnarae MacCann, *African Images in Juvenile Literature* (Jefferson: McFarland, 1996).
45. Dale Kenmuir, *Sing of Black Gold* (Pretoria: de Jager-HAUM, 1991).
46. Peter Slingsby, "Guest Spot," *Bookchat* 103 (1991): 5.
47. Dale Kenmuir, "Response to 'Guest Spot,'" *Bookchat* 104 (1992): 15.
48. Dale Kenmuir, *The Tusks and the Talisman* (Pretoria: de Jager-HAUM, 1987).
49. Marguerite Poland, *Shadow of the Wild Hare* (Cape Town: David Philip, 1986).
50. Mazisi Kunene, *The Ancestors and the Sacred Mountain* (London: Heinemann, 1982).
51. Donnarae MacCann and Yulisa Amadu Maddy, *Apartheid and Racism in South African Children's Literature 1985-1995* (London: Routledge, 2001).
52. Carolyn Parker, *Witch Woman on the Hogsback* (Pretoria: de Jager-HAUM, 1987).
53. See the discussion of *Witch Woman on the Hogsback* by Carolyn Parker and *Shadow of the Wild Hare* by Marguerite Poland in Elwyn Jenkins, *Children of the Sun*.
54. Patricia Pinnock, *The King who Loved Birds* (Grahamstown: African Sun, 1992).
55. Helen Brain, *Who's Afraid of Spiders?* (Cape Town: Human & Rousseau, 1997).
56. Klaus Kühne, *The Secret of Big Toe Mountain* (Cape Town: Human & Rousseau, 1987).
57. Alexander Prettejohn, *The Poacher of Hidden Valley* (Pretoria: Daan Retief, 1986).
58. Peter Younghusband, *Kobie and the Military Road* (Cape Town: Capricorn, 1987).
59. Lawrence Bransby, *Remember the Whales* (Pretoria, Symbol, 1991).
60. K.H. Briner, *Cassandra's Quest* (Cape Town: Human & Rousseau, 2000).
61. Elana Bregin, *Warrior of Wilderness* (Cape Town: Maskew Miller Longman, 1989).
62. Pieter Pieterse, *The Misty Mountain* (Pretoria: de Jager-HAUM, 1985).
63. Pieter Grobbelaar, *The Earth Must Be Free* (Pretoria: Daan Retief, 1984).
64. Vivienne Brown, *The Boy and the Tree* (Cape Town: Human & Rousseau, 1989).
65. Ursula McAdorey, *The Old Man of the Mountain* (Manzini: Macmillan Boleswa, 1992).
66. Peter Slingsby, *The Joining* (Cape Town: Tafelberg, 1996); *Jedro's Bane* (Cape Town: Tafelberg, 2002).
67. Wayne Booth, *The Company We Keep* (Berkeley: University of California Press, 1988).

Chapter 4

1. Jean-Philippe Wade, "English," in *European-language Writing in Sub-Saharan Africa*, Ed. Albert Gérard (Budapest: Akadémiai Kadó, 1986), 230–250, 231.
2. A.J. Coetzee, Tim Couzens and Stephen Gray, "South African Literatures to World War II," in *Gèrard*, 173–213, 205.
3. For example, Guy Butler, "Myths," in *Collected Poems* (Cape Town: David Philip, 1999), 109.
4. Elizabeth Waterston, *Children's Literature in Canada* (New York: Twayne, 1992), 38, 66.
5. Ellen van der Spuy, *A Book of Children's Stories* (Cape Town: Maskew Miller, 1931).
6. Dorothea Fairbridge, *Skiddle* (Cape Town: Maskew Miller, 1926).
7. F.A. Donnolly, *Papa Baboon* (Pretoria: van Schaik, 1933).
8. F.D. *Fact and Fancy from the Veld* (Cape Town: Juta, 1909).
9. E.G. Ridley, *Tales of the Veld Folk for the Kiddies* (Bloemfontein: A.C. White, 193–).
10. Cecil J. Shirley, *Little Veld Folk* (Cape Town: CNA, 1943).
11. Henry Juta, *Tales I told the Children* (Cape Town: Juta, 1921).
12. Herbert Leviseur, *Desert Magic* (Cape Town: CNA, 1945).
13. Graeme Harper, Ed., "Introduction," in *Comedy, Fantasy and Colonialism* (London: Continuum, 2002), 1–8, 5.
14. Sadie Merber, *Glimpses of Fairyland* (Cape Town: Juta, 1930), 23.
15. G.M. Rogers, *The Fairies in the Mealie Patch* (Cape Town: Juta, n.d.), 2.
16. Nendick Paul, *A Child in the Midst* (Pietermaritzburg: Davis, 1909), 2.
17. Victor Pohl. *Farewell the Little People* (Cape Town: Oxford University Press, 1968), n.p.
18. Enid Ablett, *Fairy Tales from the Sunny South* (Johannesburg: Voortrekkerpers), 25.
19. A.E. Bailie, *The Pixies of the South* (Pretoria: van Schaik, 1944).
20. Ella MacKenzie, *The Locust Bird and Other Stories* (Cape Town: Maskew Miller, 1923), 66.
21. Norah Perkins, *The Candle on the Windowsill*, 2nd ed. (Boksburg: Geo. Perkins, 1926).
22. Sampie de Wet, *The Monkey's Wedding* (Pretoria: van Schaik, 1939).
23. Gladie McKay, *The Little Fir Tree and Other Stories* (Cape Town: Maskew Miller, 1927?).
24. Yvonne Jooste, *Mummy, I'm Listening* (Pretoria: J.H. de Bussy, 1946).
25. Strange Library of African Studies, Catalogue (Johannesburg: Johannesburg Public Library), s.v. Jane Shaw.
26. Minnie Martin, *Tales of the African Wilds* (Durban: Knox, 1942), 17.
27. Margot le Strange, *Wideawake Rhymes for Little People* (Krugersdorp: National Council of Women, 1942), 8, 14.
28. Annette Joelson, *The Hare and the Whistles* (Cape Town: Juta, n.d.), 14.
29. Andreé-Jeanne Tötemeyer, "Trends in Children's Literature at Home and Abroad," in *Towards More Understanding: The Making and Sharing of Children's Literature in South Africa*, Ed. Isabel Cilliers, (Cape Town: Juta, 1993): 159–169, 167.
30. Madeleine Masson, *The Story of the Little Moo Cow* (Johannesburg: Simba Toys, n.d.).
31. Jay Heale, *From the Bushveld to Biko* (Grabouw: Bookchat, 1996), 15.
32. Sally Starke and Doreen Rowbottom, *The Young Karoo* (Pietermaritzburg: Shuter & Shooter, 1950), n.p.
33. Annette Joelson, *How the Ostrich Got his Name* (Cape Town: Juta, 1926), 23.
34. Phyllis Juby, *Picaninny* (Cape Town: Primavera, n.d.).
35. Esme Lewis, *Nunku the Porcupine and Other Stories* (Cape Town: Unie-Volkspers, 1939).

36. Edith King, *Veld Rhymes for Children* (London: Longmans, 1911), 28.
37. Juliet Konig (Marais Louw), *The Little Elephant Hunter and Other Stories* (Cape Town: CNA, 1944).
38. Kathleen Wilkinson, *Picaninnies: South African Fairy Tales* (Durban: The Author, 1943).
39. Jac and Mac, *Minnie Moo Cow and Her Friends on the Veld* (Wynberg: Specialty Press of S.A., 1932), 10.
40. Annette Joelson, *Field Mouse Stories* (Cape Town: Juta, 1926), 9.
41. Stephen Jay Gould, *The Hedgehog, the Fox and the Magister's Pox* (London: Cape, 2003), 165.
42. Elwyn Jenkins, *South Africa in English-language Children's Literature, 1814–1912* (Jefferson: McFarland, 2002).
43. Henry Saxby, *A History of Australian Children's Literature 1841–1941* (Sydney: Wentworth, 1969), 191.
44. Dorothy Gard'ner, *Verses for South African Children* (Pretoria: van Schaik, 1939), 36.
45. Mabel Waugh, *Verses for Tiny South Africans* (Cape Town: Maskew Miller, 1923).
46. William Branford, "A Dictionary of South African English as a Reflex of the English-speaking Cultures of South Africa," in *English-speaking South Africa Today*, Ed. André de Villiers (Cape Town: Oxford University Press, 1976), 297–316, 298.
47. Maude Bidwell, *Breath of the Veld* (Cape Town: Juta, 1923), 88.
48. I.D. du Plessis, *Tales from the Malay Quarter* (Cape Town, Maskew Miller, 1945).
49. Maureen Walsh, *May Gibbs, Mother of the Gumnuts* (North Ryde: Angus & Robertson, 1985), 1.
50. Mrs. Æneas Gunn, *The Little Black Princess of the Never-Never* (Sydney: Angus & Robertson, 1905), n.p.
51. G.M. Rogers, *Peggy's Frog Prince* (Cape Town: Juta, 1927?).
52. Margaret Herd, *Tok-Tok* (Durban: Knox, 1943), 10.
53. Emily Zinn, "Rediscovery of the Magical," *Modern Fiction Studies* 46(1) (spring 2000): 246–269, 248, 249.
54. See, for example, Elwyn Jenkins, *Children of the Sun* (Johannesburg: Ravan, 1993), 2, 140, and the concluding paragraph to the book: "Myth and fantasy were perhaps the only way until the 1970s for children's literature in South Africa to subvert the reality of racial and cultural divide in the country. The imaginative and spiritual world of the San, Khoekhoen, African and Malay peoples could be entered by white children long before the physical barriers between them could be bridged," 151. See also Andreé-Jeanne Tötemeyer, "Impact of African Mythology on South African Juvenile Literature," *South African Journal of Library and Information Science* 57(4) (1989): 393–401, 397.
55. Nadine Gordimer, "Once upon a Time," in *Jump and Other Stories* (Cape Town: David Phillip, 1991), 23–30, 30.
56. Nadine Gordimer, *July's People* (1981; Harmondsworth: Penguin, 1982), 160.
57. Shelley Davidow, *Freefalling*, (Cape Town: Maskew Miller Longman, 1991).
58. J.M. Coetzee, "Jerusalem Prize Acceptance Speech" (1987), in *Doubling the Point: Essays and Interviews*, Ed. David Attwell (Cambridge: Harvard University Press, 1992), 96–100, 99.
59. B. Northling Swemmer, *Jungle Lore and Other Stories* (Cape Town: Nasionale Pers, 1949), n.p.
60. May Henderson, *The Cock-Olly Book* (1941); *Looma, Teller of Tales* (1942); *Tortoo the Tortoise* (1943); *Mrs Mouse of Kruger Park* (1944) (Durban: Knox).
61. C.S. Stokes, *We're Telling You* (Cape Town: Sanctuary Shillings, 1943).
62. Eve Jammy, "The English Children's Book in South Africa," in *Kinder- en Jeugboeke: Referate Gelewe tydens die Haum-Daan Retiefsimposium oor Kinder-en Jeugboeke*, Ed. H. S. Coetzee and H. J. M. Retief (Pretoria: University of Pretoria, 1990), 88–96, 89.

63. Percy FitzPatrick, *The Outspan* (London: Heinemann, 1912), 54, 60.
64. James Cobban, *Cease Fire!* (London: Methuen, 1900), 243.
65. L.W. Lanham, "South African English as an Index of Social History," *English Studies in Africa* 13(1) (1970): 251–264, 263.
66. J.M. Coetzee, *White Writing* (Sandton: Radix, 1988), 7.
67. David Adey, Ridley Beeton, Michael Chapman and Ernest Pereira, *Companion to South African English Literature* (Johannesburg: Ad. Donker, 1986), 51.

Chapter 5

1. Ella MacKenzie, *The Locust Bird* (Cape Town: Maskew Miller, 1923).
2. Corinne Rey, *Tales of the Veld* (Pretoria: van Schaik, 1926).
3. Annette Joelson, *How the Ostrich Got His Name* (Cape Town: Juta, 1926), 5.
4. Carrie Rothkugel, *The Gift Book of the Fatherless Children of the South African Soldiers and Sailors* (Cape Town: Argus, 1917), 45.
5. Kathleen Wilkinson, *Picaninnies: South African Fairy Tales* (Durban: The Author, 1943), 23.
6. Pieter Grobbelaar, *Ou M'Kai Vertel* (Cape Town: John Malherbe, 1964).
7. Margaret Herd, *Tok-Tok* (Durban: Knox, 1943).
8. W.H.I. Bleek, *Specimens of Bushman Folklore* (London: George Allen, 1911); Dorothea Bleek, *The Mantis and his Friends* (Cape Town: Maskew Miller, 1924).
9. David Lewis-Williams, *Stories that Float from Afar* (Cape Town: David Philip, 2000), 26.
10. Elizabeth Helfman, *The Bushmen and their Stories* (New York: Seabury, 1971).
11. Juliet Konig (Marais Louw), *The Little Elephant Hunter* (Cape Town: CNA, 1944).
12. A.O. Vaughan, *Old Hendrik's Tales* (London: Longmans, 1904), 3.
13. Sanni Metelerkamp, *Outa Karel's Stories* (London: Macmillan, 1914).
14. G. Daniell, *Jantjie's Aunt and Other Stories* (Cape Town: Juta, 1930), 17.
15. Dudley Kidd, *The Bull of the Kraal and the Heavenly Maidens* (London: Black, 1908).
16. Dudley Kidd, *Savage Childhood: A Study of Kafir Children* (London: Black, 1906), ix.
17. Andrew Lang, Ed., *The Orange Fairy Book* (London: Constable, 1906).
18. E.J. Bourhill and J.B. Drake, *Fairy Tales from South Africa, Collected from Original Native Sources* (London: Macmillan, 1908); Lewis Marsh, *Tales of the Fairies* (London: Frowde, n.d.); Ethel McPherson, *Native Fairy Tales of South Africa* (London: Harrap, 1919); M.W. Waters, *Fairy Tales Told by Nontsomi* (London: Longmans, 1927).
19. Frank Dalby Davison, *Children of the Dark People* (Sydney: Angus & Robertson, 1936), n.p.
20. Helena Hersman and H. Lily Guinsberg, *Two Little Strangers Meet* (Cape Town: Maskew Miller, 193-) 9, 11.
21. Vicki Forrester, *The Kingdom Above the Earth* (Johannesburg: Heinemann, 1994).
22. Samantha Naidu (2001b), "The Myth of Authenticity: Folktales and Nationalism in the 'New South Africa'," *scrutiny2* 6(2) (2001): 17–26.
23. Donnarae MacCann and Yulisa Amadu Maddy, *Apartheid and Racism in South African Children's Literature, 1985-1995* (New York: Routledge, 2001).
24. See Elwyn Jenkins, "The Presentation of African Folktales in some South African English Children's Versions," in *Oral Tradition and Education*, Eds. G. Sienaert and N. Bell (Durban: University of Natal Oral Documentation and Research Centre, 1988), 191–202; N. Canonici, "The Folktale Tradition Today and Yesterday," in *Oral Studies in Southern Africa*, Ed. H.C. Groenewald (Pretoria: HSRC, 1990), 128–153; Denise Godwin, "Discovering the African Folktale in Translation," *South African Journal of African Languages* 11(4) (1991): 109–118; Susan Horsburgh, "The Translation of Zulu Folktales for English-speaking Children in South Africa" (M.A. dissertation,

University of the Witwatersrand, 1991); Kathrine van Vuuren, "A Study of Indigenous Children's Literature in South Africa" (M.A. dissertation, University of Cape Town, 1994); Naidu, 2001b; Judith Inggs, "What is a South African Folktale?" *Papers* 14(1) (2004): 15–23.

25. Marguerite Poland, *The Mantis and the Moon* (Johannesburg: Ravan, 1979); *The Wood-Ash Stars* (Cape Town: David Philip, 1983).
26. Elsa Joubert, *The Four Friends and Other Tales from Africa* (Cape Town: Tafelberg, 1987).
27. Nick Greaves, *When Hippo was Hairy* (Manzini and Durban: Bok Books, 1988); *When Lion Could Fly* (Manzini and Durban: Bok Books, 1993); *When Elephant was King* (Manzini and Durban: Bok Books, 1996).
28. Dianne Stewart, *The Zebra's Stripes*. Cape Town: Struik, 2004.
29. Valerie Stillwell, *Monsters, Heroes and Sultan's Daughters* (Cape Town: Human & Rousseau, 1989); Gcina Mhlope, *The Snake with Seven Heads* (Braamfontein: Skotaville, 1989); Nombulelo Makhuphula, *Xhosa Fireside Tales* (Johannesburg: Seriti sa Sechaba, 1988).
30. Geraldine Elliot, *The Hunter's Cave* (London: Routledge & Kegan Paul,1951), vii.
31. John Murray, "Some Literary and Ethical Issues in the Use of Indigenous Material by an Australian Children's Writer," *Literature and Theology* 10(3) (1996): 252–260, 255.
32. K. Langloh Parker, *Australian Legendary Tales* (London: Nutt, 1896), n.p.
33. Mary Grant Bruce, *The Stone-Axe of Burkammuk* (London: Ward Lock, 1922), 6.
34. I.D. du Plessis, *Tales from the Malay Quarter* (Cape Town: Maskew Miller, 1945).
35. See P. Williams and L. Chrisman, *Colonial Discourse and Post-colonial Theory* (Hemel Hempstead: Wheatsheaf, 1993).
36. Nyembwe Tshikumambila, "From Folktale to Short Story," in *European-language Writing in Sub-Saharan Africa*, Ed. Albert S. Gérard (Budapest: Akadémiai Kadó, 1986): 475–489, 476.
37. Patricia Davison, "Museums and the Reshaping of Memory," in *Negotiating the Past*, Ed. Sarah Nuttall and Carli Coetzee (Cape Town: Oxford University Press, 1998): 143–160, 143.
38. Pippa Skotnes, Ed., *Miscast* (Cape Town: University of Cape Town Press, 1996), 284; Steven Robins, "Silence in my Father's House," in Nuttall and Coetzee, 120–140, 121; Thomas Dowson and David Lewis-Williams, "Myths, Museums and Southern African Rock Art," in *Contested Images*, Eds. Thomas Dowson and David Lewis-Williams (Johannesburg: Witwatersrand University Press, 1994), 385–402; Shelly Ruth Butler, *Contested Representations* (Philadelphia: Gordon & Breach, 1999); Linda Hutcheon, *Irony's Edge* (London: Routledge, 1994).
39. Helize van Vuuren, "The Tin Shack Bushmen of Kagga Kamma," review of *In the Tradition of the Forefathers* by Hilton White (Cape Town: University of Cape Town, 1995), Alternation, 2(2) (1995): 207–211, 210.
40. Working Group of Indigenous Minorities in Southern Africa, "San Media and Research Contract" (Windhoek: WIMSA, 2001), 3.
41. Andreé-Jeanne Tötemeyer, "Impact of African Mythology on South African Juvenile Literature," *South African Journal of Library and Information Science*, 57(4) (1989): 393–401, 397.
42. Duncan Brown, "Aboriginality, Identity and Belonging in South Africa and Beyond," *English in Africa*, 28(1) (2001): 67–90, 81.
43. Gcina Mhlophe, *Stories of Africa* (Pietermaritzburg: University of Natal Press, 2003); Bob Leshoai, *Iso le Nkhono* (Braamfontein: Skotaville, 1983); Nombulelo Makhuphula, *Xhosa Fireside Tales*.
44. Dinah Mbanze, *The Magic Pot* (Cape Town: Kwela, 1999), 48.
45. Jack Cope, *Tales of the Trickster Boy* (Cape Town: Tafelberg, 1990).

46. George Manville Fenn, *Off to the Wilds* (London: Sampson Low, 1882), 157.
47. G. Stanley Hall, *Aspects of Child Life and Education* (Boston: Ginn, 1907), 288.
48. Kenneth Kidd, *Making American Boys* (Minneapolis: University of Minnesota Press, 2004), 71.
49. John Campbell, *Voyages to and from the Cape of Good Hope. Intended for the Young* (London: Religious Tract Society, 1840), 3.
50. Dudley Kidd, *Savage Childhood* (London: Black, 1906), viii.
51. Dudley Kidd, *The Essential Kaffir* (London: Black, 1904), 277.
52. Hanneke du Preez, *Kgalagadi Tales* (Alberton: Librarius Felicitas, 1984), n.p.
53. Sheila Egoff and Judith Saltman, *The New Republic of Childhood* (Toronto: Oxford University Press, 1990), 204.
54. Marguerite Poland, "Making Stars Sing," in *Towards More Understanding*, Ed. Isabel Cilliers (Cape Town: Juta, 1993), 13–20, 18.
55. Frantz Fanon, *The Wretched of the Earth* (1961; London: Penguin, 2001).
56. Ciara Ní Bhroin, "Championing Irish Literature," *Bookbird* 43(2) (2005):13–21, 21.
57. Samantha Naidu, "Transcribing Tales, Creating Cultural Identities" (M.A. dissertation, Rhodes University, 2001a); Naidu, "The Myth of Authenticity," 2001b. Naidu's scholarship is not reliable, but she has made an important contribution to debate on the subject.
58. A.C. Jordan, *Tales from South Africa* (Berkeley: University of California Press, 1973), 12.
59. Mary Phillips, *The Bushman Speaks* (Cape Town: Howard Timmins, 1961); *The Cave of Uncle Kwa* (Cape Town: Purnell, 1965).
60. Daphne Rooke, *The South African Twins* (London: Jonathan Cape, 1953).
61. Maskew Miller, *Maskew Miller's English Readers for Young South Africans, Standard I* (Cape Town: Maskew Miller, n.d.).
62. Jay Heale and Dianne Stewart, *African Myths and Legends* (Cape Town: Struik, 2001).
63. Linda Rode, Ed., *Madiba Magic* (Cape Town: Tafelberg, 2002).
64. Letters to Madiba Competition, *Letters to Madiba* (Cape Town: Maskew Miller Longman, 2001).
65. Christopher Gregorowski, *Fly, Eagle, Fly!* 2nd ed. (Cape Town: Tafelberg, 2000).
66. Penny Baillie, *Eagle Learns to Fly*, (Pretoria: Granny Frog's Tales for Tadpoles, 2002).
67. Jay Heale, "Review of *Eagle Learns to Fly*," *The Book Door* 27, (2004): 9.

Chapter 6

1. Elizabeth Waterston, *Children's Literature in Canada* (New York: Twayne, 1992), 32.
2. *Collins Encyclopedia of Music*, 2nd ed. (London: Chancellor, 1984), s.v. "Realization."
3. Harold Scheub, "Introduction," in A.C. Jordan, *Tales from South Africa* (Berkeley: University of California Press, 1973), 1–12, 12.
4. Ella MacKenzie, *The Locust Bird and Other Stories* (Cape Town: Maskew Miller, 1923), 84, 80.
5. Sadie Merber, *Glimpses of Fairyland* (Cape Town: Juta, 1930), 21.
6. Corinne Rey, *Tales of the Veld* (Pretoria: van Schaik, 1926), 50, 55.
7. G. Daniell, *Jantjie's Aunt and Other Stories* (Cape Town: Juta, 1930), 17.
8. Minnie Martin, *Tales of the African Wilds* (Durban: Knox, 1942), 83.
9. Brenda Niall, *Australia Through the Looking Glass* (Melbourne: Melbourne University Press, 1984), 214.
10. Carolyn Parker, *Witch Woman on the Hogsback* (Pretoria: de Jager-HAUM, 1987); Judy Chalmers, *The Battle of the Mountain* (Cape Town: Human & Rousseau, 1984).
11. Donnarae MacCann and Yulisa Maddy, *Apartheid and Racism in South African Children's Literature, 1985–1995* (New York: Routledge, 2001) 124.

12. Anne and Peter Cook, *The Adventures of Kalipe* (Cape Town: Via Afrika, 1957), n.p. The other books are listed in Chapters 1 and 2.
13. D.R. Sherman, *The Pride of the Hunter* (Cape Town: Romantica, 1979).
14. Dorothy Kowen, *Nyama and the Eland* (Wynberg: Kwagga, 2003).
15. Marguerite Poland, *Shadow of the Wild Hare* (Cape Town: David Philip, 1986).
16. Beryl Bowie, *Mystery at Cove Rock* (Cape Town: Tafelberg, 1991).
17. Pieter Grobbelaar, *The White Arrow* (Cape Town: Tafelberg, 1974), cover.
18. Elizabeth Helfman, *The Bushmen and their Stories* (New York: Seabury, 1971).
19. Nola Turkington and Niki Daly, *The Dancer* (Cape Town: Human & Rousseau, 1996).
20. Madeline Murgatroyd, *Tales from the Kraals* (Cape Town: Timmins, 1968).
21. Madeline Murgatroyd, *Maduma, Teller of Tales* (Cape Town: Tafelberg, 1987), cover.
22. Jenny Seed, *The Lost Prince* (Pretoria, Daan Retief, 1985); *The Strange Black Bird* (Pretoria: Daan Retief, 1986).
23. Jenny Seed, *The Bushman's Dream* (London: Hamish Hamilton, 1974).
24. Marguerite Poland, *The Mantis and the Moon* (Johannesburg: Ravan, 1979); *Once at KwaFubesi* (Johannesburg: Ravan, 1981); *Sambane's Dream* (Harmondsworth: Penguin, 1989). Samantha Naidu, in "Transcribing Tales, Creating Cultural Identities" (M.A. dissertation, Rhodes University, 2001), acknowledges that they are original, but she nevertheless includes them in her critique of folktales in translation.
25. Hamilton Wende, *The Quagga's Secret* (Durban: Gecko, 1995).
26. Barbara Meyerowitz, Jennette Copans and Tessa Welch, comp., *My Drum* (Johannesburg: Abecedarius, 1991).
27. Cicely Luck (van Straten), *The Flowers of the Thorn* (Johannesburg: Lowry, 1986).
28. Cicely van Straten, *The Great Snake of Kalungu and Other East African Stories* (Pretoria: Juventus, 1981).
29. Cicely Luck (van Straten), *Kaninu's Secret and Other East African Stories* (Pretoria: Juventus, 1981), 43.
30. Cicely van Straten, *The Fish Eagle and the Dung Beetle* (Cape Town: Human & Rousseau, 1982).
31. Cicely Luck (van Straten), *Tajewo and the Sacred Mountain* (Pretoria: Juventus, 1983); Cicely van Straten, *Torit of the Strong Right Arm* (Cape Town: Human & Rousseau, 1992); *Quest for the Sacred Stone* (Cape Town: Oxford University Press, 2000).
32. Vicki Forrester, *The Kingdom Above the Earth* (Johannesburg: Heinemann, 1994), n.p.
33. Moira Thatcher, *Tselane* (Cape Town: Tafelberg, 1986).

Chapter 7

1. Thabo Mbeki, "Speech on the Adoption of the Constitution of the Republic of South Africa," (Pretoria: Office of the Presidency, 1996).
2. Edwin Wilmsen, "First People? Images and Imaginations in South African Iconography," *Critical Arts* (1) (1995): 1–27, 19.
3. Peter Davis, *In Darkest Hollywood* (Johannesburg: Ravan, 1996); Keyan Tomaselli, "Myths, Racism and Opportunism: Film and TV Representations of the San," in *Film as Ethnography*, Eds. Ian Crawford and David Turon (Manchester: Manchester University Press, 1992), 205–221; Barbara Buntman, "'Primitives', Paintings and Paradoxes: Representations of Southern San Imagery on South African Studio Ceramics from the 1950s," in *South African Studio Ceramics: A Selection from the 1950s*, Ed. Wendy Gers (Port Elizabeth, King George V Art Gallery, 1998), 30–34; Elwyn Jenkins, *Symbols of Nationhood* (Johannesburg: South African Institute of Race Relations, 2004).

4. Elana Bregin, "Miscast: Bushmen in the Twentieth Century," *Current Writing* 13(1) (2001): 87–107, 91.

5. David Maughan Brown, "The Rehabilitation of the San in Popular Fiction," in *Race and Literature*, Ed. Charles Malan (Pinetown: Owen Burgess, 1987), 117–126, 118.

6. A.E. Voss, "The Image of the Bushman in South African English Writing of the Nineteenth and Twentieth Centuries," *English in Africa* 14(1) (1987): 21–40, 35.

7. Duncan Brown, "Aboriginality, Identity and Belonging in South Africa and Beyond," *English in Africa* 28(1) (2001): 67–90, 69.

8. Helize van Vuuren, "Bushman and Afrikaner: Cultural Interaction," *Alternation* 2(1) (1995): 151–154, 154.

9. Earlier studies were Elwyn Jenkins, "Images of the San," in *Other Worlds, Other Lives*, Eds. Myrna Machet, Sandra Olën and Thomas van der Walt (Pretoria: Unisa, 1996), 270–296; Jay Heale, "Books that Open Windows to Other Worlds," in *Peace Through Children's Books* (New Delhi: Indian Board on Books for Young People, Association of Writers and Illustrators for Children, 1998).

10. Edward Kendall, *The English Boy at the Cape* (London: Whittaker, 1835).

11. Olive Schreiner, *The Story of an African Farm* (London: Chapman & Hall, 1883).

12. Stephen Gray, *Southern African Literature* (Cape Town: David Philip, 1979), 142.

13. Malvern Van Wyk Smith, *Grounds of Contest* (Cape Town: Juta, 1990), 31.

14. G. Daniell, *Jantjie's Aunt and Other Stories* (Cape Town: Juta, 1930).

15. Corinne Rey, *Tales of the Veld* (Pretoria, van Schaik, 1926).

16. Victor Pohl, *Farewell the Little People* (Cape Town: Oxford University Press, 1968), n.p.

17. B. Schwartz, *South African Bilingual Verse* (Johannesburg: CNA, 1947), 23.

18. S.B. Hobson and G.C. Hobson, *The Lion of the Kalahari* (Pretoria: van Schaik, 1977; first published as *Skankwan van die Duine*, 1930).

19. MacDonald Hastings, *The Search for the Little Yellow Men* (London: Hulton, 1956); Candy Malherbe, *These Small People* (Pietermaritzburg: Shuter & Shooter, 1983); Alice Mertens, *Children of the Kalahari* (London: Collins, 1966); Dennis Winchester-Gould, *God's Little Bushmen* (Pretoria: Rhino, 1993).

20. Mary Phillips, *The Cave of Uncle Kwa* (Cape Town: Purnell, 1965), n.p.

21. Ursula McAdorey, *The Old Man of the Mountain* (Manzini: Macmillan Boleswa, 1992).

22. Laurens van der Post, *A Story Like the Wind* (London: Hogarth, 1972).

23. Abdul JanMohamed, "The Economy of Manichean Allegory," in *"Race," Writing and Difference*, Ed. Henry Gates (Chicago: University of Chicago Press, 1986), 78–106, 102.

24. Frances Armstrong, "Gender and Miniaturization," *English Studies in Canada* 16(4) (1990): 403–416, 403.

25. P.J. Schoeman, *Hunters of the Desert Land* (1957), revised ed. (Cape Town: Timmins, 1982).

26. Agnes Jackson, *The Bushmen of South Africa* (London: Oxford University Press, 1956), 5, 20.

27. Elizabeth Helfman, *The Bushmen and their Stories* (New York: Seabury).

28. John Coetzee, *Flint and the Red Desert* (Cape Town: Tafelberg, 1986).

29. See Robert Gordon, *The Bushman Myth* (Boulder: Westview, 1992); Paul Landau, "With Camera and Gun in Southern Africa," in *Miscast: Negotiating the Presence of the Bushmen*, Ed. Pippa Skotnes (Cape Town: University of Cape Town Press, 1996), 129–141; Edwin Wilmsen, *Land Filled with Flies* (Chicago: University of Chicago Press, 1989); Elana Bregin.

30. Enid Ablett, *Fairy Tales from the Sunny South* (Johannesburg: Vootrekkerpers, 1939), 4.

31. J.B. Wright, *Bushman Raiders of the Drakensberg 1840-1870* (Pietermaritzburg: University of Natal Press, 1971).

32. Ella MacKenzie, *The Locust Bird and Other Stories* (Cape Town: Maskew Miller, 1923), 81.

33. Elana Bregin, "Representing the Bushmen," *English in Africa* 27(1) (2000): 37–54, 49.

34. Anne and Peter Cook, *The Adventures of Kalipe* (Cape Town: Via Afrika, 1957).

35. Reginald Maddock, *The Last Horizon* (Edinburgh: Nelson, 1961).

36. Joan Nockels and Alex Wilcox, *Kabo of the Mountain* (Winterton: Drakensberg, 1988), n.p.

37. Donnarae MacCann and Yulisa Maddy, *Apartheid and Racism in South African Children's Literature, 1985-1995* (New York: Routledge, 2001), 101–104.

38. Ken Smith, *Tinde in the Mountains* (Johannesburg: Ravan, 1987).

39. Anne Harries, *The Sound of the Gora* (London: Heinemann, 1980).

40. Marguerite Poland, *The Small Clay Bull* (David Philip, 1986).

41. Jenny Seed, *The New Fire* (Cape Town: Human & Rousseau, 1983).

42. D.R. Sherman, *Pride of the Hunter* (Cape Town: Romantica, 1979).

43. Lesley Beake, *Song of Be* (Cape Town: Maskew Miller Longman, 1991).

44. Judith Rovenger, "Wonderful Ambassadors," in *Lesley Beake: Author Nomination for the Hans Christian Andersen Award 2004* (Cape Town: South African Children's Book Forum, 2004), n.p.

45. Margaret Lenta, "Goodbye Lena, Goodbye Poppie," *Ariel* 29(4)(1998): 101–118.

46. See Megan Biesele, "Religion and Folklore," in *The Bushmen*, Ed. Phillip Tobias, (Cape Town: Human & Rousseau, 1978), 162–172.

47. D.F. Jones. *Storyteller: The Many Lives of Laurens van der Post* (London: Murray, 2001).

48. M. Edward, *A Drakensberg Tale* (Cape Town: Unie-Volkspers, 195–).

49. Edna Quail, *Kattau the Hunter* (Cape Town: Oxford University Press, 1983).

50. Dianne Hofmeyr, *When Whales Go Free* (Cape Town: Tafelberg, 1988).

51. Hjalmar Thesen, *A Deadly Presence* (Cape Town: David Philip, 1982).

52. Keyan Tomaselli, "Psychospiritual Ecoscience," *Visual Anthropology* 12 (2–3), 1999, 189, cited in Elana Bregin, "Miscast: Bushmen in the Twentieth Century," *Current Writing* 13(1) (2001), 87–107, 94.

53. Victor Pohl, *Savage Hinterland* (Cape Town: Oxford University Press, 1956).

54. Gwen Westwood, *Narni of the Desert* (London: Hamish Hamilton, 1967).

55. Cicely van Straten, "Xhabbo and the Honey-guide," in *Storyland*, Ed. Jay Heale (Cape Town: Tafelberg, 1991), 63–70; Marguerite Poland, "The Broken String," in *The Small Clay Bull* (Cape Town: David Philip, 1986), 17–32.

56. Elwyn Jenkins, "Lessons from the Honey-guide," *CREArTA* 2(2) (2001): 52–59. According to the standard reference work on South African birds, the bird's ability to invoke the help of humans and animals is a fact, not a myth (*Roberts Birds of South Africa*, Cape Town: CNA, 1957, 233).

57. Marguerite Poland, *Sambane's Dream* (Harmondsworth: Penguin, 1989).

58. Marguerite Poland, *Shadow of the Wild Hare* (Cape Town: David Philip, 1986).

59. David Hook, *'Tis but Yesterday* (London: Greaves, Pass, 1911), n.p.

60. Peter Slingsby, *The Joining* (Cape Town: Tafelberg, 1996).

61. Maria Nikolajeva, *Children's Literature Comes of Age* (New York: Garland, 1996).

62. Leon de Kock, "An Impossible History," *English in Africa* 24(1) (1997): 103–117, 113.

63. Tess Cosslett, "'History from Below': Time-slip Narratives and National Identity," *The Lion and The Unicorn* 26(2) (2002): 243–253.

64. Kenneth B. Kidd, *Making American Boys* (Minneapolis: University of Minnesota Press, 2004), 61.

65. J.J. van der Post, *Agarob, Kind van die Duine* (Cape Town: Tafelberg, 1963).

66. Jill Paton Walsh, *A Chance Child* (London: Macmillan, 1978).

67. Linda Hall, "Aristocratic Houses and Radical Politics: Historical Fiction and the Time-slip Story in E. Nesbit's *The House of Arden*," *Children's Literature in Education* 29(1) (1998): 51–58, 58.

68. F. Davis, *Yearning for Yesterday* (New York: Free Press, 1979).
69. Christopher Shaw and Malcolm Chase, eds. *The Imagined Past* (Manchester: Manchester University Press, 1989).
70. Peter Slingsby, *Leopard Boy* (Cape Town: Tafelberg, 1989).
71. Judith Inggs, "Grappling with Change," *CREArTA* 3(1) (2002): 22–33, 30.
72. Michael Ondaatje, *The English Patient* (London: Bloomsbury, 1992).
73. Rufus Cook, "'Imploding Time and Geography.'" *Journal of Commonwealth Literature* 33(2) (1998): 110–125, 124.
74. Elleke Boehmer, "Endings and New Beginnings," in *Writing South Africa*, Eds. Derek Attridge and Rosemary Jolly (Cambridge: Cambridge University Press, 1998), 43–56, 53.
75. Peter Slingsby, *Jedro's Bane* (Cape Town: Tafelberg, 2002).

Chapter 8

1. Jan J. van der Post, *Agarob: Kind van die Duine* (Cape Town: Tafelberg, 1963); Dolf van Niekerk, *Karel Kousop* (Cape Town: Tafelberg, 1985).
2. Peter Slingsby, *The Joining* (Cape Town: Tafelberg, 1996), 12.
3. Jenny Seed, *The Broken Spear* (London: Hamish Hamilton, 1972), 71.
4. Enid Ablett, *Fairy Tales from the Sunny South* (Johannesburg: Vootrekkerpers, 1939), 13.
5. Kathleen Wilkinson, *Picaninnies: South African Fairy Tales* (Durban: The Author, 1943), 5.
6. Gwen Westwood, *The Red Elephant Blanket* (London: Hamish Hamilton, 1966), 7.
7. Esmé Karlson, *The Coat of Many Patches* (Durban: Knox, 1944).
8. Ann Harries, *The Sound of the Gora* (London: Heinemann, 1979), 18.
9. Ursula McAdorey, *The Old Man of the Mountain* (Manzini: Macmillan Boleswa, 1992), 42.
10. For example, Helena Hersman and H. Lily Guinsberg, *Two Little Strangers Meet* (Cape Town: Maskew Miller, 193–); Reginald Maddock, *The Last Horizon* (Edinburgh: Nelson, 1961).
11. Jenny Seed, *The Great Thirst* (London: Hamish Hamilton, 1971), 86.
12. K. Marshall, *David Goes to Zululand* (London: Nelson, 1935), 16.
13. Sadie Merber, *Glimpses of Fairyland* (Cape Town: Juta, 1930), 45.
14. Ella Mackenzie, *The Locust Bird and Other Stories* (Cape Town: Maskew Miller, 1923).
15. Luli Callinicos, *Working Life 1886-1940: Factories, Townships, and Popular Culture on the Rand* (Johannesburg: Ravan, 1987), 43.
16. D.A. Nesbitt, *Kiddies' Yarns* (Cape Town: Juta, 1926?), n.p.
17. Sally Starke and Doreen Rowbottom, *The Young Karoo* (Pietermaritzburg: Shuter & Shooter, 1950), 18.
18. Henry Juta, *Tales I Told the Children* (Cape Town: Juta, 1921).
19. Pattie Price, *The Afrikaner Little Boy: Ten Songs with Music about Small Children* (London: Methuen, 1935).
20. Edith King, *Veld Rhymes for Children* (London: Longmans, 1911), 22.
21. Dulcie Carter, *Stories from Sunny Zululand* (Durban: Knox, 1947).
22. Esmé Karlson, *Peanut Goes to School* (Durban: Knox, 1945).
23. H.A. Bryden, *The Gold Kloof* (London: Nelson, 1907).
24. Jessie Hertslet, *Mpala: The Story of an African Boy* (London: Oxford University Press, 1942); *Nono: The Story of an African Girl* (London: Oxford University Press, 1948).
25. Fay Goldie, *Zulu Boy* (London: Oxford University Press, 1968).
26. Daphne Rooke, *The South African Twins* (London: Jonathan Cape, 1953).

27. Edward Kendall, *The English Boy at the Cape* (London: Whittaker, 1835).
28. Alba Bouwer, *Stories van Rivierplaas* (Cape Town: Tafelberg, 1955).
29. Gail Ching-Liang Low, "White Skins/Black Masks: The Pleasures and Politics of Imperialism," *New Formations* 9 (1989): 83–103, 90.
30. Lesley Beake, *A Cageful of Butterflies* (Cape Town: Maskew Miller Longman, 1989).
31. Robert Hill, *Forever in the Land* (Cape Town: Tafelberg, 1991), 25.
32. Patricia Wrightson, *The Rocks of Honey* (Sydney: Angus & Robertson, 1961), 75.
33. Ann Dymond, *Borderline* (Pretoria: Daan Retief, 1986).
34. Catherine Annandale, *Tongelo* (Johannesburg: Perskor, 1976).
35. Sheila Gordon, *Waiting for the Rain* (New York: Bantam, 1989).
36. Michael Williams, *Into the Valley* (Cape Town: Tafelberg, 1990).
37. Lawrence Bransby, *Outside the Walls* (Johannesburg: Heinemann, 1995).
38. Kenneth B. Kidd, *Making American Boys* (Minneapolis: University of Minnesota Press, 2004), 84.
39. Robin Malan, *The Sound of New Wings* (Cape Town: Maskew Miller Longman, 1998).
40. Peter Slingsby, *Jedro's Bane* (Cape Town: Tafelberg, 2002).

Chapter 9

1. Dorothea Fairbridge, *Skiddle* (Cape Town: Maskew Miller, 1926). See Chapter 6.
2. Jay Heale, "South African Children's Literature in English," *Bookchat* 102 (1991): 19; Andreé-Jeanne Tötemeyer, "Trends in Children's Literature at Home and Abroad," in *Towards More Understanding*, Ed. Isabel Cilliers (Cape Town: Juta, 1993), 159–169, 168.
3. Peter Davis, *In Darkest Hollywood* (Johannesburg: Ravan, 1996), 21–31.
4. Michael Chapman, *Southern African Literatures* (London: Longman, 1996), 209.
5. Iris Clinton, *Ridge of Destiny* (London: Edinburgh House, 1956).
6. M.B. Sewitz, "Children's Books in English in an African Setting, 1914–1964" (Research project, University of the Witwatersrand, 1965), 57.
7. Juliet Marais Louw, *Sipho and the Yellow Plastic Purse* (Johannesburg: Perskor, 1977).
8. Beverley Naidoo, *Journey to Jo'burg* (Harlow: Longman, 1985).
9. Lesley Beake, *Serena's Story* (Cape Town: Maskew Miller Longman, 1990).
10. Es'kia Mphahlele, *Down Second Avenue* (London: Faber, 1959).
11. James Cahill, *M'Bonga's Trek* (London: Lutterworth, 1952).
12. Kitty Ritson, *Tessa in South Africa* (London: Nelson, 1955).
13. Maud Reed, *Candy Finds the Clue* (London: Epworth, 1958).
14. Dorothy Wager, *Umhlanga* (Durban: Knox, 1946).
15. Jane Shaw, *Venture to South Africa* (London: Nelson), 64.
16. Iris Clinton, *The Clarkes Go South* (London: Livingstone, 1951).
17. Lesley Beake, *Harry Went to Paris* (London: Puffin, 1989).
18. Norman Silver, *No Tigers in Africa* (London: Faber, 1990).
19. Robin Saunders, *Dear Ludwig* (Cape Town: Maskew Miller Longman, 1998).
20. Janet Smith, *Joe Cassidy and the Red Hot Cha-Cha* (Cape Town: Maskew Miller Longman, 1994).
21. Malvern van Wyk Smith, *Grounds of Contest* (Cape Town: Juta, 1990), 37.
22. The way young adult fiction dealt with political struggle has been analyzed elsewhere. See, for example, Elwyn Jenkins, *Children of the Sun* (Johannesburg: Ravan, 1993), 129–152; Donnarae MacCann and Yulisa Maddy, *Apartheid and Racism in South African Children's Literature, 1985–1995* (New York: Routledge, 2001); Peter Midgley, "Review of MacCann and Maddy," H-Net: Humanities and Social Sciences Online,

http://www.h-net.org/reviews (Posted 11 Sept. 2002); Judith Bentley and Peter Midgley, "Coming of Age in the New South Africa," *The Alan Review* 27(2) (2000): 52–58. The work of MacCann and Maddy must be treated with great caution: it is factually inaccurate and logically and theoretically flawed.

23. Linda Rode and Jakes Gerwel, comp., *Crossing Over: New Writing for a New South Africa* (Cape Town: Kwela, 1995), n.p.
24. Judith Inggs, "The Changing Construct of the Child in Contemporary South African English Children's Fiction" (Paper delivered at the conference of the International Research Society for Children's Literature, Warmbaths, 23 August 2001).
25. Wendy Michaels, "The Realistic Turn," *Papers* 14(1) (2004): 49–59, 57.
26. Mike Featherstone, *Consumer Culture and Postmodernism* (London: Sage, 1991), 45.
27. Lawrence Bransby, *Outside the Walls* (Johannesburg: Heinemann, 1995).
28. Beryl Bowie, *Pedal Me Faster* (Cape Town: Maskew Miller Longman, 1995), 4, 5.
29. Dianne Hofmeyr, *Blue Train to the Moon* (Cape Town: Maskew Miller Longman, 1993); *Boikie You Better Believe It* (Cape Town: Tafelberg, 1994).
30. Sarah Britten, *The Worst Year of My Life — So Far* (Cape Town: Tafelberg, 2000); *Welcome to the Martin Tudhope Show!* (Cape Town: Tafelberg, 2002).
31. Gail Smith, *Way to Go!* Cape Town: Tafelberg, 1995.
32. Dawn Garisch, *Not Another Love Story* (Johannesburg: Heinemann, 1994), 95.
33. Robin Malan, *The Sound of New Wings* (Cape Town: Maskew Miller Longman, 1998).
34. Shelley Davidow, *Freefalling* (Cape Town: Maskew Miller Longman, 1991), 78.
35. Chris du Toit, *Madiba, The Story of Nelson Mandela* (Cape Town: Actua Press, 1998).
36. Hugh Lewin, *The Picture that Came Alive* (Oxford: Heinemann, 1992).
37. Michael Williams, *The Eighth Man* (Cape Town: Oxford University Press, 2002).
38. Michael Williams, *Crocodile Burning* (New York: Dutton, 1992).
39. Anne Schlebusch, *Dance Idols* (Cape Town: New Africa Books, 2003).
40. Robin Malan, series Ed., *Siyagruva* Series (Cape Town: New Africa Books); Robin Malan, "Siyagruva: Developing a Teen Fiction Series for Africa" (Presentation at the 29th Congress of the International Board on Books for Young People, Cape Town, 8 September 2004).
41. Jenny Robson, *Mellow Yellow* (Cape Town: Tafelberg, 1994); *Dark Waters* (Cape Town: Tafelberg, 1995); Jane Rosenthal, *Wake Up Singing* (Cape Town: Maskew Miller Longman, 1990).
42. C. de Bosdari, *Ten Tickeys* (Cape Town: Balkema, 1954); Maretha Maartens, *Sidwell's Seeds* (Cape Town: Tafelberg, 1985); Reviva Schermbrucker, *Charlie's House* (Cape Town: David Philip, 1989); Zachariah Rapola, *Stanza on the Edge* (Cape Town: Maskew Miller Longman, 2001).
43. Mosibudi Mangena, *A Twin World* (Cape Town: Maskew Miller Longman, 1996).
44. Niki Daly, *What's Cooking, Jamela?* (New York: Farrar, Straus & Giroux, 2001), published in South Africa as *Yebo, Jamela!* (Cape Town: Tafelberg, 2001).
45. Niki Daly, *Not So Fast, Songololo* (Cape Town: Human & Rousseau, 1985).
46. Jay Heale, *South African Authors and Illustrators* (Grabouw: Bookchat, 1994), 14; *From the Bushveld to Biko* (Grabouw: Bookchat, 1996), 29.
47. Andreé-Jeanne Tötemeyer, "The Visual Portrayal of Black People in South African Children's and Juvenile Literature," in *Far Far Away*, Ed. Marianne Hölscher (Cape Town: South African National Gallery, 1986), 36-46, 45.
48. Sadie Merber, *Glimpses of Fairyland* (Cape Town: Juta, 1930), 50. See Chapter 8.
49. Ingrid Mennen and Niki Daly, *Ashraf of Africa* (Cape Town: David Philip, 1990).
50. Patricia Pinnock, *Skyline* (Cape Town: David Philip, 2000).

BIBLIOGRAPHY

Primary Sources

Ablett, Enid. *Fairy Tales from the Sunny South*. Johannesburg: Voortrekkerpers, 1939.

Annandale, Catherine. *Tongelo*. Johannesburg: Perskor, 1976.

Argyle, K. *Stories from the Game Reserve*. Cape Town, Oxford University Press, 1985.

Bailey, Dennis. *Khetho*. Johannesburg: Heinemann, 1994.

Bailie, A.E. *The Pixies of the South*. Pretoria: van Schaik, 1944.

Baillie, Penny. *Eagle Learns to Fly*. Pretoria: Granny Frog's Tales for Tadpoles, 2002.

Baldwin, May. *Corah's School Chums*. London: Chambers, 1912.

Beake, Lesley. *A Cageful of Butterflies*. Cape Town: Maskew Miller Longman, 1989.

———*Harry Went to Paris*. London: Puffin, 1989.

———*Serena's Story*. Cape Town: Maskew Miller Longman, 1990.

———*Song of Be*. Cape Town: Maskew Miller Longman, 1991.

Bennett, Jack. *Jamie*. London: Michael Joseph, 1963. Republished. Boston: Little, Brown, 1963. 2nd, revised ed. Cape Town: Tafelberg, 1990.

———*Mister Fisherman*. London: Michael Joseph, 1964.

———*The Voyage of the Lucky Dragon*. London: Angus & Robertson, 1981.

Bevan, Marjorie. *Anne of the Veld*. London: Nelson, 192–.

Bidwell, Maude. *Breath of the Veld: A Story or a Play*. Cape Town: Juta, 1923.

Bleek, Dorothea. *The Mantis and his Friends*. Cape Town: Maskew Miller, 1924.

Bleek, W.H.I. *Specimens of Bushman Folklore*. London: George Allen, 1911.

Bolus, Harriet. *Elementary Lessons in Systematic Botany*. Cape Town: Maskew Miller, 1919.

Bongela, K.S. *The Silent People*. Cape Town: Maskew Miller Longman, 1983.

Bourhill, E.J. and J.B. Drake. *Fairy Tales from South Africa, Collected from Original Native Sources*. London: Macmillan, 1908.

Bouwer, Alba. *Stories van Rivierplaas*. Cape Town: Tafelberg, 1955.

Bower, Lola. *Zulu Boy*. London: Hutchinson, 1960.

Bowie, Beryl. *Mystery at Cove Rock*. Cape Town: Tafelberg, 1991.

———*Pedal Me Faster*. Cape Town: Maskew Miller Longman, 1995.

Brain, Helen. *Who's Afraid of Spiders?* Cape Town: Human & Rousseau, 1997.

Bransby, Lawrence. *Remember the Whales*. Pretoria: Symbol, 1991.

———*Outside the Walls*. Johannesburg: Heinemann, 1995.

Bregin, Elana. *Warrior of Wilderness*. Cape Town: Maskew Miller Longman, 1989.

Britten, Sarah. *The Worst Year of My Life — So Far*. Cape Town: Tafelberg, 2000.

———*Welcome to the Martin Tudhope Show!* Cape Town: Tafelberg, 2002.

Brown, Vivienne. *The Boy and the Tree*. Cape Town: Human & Rousseau, 1989.

Bruce, Mary Grant. *The Stone-Axe of Burkammuk*. London: Ward Lock, 1922.

Bryden, H.A. *Animals of Africa*. London: Sands, 1900.

———*The Gold Kloof*. London: Nelson, 1907.

Butler, Guy. *Collected Poems*. Cape Town: David Philip, 1999.

Cahill, James. *M'Bonga's Trek*. London: Lutterworth, 1952.

Campbell, Roy. *The Mamba's Precipice*. London: Frederick Muller, 1953.

Carey-Hobson, Mary. *The Farm in the Karoo; or, What Charlie Vyvyan and his Friends Saw in South Africa*. London: Juta, Heelis, 1883.

Carter, Dulcie. *Stories from Sunny Zululand*. Durban: Knox, 1947.

Chalmers, Judy. *The Battle of the Mountain*. Cape Town: Human & Rousseau, 1984.

Clinton, Iris. *The Clarkes Go South*. London: Livingstone, 1951.

———*Ridge of Destiny*. London: Edinburgh House, 1956.

Cloete, Stuart. "The Claws of the Cat." In *The Soldiers' Peaches and Other South African Stories*, 154–173. London: Collins, 1959. Reprinted in *Close to the Sun*, Ed. G.E. de Villiers, 118–132. Johannesburg: Macmillan, 1979; and in *Africana Short Stories*, Ed. J.W. Loubser, 113–126. Alberton: Varia Books, 1969.

Cobban, James *Cease Fire!* London: Methuen, 1900.

Coetzee, Baffie. *Children of Mount Imperani*. Pretoria: Daan Retief, 1987.

Coetzee, John. *Flint and the Red Desert*. Cape Town: Tafelberg, 1986.

Cook, Anne and Peter. *The Adventures of Kalipe*. Cape Town: Via Afrika, 1957.

Cope, Jack. *Tales of the Trickster Boy*. Cape Town: Tafelberg, 1990.

Daly, Niki. *Not So Fast, Songololo*. Cape Town: Human & Rousseau, 1985.

———*What's Cooking, Jamela?* New York: Farrar, Straus & Giroux, 2001. Published in South Africa as *Yebo, Jamela!* Cape Town: Tafelberg, 2001.

Daniell, G. *Jantjie's Aunt and Other Stories*. Cape Town: Juta, 1930.

Davidow, Shelley. *Freefalling*. Cape Town: Maskew Miller Longman, 1991.

Davison, Frank Dalby. *Children of the Dark People*. Sydney: Angus & Robertson, 1936.

de Bosdari, C. *Ten Tickeys*. Cape Town: Balkema, 1954.

de Wet, Sampie. *The Monkey's Wedding and Other Stories for Children*. Pretoria: van Schaik, 1939.

Dederick, Sheila. *Tickey*. Cape Town: Oxford University Press, 1965.

Dladla, Mboma. *The Story of Mboma*. Johannesburg: Ravan, 1979.

Donnolly, F.A. *Papa Baboon*. Pretoria: van Schaik,1933.

du Plessis, I.D. *Tales from the Malay Quarter*. Cape Town, Maskew Miller, 1945.

du Preez, Francois. *Mystery at Rushing Waters*. Johannesburg: Afrikaanse Pers-Boekhandel, 1964.

du Preez, Hanneke. *Kgalagadi Tales*. Alberton: Librarius Felicitas, 1984.

du Toit, Chris. *Madiba, The Story of Nelson Mandela* Cape Town: Actua Press, 1998.

Dymond, Ann. *Borderline*. Pretoria: Daan Retief, 1986.

Edward, M. *A Drakensberg Tale*. Cape Town: Unie-Volkspers, 195-.

Eliovson, Sima. *Little Umfaan: The Story of a Road*. Johannesburg: The Author, 1952?

Elliot, Geraldine. *The Hunter's Cave*. London: Routledge & Kegan Paul, 1951.

F.D. [F. Dawson]. *Fact and Fancy from the Veld*. Cape Town: Juta, 1909.

Fairbridge, Dorothea. *Skiddle*. Cape Town: Maskew Miller, 1926.

Fenn, George Manville. *Off to the Wilds*. London: Sampson Low, 1882.

Ferreira, Anton. *Sharp, Sharp, Zulu Dog*. Johannesburg: Jacana, 2003. First published as *Zulu Dog*. New York: Farrar, Straus and Giroux, 2002.

Fincher, Nellie. *The Chronicles of Peach Grove Farm: A Story for S. African Children*. Pietermaritzburg: Times Printing and Publishing, 1910.

FitzPatrick, Percy. *Jock of the Bushveld*. London: Longmans, Green, 1907.

———*The Outspan*. London: Heinemann, 1912.

Fitzsimons, Frederick. *The Monkeyfolk of South Africa*. 2nd ed. London: Longmans, 1924.

Flemming, Leonard. *A Fool on the Veld*. Cape Town: Argus, 1916.

Forrester, Vicki. *The Kingdom Above the Earth*. Johannesburg: Heinemann, 1994.

Franz, G.H. *Tau, the Chieftain's Son*. Dundee, Natal: Ebenezer, 1929.

Gard'ner, Dorothy. *Verses for South African Children, Grown Up or Otherwise*. Pretoria: van Schaik, 1939.

Garisch, Dawn. *Not Another Love Story*. Johannesburg: Heinemann, 1994.

Goldie, Fay. *Zulu Boy*. London: Oxford University Press, 1968.

Gordimer, Nadine. *July's People*. 1981. Harmondsworth: Penguin, 1982.

———"Once upon a Time." In *Jump and Other Stories*, 22–30. Cape Town: David Phillip, 1991.

Gordon, Sheila. *Waiting for the Rain*. 1987. New York: Bantam, 1989.

Greaves, Nick. *When Hippo was Hairy*. Manzini and Durban: Bok Books, 1988.

———*When Lion Could Fly*. Manzini and Durban: Bok Books, 1993.

———*When Elephant was King*. Manzini and Durban: Bok Books, 1996.

Green, Edith. *The Cape Cousins*. London: Wells Gardner, Darton, 1902.

Gregorowski, Christopher. *Fly, Eagle, Fly!* 2nd ed. Cape Town: Tafelberg, 2000.

Grobbelaar, Pieter. *Ou M'Kai Vertel*. Cape Town: John Malherbe, 1964.

———*The White Arrow*. Cape Town: Tafelberg, 1974.

———*The Earth Must Be Free*. Pretoria: Daan Retief, 1984.

Gunn, Mrs. Æneas. *The Little Black Princess of the Never-Never*. Sydney: Angus & Robertson, 1905.

Haig-Brown, Roderick. 1943. *Starbuck Valley Winter*. London: Collins, 1965.

Harries, Anne. *The Sound of the Gora*. London: Heinemann, 1980.

Hastings, MacDonald. *The Search for the Little Yellow Men*. London: Hulton, 1956.

Heale, Jay and Dianne Stewart. *African Myths and Legends*. Cape Town: Struik, 2001.

Helfman, Elizabeth. *The Bushmen and their Stories*. New York: Seabury, 1971.

Henderson, May. *The Cock-Olly Book*. Durban: Knox, 1941.

———*Looma, Teller of Tales*. Durban: Knox, 1942.

———*Tortoo the Tortoise*. Durban: Knox, 1943.

———*Mrs Mouse of Kruger Park*. Durban: Knox, 1944.

Herbst, William. *From Beacon to Beacon*. Johannesburg: Voortrekkerpers, 1959?.

Herd, Margaret. *Tok-Tok: Stories for Very Young S. Africans*. Durban: Knox, 1943.

Hersman, Helena and H. Lily Guinsberg. *Two Little Strangers Meet*. Cape Town: Maskew Miller, 193–.

Hertslet, Jessie. *Mpala: The Story of an African Boy*. London: Oxford University Press, 1942.

———*Kana and His Dog*. Cape Town: African Bookman, 1946.

———*Nono: The Story of an African Girl*. London: Oxford University Press, 1948.

Heyns, Werner. *Ramini: Smugglers' core*. Johannesburg: Afrikaanse Pers-Boekhandel, 1963.

———*Ramini of the Bushveld*. Pretoria: Voortrekkerpers, 1963.

Hill, Robert. *Forever in the Land*. Cape Town: Tafelberg, 1991.

Hobson, S.B. and G.C. Hobson. *The Lion of the Kalahari* Introduced and translated by Esther Linfield, 1930. Pretoria: van Schaik, 1977. First published as *Skankwan van die Duine*.

Hofmeyr, Dianne. *When Whales Go Free*. Cape Town: Tafelberg, 1988.

———*Blue Train to the Moon*. Cape Town: Maskew Miller Longman, 1993.

———*Boikie You Better Believe It*. Cape Town: Tafelberg, 1994.

Hook, David. *'Tis but Yesterday*. London: Greaves, Pass, 1911.

Hoppé, Charles. *Sons of the African Veld*. New York: McBride, 1947.

Jac and Mac. *Minnie Moo Cow and Her Friends on the Veld*. Wynberg: Specialty Press of S.A., 1932.

Jackson, Agnes. *The Bushmen of South Africa*. London: Oxford University Press, 1956.

Joelson, Annette. *Field Mouse Stories*. Cape Town: Juta, 1926.

———*How the Ostrich got his Name and Other South African Stories for Children*. Cape Town: Juta, 1926.

—*The Hare and the Whistles*. Cape Town: Juta, n.d.

Jooste, Yvonne. *Mummy, I'm Listening*. Pretoria: J.H. de Bussy and Cape Town: HAUM, 1946.

Jordan, A.C. *Tales from South Africa*. Berkeley: University of California Press, 1973.

Joubert, Elsa. *The Four Friends and Other Tales from Africa*. Cape Town: Tafelberg, 1987.

Juby, Phyllis. *Picaninny: South African Versions of Popular Nursery Rhymes*. Cape Town: Primavera, n.d.

Juta, Henry. *Tales I Told the Children*. Cape Town: Juta, 1921.

Juta, Jan. *Look Out for the Ostriches*. Cape Town: Dassie, 1949.

Karlson, Esmé. *The Coat of Many Patches*. Durban: Knox, 1944.

———*Peanut Goes to School*. Durban: Knox, 1945.

Keats, Felicity, *Rudolph's Valley*. Cape Town: Tafelberg, 1991.

Kendall, Edward. *The English Boy at the Cape*. 3 vols. London: Whittaker, 1835.

Kenmuir, Dale. *The Tusks and the Talisman*. Pretoria: de Jager-HAUM, 1987.

———*Song of the Surf*. Cape Town: Maskew Miller Longman, 1988.

———*Sing of Black Gold*. Pretoria: de Jager-HAUM, 1991.

———*The Catch*. Cape Town: Maskew Miller Longman, 1993.

Kidd, Dudley. *The Bull of the Kraal and the Heavenly Maidens*. London: Black, 1908.

King, Edith. *Veld Rhymes for Children*. London: Longmans, 1911.

King (Goldie), Fay. *Friends of the Bushveld*. London: Cape, 1954.

Klerck, George. *At the Foot of the Koppie*. Cape Town: Maskew Miller, 1929.

Konig (Marais Louw), Juliet. *South Wind*. Cape Town: CNA, 1943.

———*The Little Elephant Hunter and Other Stories*. Cape Town: CNA, 1944.

Kowen, Dorothy. *Nyama and the Eland*. Wynberg: Kwagga, 2003.

Kühne, Klaus. *The Secret of Big Toe Mountain*. Cape Town: Human & Rousseau, 1987.

Kunene, Mazizi. *The Ancestors and the Sacred Mountain*. London: Heinemann, 1982.

Lang, Andrew, Ed. *The Orange Fairy Book*. London: Constable, 1906.

le Strange, Margot. *Wideawake Rhymes for Little People*. Krugersdorp: National Council of Women, 1942.

Leshoai, Bob. *Iso le Nkhono: African Folktales for Children*. Braamfontein: Skotaville, 1983.

Letters to Madiba Competition. *Letters to Madiba*. Cape Town: Maskew Miller Longman, 2001.

Levick, W.M. *Dry River Farm*. London: Dent, 1955.

———*River Camp*. London: Dent, 1960.

Lewin, Hugh. *The Picture that Came Alive*. Oxford: Heinemann, 1992.

Lewis, Esme. *Nunku the Porcupine and Other Stories*. Cape Town: Unie-Volkspers, 1939.

———*Sipho and the Yellow Plastic Purse*. Johannesburg: Perskor, 1977.

Luck (van Straten), Cicely. *Kaninu's Secret and Other East African Stories*. Pretoria: Juventus, 1981.

———*Tajewo and the Sacred Mountain*. Pretoria: Juventus, 1983.

———*The Flowers of the Thorn*. Johannesburg: Lowry, 1986.

Maartens, Maretha. *Sidwell's Seeds*. Cape Town: Tafelberg, 1985.

Mabetoa, Maria. *Our Village Bus*. Johannesburg: Ravan, 1985.

MacKay, James. *Some South African Insects, Described in Rhyme with Nature Notes for a Southern Clime*. Durban: Davis, 1915.

MacKenzie, Ella. *The Locust Bird and Other Stories*. Cape Town: Maskew Miller, 1923.

Maddock, Reginald. *The Last Horizon*. Edinburgh: Nelson, 1961.

Makhuphula, Nombulelo. *Xhosa Fireside Tales*. Johannesburg: Seriti sa Sechaba, 1988.

Malan, Robin. *The Sound of New Wings*. Cape Town: Maskew Miller Longman, 1998.

———, series Ed. *Siyagruva Series*. Cape Town: New Africa Books.

Malherbe, Candy. *These Small People*. Pietermaritzburg: Shuter & Shooter,1983.

Mangena, Mosibudi. *A Twin World*. Cape Town: Maskew Miller Longman, 1996.

Marchant, Bessie. *Molly of One Tree Bend*. London: Butcher, 1910.

———*A Girl of Distinction*. London: Blackie, 1912.

———*Laurel the Leader*. London: Blackie, n.d.

Marsh, Lewis. *Tales of the Fairies*. London: Frowde, n.d.

Marshall, K. *David Goes to Zululand*. London: Nelson, 1935.

Martin, Minnie. *Tales of the African Wilds*. Durban: Knox, 1942.

Maskew Miller. *Maskew Miller's English Readers for Young South Africans, Standard I*. Cape Town: Maskew Miller, n.d.

Masson, Madeleine. *The Story of the Little Moo Cow*. Johannesburg: Simba Toys, n.d.

Mbanze, Dinah. *The Berry Basket*. Cape Town: Kwela, 1999.

———*The Magic Pot*. Cape Town: Kwela, 1999.

McAdorey, Ursula. *The Old Man of the Mountain*. Manzini: Macmillan Boleswa, 1992.

McKay, Gladie. *The Little Fir Tree and Other Stories*. Cape Town: Maskew Miller, 1927?

McPherson, Ethel. *Native Fairy Tales of South Africa*. London: Harrap, 1919.

Mennen, Ingrid and Niki Daly. *Ashraf of Africa*. Cape Town: David Philip, 1990.

Merber, Sadie. *Glimpses of Fairyland*. Cape Town: Juta, 1930.

Mertens, Alice. *Children of the Kalahari*. London: Collins, 1966.

Metelerkamp, Sanni. *Outa Karel's Stories*. London: Macmillan, 1914.

Meyerowitz, Barbara, Jennette Copans and Tessa Welch, comp. *My Drum I and II*. Johannesburg: Abecedarius, 1991.

Mhlope, Gcina. *The Snake with Seven Heads*. Braamfontein: Skotaville, 1989.

———*Stories of Africa*. Pietermaritzburg: University of Natal Press, 2003.

Millin, Sarah Gertrude. *The South Africans*. London: Constable, 1926.

Mphahlele, Es'kia, *Down Second Avenue*. London: Faber, 1959.

———*Father Come Home*. Johannesburg: Ravan, 1984.

———"The Dream of Our Time." In *Storyland*, Ed. Jay Heale, 85-90. Cape Town, Tafelberg, 1991.

Munitich, Brenda. *Ben's Buddy*. Pretoria: de Jager-HAUM, 1987.

———*Thoko*. Cape Town: Tafelberg, 1995.

Murgatroyd, Madeline. *Tales from the Kraals*. Cape Town: Timmins, 1968.

———*Maduma, Teller of Tales*. Cape Town: Tafelberg, 1987.

Naidoo, Beverley. *Journey to Jo'burg*. Harlow: Longman, 1985.

Ndebele, Njabulo. *Bonolo and the Peach Tree*. Johannesburg: Ravan, 1992.

Nesbitt, D.A. *Kiddies' Yarns*. Cape Town: Juta, 1926?

Nockels, Joan and Alex Wilcox. *Kabo of the Mountain*. Winterton: Drakensberg, 1988.

Norman, Dorothy, comp. *A Bird-book for South African Children*. Cape Town: Juta, 191–.

Nortje, P.H. *The Green Ally*. London: Oxford University Press, 1963.

———*Wild Goose Summer*. London: Oxford University Press, 1964.

Ondaatje, Michael. *The English Patient*. London: Bloomsbury, 1992.

Parker, Carolyn. *Witch Woman on the Hogsback*. Pretoria: de Jager-HAUM, 1987.

Parker, K. Langloh. *Australian Legendary Tales*. London: Nutt, 1896.

Paul, Nendick. *A Child in the Midst*. Pietermaritzburg: Davis, 1909.

Perkins, Norah. *The Candle on the Windowsill: A Romance of Childhood*. 2nd ed. Boksburg: Geo. Perkins, 1926.

Philip, Marie. *Caravan Caravel*. Cape Town: David Philip, 1973.

Phillips, Mary. *The Bushman Speaks*. Cape Town: Howard Timmins, 1961.

———*The Cave of Uncle Kwa*. Cape Town: Purnell, 1965.

Phiri, David. *Tikki's Wildlife Adventure*. Cape Town: Houston, 1995.

Pieterse, Pieter. *The Misty Mountain*. Pretoria: de Jager-HAUM, 1985.

Pinnock, Patricia. *The King who Loved Birds*. Grahamstown: African Sun, 1992.

———*Skyline*. Cape Town: David Philip, 2000.

Pohl, Victor. *Savage Hinterland*. Cape Town, Oxford University Press, 1956.

———*Farewell the Little People*. Cape Town: Oxford University Press, 1968.

Poland, Marguerite. *The Mantis and the Moon*. Johannesburg: Ravan, 1979.

———*Once at KwaFubesi*. Johannesburg: Ravan, 1981.

———*The Wood-Ash Stars*. Cape Town: David Philip, 1983.

———"The Broken String." In *The Small Clay Bull*, 17–32. Cape Town: David Philip, 1986.

———*Shadow of the Wild Hare*. Cape Town: David Philip, 1986.

———*The Small Clay Bull*. David Philip, 1986.

———*Sambane's Dream*. Harmondsworth: Penguin, 1989.

Prettejohn, Alexander. *The Poacher of Hidden Valley*. Pretoria: Daan Retief, 1986.

Price, Pattie. *The Afrikaner Little Boy: Ten Songs with Music about Small Children*. London: Methuen, 1935.

Pringle, Thomas. *African Poems of Thomas Pringle*. Edited by Ernest Pereira and Michael Chapman. Pietermaritzburg: University of Natal Press, 1989.

Quail, Edna. *Kattau the Hunter*. Cape Town: Oxford University Press, 1983.

Raath, George and Lorrie. *Chums of Meredrift School*. Johannesburg: Afrikaanse Pers-Boekhandel, n.d.

Rapola, Zachariah. *Stanza on the Edge*. Cape Town: Maskew Miller Longman, 2001.

Reed, Maud. *Candy Finds the Clue*. London: Epworth, 1958.

Reid, Thomas Mayne. *The Bush Boys*. London: David Bogue, 1856.

Rey, Corinne. *Tales of the Veld*. Pretoria: van Schaik, 1926.

Ridley, E.G. *Tales of the Veld Folk for the Kiddies*. Bloemfontein: A.C. White, 193–.

Ritson, Kitty. *Tessa in South Africa*. London: Nelson, 1955.

Robson, Jenny. *Mellow Yellow*. Cape Town: Tafelberg, 1994.

———*Dark Waters*. Cape Town: Tafelberg, 1995.

Rode, Linda, Ed. *Madiba Magic*. Cape Town: Tafelberg, 2002.

Rogers, G.M. *Peggy's Frog Prince*. Cape Town: Juta, 1927?

———"Snow," *The Brave Little Kaffir Boy*. Cape Town: Juta, 1927?

———*The Fairies in the Mealie Patch*. Cape Town: Juta, n.d.

Rooke, Daphne. *The South African Twins*. London: Jonathan Cape, 1953. 2nd ed. *Twins in South Africa*. Boston: Houghton Mifflin, 1955.

Rosenthal, Jane. *Wake Up Singing*. Cape Town: Maskew Miller Longman, 1990.

Rothkugel, Carrie. *The Gift Book of the Fatherless Children of the South African Soldiers and Sailors*. Cape Town: Argus, 1917.

Roux, Edward. *The Veld and the Future*. Cape Town: African Bookman,1946.

Saunders, Robin. *Dear Ludwig*. Cape Town: Maskew Miller Longman, 1998.

Savory, Phyllis. *Xhosa Fireside* Tales. Reprinted in *African Fireside Tales*, 15–102. Cape Town: Timmins, 1982.

Schermbrucker, Reviva. *Charlie's House*. Cape Town: David Philip, 1989.

Schlebusch, Anne. *Dance Idols*. Cape Town: New Africa Books, 2003.

Schoeman, P.J. *Hunters of the Desert Land*. 1957. Revised ed. Cape Town: Timmins, 1982.

Schreiner, Olive. *The Story of an African Farm*. London: Chapman & Hall, 1883.

Schwartz, B. *South African Bilingual Verse*. Johannesburg: CNA, 1947.

Seed, Jenny. *The Great Thirst*. London: Hamish Hamilton, 1971.

———*The Broken Spear*. London: Hamish Hamilton, 1972.

———*The Bushman's Dream*. London: Hamish Hamilton, 1974.

———*The New Fire*. Cape Town: Human & Rousseau, 1983.

———*The Lost Prince*. Pretoria, Daan Retief, 1985.

———*The Strange Black Bird*. Pretoria: Daan Retief, 1986.

Shaw, Jane. *Venture to South Africa*. London: Thomas Nelson, 1960.

Sherman, D.R. *The Pride of the Hunter*. Cape Town: Romantica, 1979.

Shirley, Cecil J. *Little Veld Folk*. Cape Town: CNA, 1943.

Silver, Norman. *No Tigers in Africa*. London: Faber, 1990.

Skaife, Sydney. *The Strange Adventures of John Harmer*. Cape Town: Maskew Miller, 1928.

Slingsby, Peter. *Leopard Boy*. Cape Town: Tafelberg, 1989.

———*The Joining*. Cape Town: Tafelberg, 1996.

———*Jedro's Bane*. Cape Town: Tafelberg, 2002.

Smith, Gail. *Way to Go!* Cape Town: Tafelberg, 1995.

Smith, Janet. *Joe Cassidy and the Red Hot Cha-Cha*. Cape Town: Maskew Miller Longman, 1994.

Smith, Ken. *Tinde in the Mountains*. Johannesburg: Ravan, 1987.

Smith, Pauline. *Platkops Children*. 1935. Cape Town: Balkema, 1981.

Spettigue, Jane. *An Africander Trio*. London: Blackie, 1898.

———*A Trek and a Laager*. London: Blackie, 1900?

Starke, Sally. *Little Huts That Grow in the Veld*. Cape Town: CNA, 1943.

Starke, Sally and Doreen Rowbottom. *The Young Karoo*. Pietermaritzburg: Shuter & Shooter, 1950.

Stewart, Dianne. *The Zebra's Stripes*. Cape Town: Struik, 2004.

Stillwell, Valerie. *Monsters, Heroes and Sultan's Daughters*. Cape Town: Human & Rousseau, 1989.

Stimie, C.M. *Children of the Camdeboo*. Johannesburg: Afrikaanse Pers-Boekhandel, 1964.

Stokes, C.S. *We're Telling You*. Cape Town: Sanctuary Shillings, 1943.

Stranger, L.D. *The Odd One Out*. London: Nelson, 193–.

Stredder, Eleanor. *Jack and His Ostrich*. London: Nelson, 1890.

Swemmer, B. Northling. *Jungle Lore and Other Stories*. Cape Town: Nasionale Pers, 1949.

Taylor, Isaac. *Scenes in Africa, For the Amusement and Instruction of Little Tarry-at-Home Travellers*. London: Harris, 1820.

Thatcher, Moira. *Tselane*. Cape Town: Tafelberg, 1986.

Thesen, Hjalmar. *A Deadly Presence*. Cape Town: David Philip, 1982.

Turkington, Nola and Niki Daly. *The Dancer*. Cape Town: Human & Rousseau, 1996.

van der Post, Jan J. *Agarob: Kind van die Duine*. Cape Town: Tafelberg, 1963.

van der Post, Laurens. *The Hunter and the Whale*. London: Hogarth, 1967.

———*A Story Like the Wind*. London: Hogarth, 1972.

van der Spuy, Ellen. *A Book of Children's Stories*. Cape Town: Maskew Miller, 1931.

van Niekerk, Dolf. *Karel Kousop*. Cape Town: Tafelberg, 1985.

van Straten, Cicely. *The Great Snake of Kalungu and Other East African Stories*. Pretoria: Juventus, 1981.

———*The Fish Eagle and the Dung Beetle*. Cape Town: Human & Rousseau, 1982.

———*Quest for the Sacred Stone*. Cape Town: Oxford University Press, 2000.

———"Xhabbo and the Honey-guide." In *Storyland*, Ed. Jay Heale, 63-70. Cape Town: Tafelberg, 1991.

———*Torit of the Strong Right Arm*. Cape Town: Human & Rousseau, 1992.

Vaughan, A.O. *Old Hendrik's Tales*. London: Longmans, 1904.

Vaughan, Iris. *The Diary of Iris Vaughan*. Johannesburg: CNA, 1958.

Wager, Dorothy. *Umhlanga*. Durban: Knox, 1946.

Walsh, Jill Paton. *A Chance Child*. London: Macmillan, 1978.

Waters, M.W. *Fairy Tales Told by Nontsomi*. London: Longmans, 1927.

Waugh, Mabel. *Verses for Tiny South Africans*. Cape Town: Maskew Miller, 12.

Wende, Hamilton. *The Quagga's Secret*. Durban: Gecko, 1995.

Westwood, Gwen. *The Red Elephant Blanket*. London: Hamish Hamilton, 1966.

———*Narni of the Desert*. London: Hamish Hamilton, 1967.

Wilkinson, Kathleen. *Picaninnies: South African Fairy Tales*. Durban: The Author, 1943.

Williams, Michael. *Into the Valley*. Cape Town: Tafelberg, 1990.

————*Crocodile Burning.* New York: Dutton, 1992.

————*The Eighth Man.* Cape Town: Oxford University Press, 2002.

Winchester-Gould, Dennis. *God's Little Bushmen.* Pretoria: Rhino, 1993.

Wright, E. Owen. *Backveld Born.* Bloemfontein: A.C. White, n.d.

Wrightson, Patricia. *The Rocks of Honey.* Sydney: Angus & Robertson, 1961.

Younghusband, Peter. *Kobie and the Military Road.* Cape Town: Capricorn, 1987.

Secondary Sources, Critical Works, Bibliographies and Catalogs

Adey, David, Ridley Beeton, Michael Chapman and Ernest Pereira. *Companion to South African English Literature.* Johannesburg: Ad Donker, 1986.

Allen, Geoffrey. "Touching Eastern Cape Tale." *Eastern Province Herald,* 6 June 1990.

Armstrong, Frances. "Gender and Miniaturization." *English Studies in Canada* 16(4) (1990): 403–416.

Bentley, Judith and Peter Midgley. "Coming of Age in the New South Africa." *The Alan Review* 27(2) (2000): 52–58.

Bevan, Joan. "Children's Literature in English." In *Catalogue for the Exhibition of South African Children's and Youth Books,* Ed. M.A.G. Swart, 32–34. Potchefstroom: South African Library Association, 1978.

Biesele, Megan. "Religion and Folklore." In *The Bushmen,* Ed. Phillip Tobias, 162–172. Cape Town: Human & Rousseau, 1978.

Boehmer, Elleke. "Endings and New Beginnings." In *Writing South Africa,* Eds. Derek Attridge and Rosemary Jolly, 43–56. Cambridge: Cambridge University Press, 1998.

Booth, Wayne. *The Company We Keep.* Berkeley: University of California Press, 1988.

Branford, William. "A Dictionary of South African English as a Reflex of the English-speaking Cultures of South Africa." In *English-speaking South Africa Today,* Ed. André de Villiers, 297-316. Cape Town: Oxford University Press, 1976.

Brantlinger, Patrick. *Rule of Darkness.* Ithaca: Cornell University Press, 1988.

Bregin, Elana. "Representing the Bushmen." *English in Africa* 27(1) (2000): 37–54.

————"Miscast: Bushmen in the Twentieth Century." *Current Writing* 13(1) (2001): 87–107.

Brown, Duncan. "Aboriginality, Identity and Belonging in South Africa and Beyond." *English in Africa,* 28(1) (2001): 67–90.

Bunn, David. "Comparative Barbarism." In *Texts, Theory, Space,* Eds. Kate Dorian-Smith, Liz Gunner and Sarah Nuttall, 37–52. London: Routledge, 1996.

Buntman, Barbara. "'Primitives,' Paintings and Paradoxes: Representations of Southern San Imagery on South African Studio Ceramics from the 1950s." In *South African Studio Ceramics: A Selection from the 1950s,* Ed. Wendy Gers, 30–34. Port Elizabeth: King George V Art Gallery, 1998.

Butler, Shelly Ruth. *Contested Representations.* Philadelphia: Gordon & Breach, 1999.

Callinicos, Luli. *Working Life 1886-1940: Factories, Townships, and Popular Culture on the Rand.* Johannesburg: Ravan, 1987.

Campbell, John. *Voyages to and from the Cape of Good Hope. Intended for the Young.* London: Religious Tract Society, 1840.

Canonici, N. "The Folktale Tradition Today and Yesterday." In *Oral Studies in Southern Africa,* Ed. H.C. Groenewald, 128–153. Pretoria: HSRC, 1990.

Carpenter, Humphrey and Mari Prichard. *The Oxford Companion to Children's Literature.* Oxford: Oxford University Press, 1984.

Carruthers, Jane. *Diverging Environments.* Boston, Mass.: African Studies Association, 1993.

———*The Kruger National Park*. Pietermaritzburg: University of Natal Press, 1995.

Chapman, Michael. *Southern African Literatures*. London: Longman, 1996.

Ching-Liang Low, Gail. "White Skins/Black Masks: The Pleasures and Politics of Imperialism." *New Formations* 9 (1989): 83–103.

Coetzee, A.J., Tim Couzens and Stephen Gray. "South African Literatures to World War II." In *European-language Writing in Sub-Saharan Africa*, Ed. Albert S. Gérard, 173–213. Budapest: Akadémiai Kadó, 1986.

Coetzee, J.M. *White Writing*. Sandton: Radix, 1988.

———"Jerusalem Prize Acceptance Speech." 1987. In *Doubling the Point: Essays and Interviews*, Ed. David Attwell, 96–100. Cambridge: Harvard University Press, 1992.

Collins Encyclopedia of Music. 2nd ed. London: Chancellor, 1984.

Cook, Rufus. "'Imploding Time and Geography': Narrative Compression in Michael Ondaatje's *The English Patient*." *Journal of Commonwealth Literature* 33(2) (1998): 110–125.

Cosslett, Tess. "'History from Below': Time-slip Narratives and National Identity." *The Lion and The Unicorn* 26(2) (2002): 243–253.

Davies, Shirley. *Reading Roundabout: A Review of South African Children's Literature*. Pietermaritzburg: Shuter & Shooter, 1992.

Davis, F. *Yearning for Yesterday: A Sociology of Nostalgia*. New York: Free Press, 1979.

Davis, Peter. *In Darkest Hollywood: Exploring the Jungles of Cinema's South Africa*. Randburg: Ravan, 1996.

Davison, Patricia. "Museums and the Reshaping of Memory." In *Negotiating the Past: The Making of Memory in South Africa*, Eds. Sarah Nuttall and Carli Coetzee, 143–160. Cape Town: Oxford University Press, 1998.

de Kock, Leon. "An Impossible History." *English in Africa* 24(1) (1997): 103–117.

Dewes, Jack. "Journalism gave PE-born Author Work Discipline." *Weekend Post*, 31 May 1990.

Dowson, Thomas and David Lewis-Williams. "Myths, Museums and Southern African Rock Art." In *Contested Images: Diversity in Southern African Rock Art Research*, Eds. Thomas Dowson and David Lewis-Williams, 385–402. Johannesburg: Witwatersrand University Press, 1994.

Egoff, Sheila and Judith Saltman. *The New Republic of Childhood: A Critical Guide to Canadian Children's Literature in English*. Toronto: Oxford University Press, 1990.

Fanon, Frantz. *The Wretched of the Earth*. 1961. London: Penguin, 2001.

Featherstone, Mike. *Consumer Culture and Postmodernism*. London: Sage, 1991.

Godwin, Denise. "Discovering the African Folktale in Translation." *South African Journal of African Languages* 11(4) (1991): 109–118.

Gordon, Robert. *The Bushman Myth*. Boulder: Westview, 1992.

Gould, Stephen Jay. *The Hedgehog, the Fox and the Magister's Pox*. London: Cape, 2003.

Gray, Stephen. *Southern African Literature*. Cape Town: David Philip, 1979.

Hall, G. Stanley. *Aspects of Child Life and Education*. Boston: Ginn, 1907.

Hall, Linda. "Aristocratic Houses and Radical Politics: Historical Fiction and the Time-slip Story in E. Nesbit's *The House of Arden*." *Children's Literature in Education* 29(1) (1998): 51–58.

Halliday, Hilda. "South African Writing for Children." *Crux* 8(3) (1974): 57–60.

Harper, Graeme, Ed. "Introduction." In *Comedy, Fantasy and Colonialism*, 1–8. London: Continuum, 2002.

Heale, Jay. *Young Africa Booklist*. Glasgow: Blackie, and Cape Town: Book Promotions, 1985.

———"South African Children's Literature in English." *Bookchat* 102 (1991): 19.

———*South African Authors and Illustrators*. Grabouw: Bookchat, 1994.

———*From the Bushveld to Biko: The Growth of South African Children's Literature in English from 1907 to 1992 Traced through 110 Notable Books*. Grabouw: Bookchat, 1996.

———"Books that Open Windows to Other Worlds." In *Peace Through Children's Books*. New Delhi: Indian Board on Books for Young People, Association of Writers and Illustrators for Children, 1998.

———"Review of *Eagle Learns to Fly*." *The Book Door* 27, (2004): 9.

Hillier, Bevis. *The Style of the Century, 1900-1980*. London: Herbert, 1983.

Hofmeyr, Dianne. "A Greening for our Children." *Weekly Mail*, 3–9 November 1989.

Horsburgh, Susan. "The Translation of Zulu Folktales for English-speaking Children in South Africa." M.A. dissertation, University of the Witwatersrand, 1991.

Hutcheon, Linda. *Irony's Edge*. London: Routledge, 1994.

Inggs, Judith. "The Changing Construct of the Child in Contemporary South African English Children's Fiction." Paper delivered at the conference of the International Research Society for Children's Literature, Warmbaths, 23 August 2001.

———"Grappling with Change: The English Language Youth Novel in South Africa." *CREArTA* 3(1) (2002): 22–33.

———"What is a South African Folktale?" *Papers* 14(1) (2004): 15–23.

Jammy, Eve. "The English Children's Book in South Africa." In *Kinder- en Jeugboeke: Referate Gelewe tydens die Haum-Daan Retiefsimposium oor Kinder- en Jeugboeke*, Eds. H.S. Coetzee and H.J.M. Retief, 88–96. Pretoria: University of Pretoria, 1990.

JanMohamed, Abdul. "The Economy of Manichean Allegory." In *"Race," Writing and Difference*, Ed. Henry Gates, 78–106. Chicago: University of Chicago Press, 1986.

Jenkins, Elwyn. "The Presentation of African Folktales in some South African English Children's Versions." In *Oral Tradition and Education*, Eds. G. Sienaert and N. Bell, 191–202. Durban: University of Natal Oral Documentation and Research Centre, 1988.

———*Children of the Sun: Selected Writers and Themes in South African Children's Literature*. Johannesburg: Ravan, 1993.

———"Images of the San." In *Other Worlds, Other Lives*, Eds. Myrna Machet, Sandra Olën and Thomas van der Walt, 270–296. Pretoria: Unisa, 1996.

———"Lessons from the Honey-guide." *CREArTA* 2(2) (2001): 52–59.

———*South Africa in English-language Children's Literature, 1814-1912*. Jefferson: McFarland, 2002.

———*Symbols of Nationhood*. Johannesburg: South African Institute of Race Relations, 2004.

Jones, D.F. *Storyteller: The Many Lives of Laurens van der Post*. London: Murray, 2001.

Kenmuir, Dale. "Response to 'Guest Spot.'" *Bookchat* 104 (1992): 15.

Kidd, Dudley. *The Essential Kaffir*. London: Black, 1904.

———*Savage Childhood: A Study of Kafir Children*. London: Black, 1906.

Kidd, Kenneth B. *Making American Boys: Boyology and the Feral Tale*. Minneapolis: University of Minnesota Press, 2004.

Kristeva, Julia. *Powers of Horror*. New York: Columbia University Press, 1982.

Kruger, J.A. *Kinderkeur: 'n Gids tot Bekroonde Suid-Afrikaanse kleuter-, kinder- en jeugboeke tot 1989*. Pretoria: Unisa, 1991.

Landau, Paul. "With Camera and Gun in Southern Africa." In *Miscast: Negotiating the Presence of the Bushmen*, Ed. Pippa Skotnes, 129–141. Cape Town: University of Cape Town Press, 1996.

Lanham, L.W. "South African English as an Index of Social History." *English Studies in Africa* 13(1) (1970): 251–264.

Lenta, Margaret. "Goodbye Lena, Goodbye Poppie." *Ariel* 29(4) (1998): 101–118.

———"Postcolonial Children and Parents: Pauline Smith's *Platkops Children*." *English in Africa* 27(2) (2000): 29–43.

Lewis-Williams, David. *Stories that Float from Afar: Ancestral Folklore of the San of South Africa*. Cape Town: David Philip, 2000.

Louw, Anna. "The English Children's Book of South African Origin." In *Papers Presented at the First Symposium on Children's Literature*, 16–26. Potchefstroom: Institute for Research in Children's Literature, Potchefstroom University for CHE, 1979.

MacCann, Donnarae, "The Sturdy Fabric of Cultural Imperialism: Tracing its Patterns in Contemporary Children's Novels." *Children's Literature* 33 (2005): 185–208.

MacCann, Donnarae and Yulisa Amadu Maddy. *Apartheid and Racism in South African Children's Literature, 1985-1995*. New York: Routledge, 2001.

MacKenzie, John. *The Empire of Nature*. Manchester: Manchester University Press, 1988.

———"Empire and the Ecological Apocalypse." In *Ecology and Empire*, Eds. Tom Griffiths and Libby Robin, 215–228. Edinburgh: Keele University Press, 1997.

Maddy, Yulisa and Donnarae MacCann. *African Images in Juvenile Literature*. Jefferson: McFarland, 1996.

Malan, Robin. "Siyagruva: Developing a Teen Fiction Series for Africa." Presentation at the 29th Congress of the International Board on Books for Young People, Cape Town, 8 September 2004.

Martin, Julia. "Long Live the Fresh Air! Long Live!" *scrutiny2* 2(2) (1997): 10–29.

Maughan Brown, David. "The Rehabilitation of the San in Popular Fiction." In *Race and Literature*, Ed. Charles Malan, 117–126. Pinetown: Owen Burgess, 1987.

Mbeki, Thabo. "Speech on the Adoption of the Constitution of the Republic of South Africa." Pretoria: Office of the Presidency, 1996.

Michaels, Wendy. "The Realistic Turn: Trends in Recent Australian Young Adult Fiction." *Papers* 14(1) (2004): 49–59.

Midgley, Peter. "Review of MacCann, Donnarae and Yulisa Amadu Maddy. *Apartheid and Racism in South African Children's Literature, 1985-1995*." H-Net: Humanities and Social Sciences Online. http://www.h-net.org/reviews. Posted 11 September 2002.

Moya, Fikile-Ntsikelelo. "Of Sacred Cows.... Interview with Wole Soyinka." *Mail & Guardian*, 22–28 July 2005.

Murray, John. "Some Literary and Ethical Issues in the Use of Indigenous Material by an Australian Children's Writer." *Literature and Theology* 10(3) (1996): 252–260.

Naidu, Samantha. "Transcribing Tales, Creating Cultural Identities." M.A. dissertation, Rhodes University, 2001.

———"The Myth of Authenticity: Folktales and Nationalism in the 'New South Africa'." *scrutiny2* 6(2) (2001): 17–26.

National Arts Council. "Voices in Action: Towards Developing a National South African Literature." Unpublished proceedings of the conference of the National Arts Council. Pretoria, 21–23 June 2002.

National Library. *Amandla eBali*. Cape Town: National Library, 2004.

Ní Bhroin, Ciara. "Championing Irish Literature." *Bookbird* 43(2) (2005): 13–21.

Niall, Brenda. *Australia Through the Looking Glass: Children's Fiction 1830-1980*. Melbourne: Melbourne University Press, 1984.

Nikolajeva, Maria. *Children's Literature Comes of Age*. New York: Garland, 1996.

Poland, Marguerite. "Making Stars Sing." In *Towards More Understanding: The Making and Sharing of Children's Literature in Southern Africa*, Ed. Isabel Cilliers, 13–20. Cape Town: Juta, 1993.

Pretoria News. "*e'Lollipop* Makes a Return." 6 May 2004.

Roberts Birds of South Africa. Cape Town: CNA, 1957.

Robins, Steven. "Silence in my Father's House." In *Negotiating the Past: The Making of Memory in South Africa*, Ed. Sarah Nuttall and Carli Coetzee, 120–140. Cape Town: Oxford University Press, 1998.

Rode, Linda and Jakes Gerwel, comp. *Crossing Over: New Writing for a New South Africa*. Cape Town: Kwela, 1995.

Rovenger, Judith. "Wonderful Ambassadors." In *Lesley Beake: Author Nomination for the Hans Christian Andersen Award 2004*, n.p. Cape Town: South African Children's Book Forum, 2004.

Saxby, Henry. *A History of Australian Children's Literature 1841-1941*. Sydney: Wentworth, 1969.

Scanlon, Margaret and David Buckingham. "Deconstructing Dinosaurs: Imagery, Fact, and Fiction in Information Books." *Bookbird* 41(1)(2003): 14–20.

Scheub, Harold. "Introduction." In A.C. Jordan, *Tales from South Africa*, 1–12. Berkeley: University of California Press, 1973.

Scholten, Sheila. "*Platkops Children* — The Childhood Sketches of Pauline Smith: A Commentary." In *Pauline Smith*, Ed. Dorothy Driver, 138–43. Johannesburg: McGraw-Hill, 1983.

Sewitz, M. "Children's Books in English in an African Setting: 1914–1964." Research project, University of the Witwatersrand, 1965.

Shaw, Christopher and Malcolm Chase, Eds. *The Imagined Past: History and Nostalgia*. Manchester: Manchester University Press, 1989.

Skotnes, Pippa, Ed. *Miscast: Negotiating the Presence of the Bushmen*. Cape Town: University of Cape Town Press, 1996.

Slingsby, Peter. "Guest Spot." *Bookchat* 103 (1991): 5.

Smith, Anna. "Children's Books." In *English and South Africa*, Ed. Alan Lennox-Short, 125–129. Cape Town: Nasou, 197-.

Snyman, Maritha. "Die Afrikaanse Jeugreeksboek." In *Van Patrys-hulle tot Hanna Hoekom: 'n Gids tot die Afrikaanse Kinder- en Jeugboek*. Eds. Gretel Wybenga and Maritha Snyman, 89-112. Pretoria: LAPA, 2005.

South African Institute of Race Relations, *Fast Facts* 2 (2005): 1.

Stanton, P.J. "Bibliography of Books in English Especially Suited to South African Children." Research project, University of Cape Town, 1946.

Strange Library of African Studies. Catalog. Johannesburg: Johannesburg Public Library.

Tomaselli, Keyan. "Myths, Racism and Opportunism: Film and TV Representations of the San." In *Film as Ethnography*, Eds. Ian Crawford and David Turon, 205–221. Manchester: Manchester University Press, 1992.

———"Psychospiritual Ecoscience." *Visual Anthropology* 12 (2–3) (1999).

Tötemeyer, Andreé-Jeanne. "The Visual Portrayal of Black People in South African Children's and Juvenile Literature." In *Far Far Away*, Ed. Marianne Hölscher, 36–46. Cape Town: South African National Gallery, 1986.

———"Impact of African Mythology on South African Juvenile Literature." *South African Journal of Library and Information Science* 57(4) (1989): 393–401.

———"Trends in Children's Literature at Home and Abroad." In *Towards More Understanding: The Making and Sharing of Children's Literature in South Africa*, Ed. Isabel Cilliers, 159–169. Cape Town: Juta, 1993.

Tshikumambila, Nyembwe. "From Folktale to Short Story." In *European-language Writing in Sub-Saharan Africa*, Ed. Albert S. Gérard, 475–489. Budapest: Akadémiai Kadó, 1986.

van Vuuren, Helize. "Bushman and Afrikaner: Cultural Interaction." *Alternation* 2(1) (1995): 151–154.

———"The Tin Shack Bushmen of Kagga Kamma." Review of *In the Tradition of the Forefathers* by Hilton White (Cape Town: University of Cape Town, 1995). *Alternation*, 2(2) (1995): 207–211.

van Vuuren, Kathrine. "A Study of Indigenous Children's Literature in South Africa." M.A. dissertation, University of Cape Town, 1994.

van Wyk Smith, Malvern. *Grounds of Contest: A Survey of South African English Literature*. Cape Town: Juta, 1990.

Voss, A.E. "The Image of the Bushman in South African English Writing of the Nineteenth and Twentieth Centuries." *English in Africa* 14(1) (1987): 21–40.

Wade, Jean-Philippe. "English." In *European-language Writing in Sub-Saharan Africa*, Ed. Albert Gérard, 230–250. Budapest: Akadémiai Kadó, 1986.

Walsh, Maureen. *May Gibbs, Mother of the Gumnuts*. North Ryde: Angus & Robertson, 1985.

Waterston, Elizabeth. *Children's Literature in Canada*. New York: Twayne, 1992.

Watts, H.L. "A Social and Demographic Portrait of English-speaking White South Africans." In *English-speaking South Africa Today*, Ed. André Villiers, 41–90. Cape Town: Oxford University Press, 1976.

Webster, Mary. "Daphne Rooke." In *English and South Africa*, Ed. Alan Lennox-Short, 67–69. Cape Town, Nasou, 197–.

Williams, P. and L. Chrisman. *Colonial Discourse and Post-colonial Theory*. Hemel Hempstead: Wheatsheaf, 1993.

Wilmsen, Edwin. *Land Filled with Flies: A Political Economy of the Kalahari*. Chicago: University of Chicago Press, 1989.

———"First People? Images and Imaginations in South African Iconography." *Critical Arts* (1) (1995): 1–27.

Working Group of Indigenous Minorities in Southern Africa. "San Media and Research Contract." Windhoek: WIMSA, 2001.

Wright, J.B. *Bushman Raiders of the Drakensberg 1840-1870*. Pietermaritzburg: University of Natal Press, 1971.

Wybenga, Gretel and Maritha Snyman, Eds. *Van Patrys-hulle tot Hanna Hoekom: 'n Gids tot die Afrikaanse Kinder- en Jeugboek*. Pretoria: LAPA, 2005.

Wylie, Dan. "Elephants and Compassion: Ecological Criticism and Southern African Hunting Literature." *English in Africa* 28(2) (2001): 79–100.

Zinn, Emily. "Rediscovery of the Magical: On Fairy Tales, Feminism, and the new South Africa." *Modern Fiction Studies* 46(1) (spring 2000): 246–269.

INDEX

Bold numbers indicate illustrations.

For Product Safety Concerns and Information please contact our EU
representative GPSR@taylorandfrancis.com
Taylor & Francis Verlag GmbH, Kaufingerstraße 24, 80331 München, Germany

* 9 7 8 1 1 3 8 8 3 3 3 2 6 *